Absurdity and Meaning in Contemporary Philosophy and Jewish Thought

There is a lively discussion in contemporary philosophy that explores the meaning of life or, more modestly, meaning in life. Philosophers, for the most part, assume that religion has little to contribute to this inquiry. They believe that the Western religions, such as Judaism, have doctrinaire beliefs which have become implausible and can no longer satisfy the search for meaning. In this book, Alan L. Mittleman argues that this view is misconceived. He offers a presentation of core Jewish beliefs by using classical and contemporary texts that address the question of the meaning of life in a philosophical spirit. That spirit includes profound self-questioning and self-criticism. Such beliefs are not doctrinaire: Jewish sources, such as the biblical Book of Ecclesiastes, are, in fact, open to an absurdist reading. Mittleman demonstrates that both philosophy and Judaism are prone to ineliminable doubts and perplexities. Far from pre-empting a conversation, they promote honest dialogue.

ALAN L. MITTLEMAN is Aaron Rabinowitz and Simon H. Rifkind Emeritus Professor of Jewish Philosophy at The Jewish Theological Seminary of America. He is the author of *Hope in a Democratic Age* (Oxford University Press, 2009) and *Does Judaism Condone Violence? Holiness and Ethics in the Jewish Tradition* (Princeton University Press, 2018).

Absurdity and Meaning in Contemporary Philosophy and Jewish Thought

ALAN L. MITTLEMAN
The Jewish Theological Seminary of America

Shaftesbury Road, Cambridge CB2 8EA, United Kingdom

One Liberty Plaza, 20th Floor, New York, NY 10006, USA

477 Williamstown Road, Port Melbourne, VIC 3207, Australia

314–321, 3rd Floor, Plot 3, Splendor Forum, Jasola District Centre, New Delhi – 110025, India

103 Penang Road, #05–06/07, Visioncrest Commercial, Singapore 238467

Cambridge University Press is part of Cambridge University Press & Assessment, a department of the University of Cambridge.

We share the University's mission to contribute to society through the pursuit of education, learning and research at the highest international levels of excellence.

www.cambridge.org
Information on this title: www.cambridge.org/9781009098267

DOI: 10.1017/9781009099400

First published 2023

A catalogue record for this publication is available from the British Library

A Cataloging-in-Publication data record for this book is available from the Library of Congress

ISBN 978-1-009-09826-7 Hardback

Contents

Acknowledgments

Some wonderful people and institutions helped me to think about and write this book. My academic home, the Jewish Theological Seminary (JTS), in addition to being a congenial environment to work on questions of meaning, religion, and philosophy also gave me a yearlong sabbatical at a critical point in the work. That sabbatical was also made possible by the Madison Program in American Ideals and Institutions at Princeton University, which granted me a fellowship in 2020–2021. Although the worst of the pandemic precluded in person meetings, my cohort met weekly online. I got to share many ideas and an early draft among friends. Thanks also go to my students at JTS who signed up for a course I taught twice on "The Meaning of Life in Modern Jewish Thought." This was invaluable for gaining greater clarity about the issues and translating between often abstruse philosophical metalevel discussions and the concerns of actual human beings. I thank my editor at Cambridge University Press, Beatrice Rehl, for her encouragement and the anonymous readers, who helped me to refine the project. For advice and insight into the Book of Ecclesiastes, I had a number of fruitful discussions with Tamara Eskenazi. Other helpful discussion partners were Todd Moody, Catherine Chalier, Benjamin Schvarcz, Yoni Brafman, Arthur Kover, Amanda Greene, Alex Green, Tom Angier, the late Richard Claman, Alan Astrow, Jonathan Moss, Michael Morgan, Leora Batnitzky, Tzvi Novick, Paul Steiner, and Arnie Eisen. I am deeply grateful to my partner, Annette Aronowicz, who carefully read the entire manuscript (twice!) and offered penetrating comments, criticism – and ongoing moral support.

I dedicate the book to my late wife, Patti Mittleman (1959–2018). By emphasizing the ethical dimensions of meaning, I tried to capture something of Patti's spirit and moral passion. Her life was marked by great seriousness, courage, love, devotion, and unflagging energy despite harsh health challenges. My sons, Ari and Joel, and I miss her deeply. I dedicate this book as well to my terrific grandchildren, Adrian and Eden Shira Mittleman-Levin and Eliora Galit Mittleman. They bring great light to my life. May they live meaningful lives in a world worthy of their promise.

Introduction

Religious thought addresses problems, typically problems of an existential nature, if this peculiar modern term may be allowed. "Existential problems" are generated in response to human life as a whole. They respond to universal human themes, dilemmas, perplexities, and anxieties. Why are we here? Do we have a purpose? What is of value? Is what is of value to me truly of value? What is the significance, if any, of my life? How does it make sense if, indeed, it does? The slippage from "we" to "me" is intentional. Individuals capable of reflection put such questions to themselves, but they do so within a cultural context – a world of shared meanings. The endless diversity of cultures notwithstanding, we share the human condition that prompts the questions. Yet even within that larger framework, the search for answers takes us back to our own personal condition. Whatever counts as an answer must be something that you or I in our particularity must be able to live with or by.

Perhaps it wasn't always so. When the great religions were the dominant civilization shaping forces, when life took place within their protective atmospheres, the questions might not have arisen with much urgency. Perhaps religious thought "solved" the problems. I doubt, however, that that was the case. At least within the great traditions, with their complex literatures, religious thought was and is irreducibly heterogenous, even conflictual. Traditions are typically traditions of argument. The Jewish tradition, at least, did not relieve individuals of the burden of sensemaking and of struggling with discrepant texts and teachings. Even in less conflictual traditions, not everyone is content to go along with a consensus, especially if the consensus is buttressed by powerful institutions. At least some human hearts rebel against coercion. Our peculiar modern restlessness notwithstanding, there is something intrinsically restless about the human mind; its questioning – sparked by wonder – is irrepressible. The problems that religious thought means to solve always give rise to new problems. Religious thought is a mode of engagement with existential problems. These problems may slumber, but they never fall soundly asleep.

This is no less true in our self-professed secular age. Secularity is an orientation consciously shaped by contrast with modes of life informed by religion. But the contrast is neither exhaustive nor tidy. Secular approaches to existential problems often reiterate the dilemmas explored by religious thought, as if there were only so many possibilities human minds can envisage vis-à-vis fundamental problems. Secular approaches may bracket crucial religious concepts or commitments – God, most prominently – but they too have their gods, their polytheisms, and their monotheisms. They have their institutional orthodoxies, high priests, prophets, tricksters, and pious fools. They too, when cynical or shallow, capitalize on credulity and, when earnest, ask for trust.

When self-consciously secular thinkers turn to the problems of value and meaning, they try to solve them within an "immanent frame."[1] They eschew transcendence, whether refined (as in Plato's "good beyond being" or Paul Tillich's "ultimate concern") or crude (as in the blunt supernaturalism of literalist believers). But transcendence does not leave them alone. They too need skyhooks. Their proposals for meaning, if they don't bottom out in just-so stories or cultural conventions, require the invocation of secular mysteries. The leap from what nature has selected us to be to how we ought, therefore, to live is also a leap of faith. It is an open question whether the secular is truly an alternative to the religious. We can use the binary opposition without entirely endorsing it.

This book is an analysis and critique of both a body of religious thought, drawn primarily from Judaism, and of a field within secular thought – contemporary philosophical work in the analytic tradition on existential problems. (I draw from contemporary Anglo-American philosophy because I wish to enter the current conversation among writers on meaning.) The book looks – selectively, to be sure – at how Jewish thought has responded over the millennia to the problem of meaning. It brings that tradition of reflection, as mediated by academic scholarship, into conversation with the contemporary philosophical turn to the same cluster of questions. I try to show that, as different as these traditions are, at the base of each, there remains ineliminable perplexity. Each tradition reveals a gap between its claims and the mystery of human existence that the claims seek to illuminate. Accepting perplexity while confidently holding on to the tradition that generates it but cannot succeed in dispelling it is *absurd*. I use the terms "absurdity" or "the absurd" to indicate this paradoxical situation. The paradox is not a logical one; it is existential. It has to do with the commitments we make and live by, their irremediable conceptual problems notwithstanding.

Judaism, despite its robust faith in a God who creates, reveals, and redeems, preserves unsettling doubts about the meaning of creation, revelation, and redemption – as well as about the power of the God who is the agent of these acts. I take creation, revelation, and redemption to be concepts that make meaning from the facts of human experience and the values revealed by it. The concepts are expressed in stories that Jews have told for millennia. When the stories are analyzed conceptually, however, innumerable doubts and perplexities arise. Continuing to affirm the truth, however metaphorical, of the story while acknowledging the doubts requires a sense of the absurd. Judaism's core affirmations about the meaning of human life butt up against absurdity, sometimes acknowledged, sometimes just out of view. Judaism can be a balancing act on what Martin Buber called "a narrow ridge."[2] This is especially true for modern Jews and modern Judaism.

Similarly, modern philosophical thought in its struggle to ground a livable answer to the meaning of (or more modestly – itself a retreat or concession – the meaning *in*) human life also comes up against the absurd. We are told, by some science-oriented philosophers, that we are just social primates or just brains; that our values and the cultures that express them are just survival mechanisms, naturally selected within our ancestors' environmental niches. Yet the seeming realism of such commonplaces is not realistic enough to accommodate our felt experience of what it is like to be human beings. The philosophers' proposals for values, for how we are to live, are often based on reasons that compound rather than relieve our perplexity. (One philosopher, whom we will treat in Chapter 2, for example, essentially argues: Well-functioning brains need pleasure, work, and connection so live in such a way as to maximize pleasure, work, and connection! Could one live meaningfully within such a biological straitjacket? The struggle to persuade ourselves that we are "just brains" presupposes that we are more than just brains.[3]) Some philosophers are honest about the deep schism between biologizing and humanizing stories about human life.[4] They sense the absurdity of the schism and yet persevere in maintaining it. Others try to define the human down and deny absurdity. Still others accept absurdity but give up on the tension and embrace nihilism: the ultimate meaninglessness of life. Philosophers too walk that narrow ridge.

Is a conversation between these different groups of seekers possible? This book attempts to motivate one. It explores the existential problem of meaning in both Judaism and philosophy. It invites a reconsideration of the role of absurdity in both. I write as a Jew with religious commitments, who is also a philosopher with no small measure of skepticism toward my religious commitments *and* toward my philosophical influences. I have come to accept absurdity as an unwelcome guest but one that cannot be turned away. Nonetheless, I do try to turn away an even more unwelcome one, nihilism. The two are not the same, I will argue. Absurdity is an ongoing concomitant of commitment; it leaves the doors of discovery open. Nihilism locks the doors.

The fundamental, ineliminable perplexity at the root of thought shakes some of Judaism's claims, as it does those of philosophy. For both, there are, at bottom, aporias. Given this, I claim that a self-aware, self-critical Judaism can be an ally of philosophy, not a zero-sum competitor. Many works of contemporary philosophy of meaning reject such irenicism. I hope to show, at least obliquely, that they are wrong to do so.

Of course, our basic perplexity, or to be blunt, our ignorance, should not bring on the night in which all cows are black. It shouldn't level distinctions between better and worse worldviews, explanations, values, or modes of being. At some point, we have to choose those views that best preserve what we – and the traditions within whose horizon we live – take to be the noble, courageous, humane, and true. Such are the touchstones of a meaningful life. Nonetheless, nagging doubts about the soundness of our choices may remain. Doubt at this level may be a permanent feature of our condition. But unless we repudiate meaningfulness altogether – unless we opt for nihilism – we must take a risk and commit. Our commitments are neither as well-grounded as we would like nor entirely as arbitrary as we might fear. I think that we can find good (but not unimpeachable) reasons, for grounding a meaningful life. I do not think that we are condemned to brute decisionism. This book is an essay on these dilemmas.

* * *

To begin, let us not address meaning head-on but rather its contrary, meaninglessness. I do not take meaninglessness to be our original condition in the sense that the universe per se is meaningless and our efforts to find meaning in it are human projections onto an infinity of brute facts. On that view, rock bottom reality is meaningless, full stop. Claims to the contrary are delusional. The ubiquity of such a view in the contemporary literature notwithstanding, I think it claims more than it can know. It posits a world-in-itself, untouched by mind, uninfected by value, even those epistemic values by which we could know such a world. I don't see how we could know that "the universe" is a value-free collection of empirical furniture/brute facts such that all values and meanings are inessential, humanly imposed additions. Thus, rather than blaming the universe for our crises of meaning, I take meaninglessness to be a condition *within* human experience. Something that once had worth – life as such and the projects meant to protect and sustain it – has lost that worth. We might invoke some metaphysical view of the universe as a reason for the loss of meaning, but such reasoning already assumes meaningful human practices, such as reason-giving, justification, etc. The dogmatic assumption that the universe in itself lacks value and meaning is overly hasty. It is nihilistic. Nihilism, for all of its assumed certainty, is question-begging.

Meaninglessness is a token of something we have lost. It is a sign that our world has fallen apart. The props of the world – selfhood, customs, traditions, norms, and hopes – have weakened and tottered. The authority of received wisdom has lapsed. One lives a life that one can no longer understand insofar as the markers of intelligibility have been removed. Just as one experiences shock and disorientation at the death of a loved one, so the loss of meaning deranges and discomfits. Reality is no longer what it was, and the new reality is pressing, insistent, and opaque. It is both unclear how to go on and, more fundamentally, whether one can or should. The significance and self-evidence of the world have been lost. Does one have the strength to make a new world? What, after all, would be the point? Meaninglessness is worldlessness. It is a whirlpool stirring itself into dissolution. How does this happen? How does the familiar and meaningful become foreign and unjustified?

THE CRISIS OF MEANING IN TOLSTOY

Let us consider two approaches to these questions, both drawn from the work of the great Russian writer, Leo Tolstoy. (Although not alone among nineteenth-century authors who grapple with meaning and nihilism, Tolstoy does so explicitly, hence my choice of him.)

Tolstoy's novella, *The Death of Ivan Ilych*, is a classic fictional portrayal of a crisis of meaning. Ivan Ilych is an ordinary, unimaginative man, neither appealing nor repellant. He is a lawyer in a Russian province, a careerist who has climbed the ladder to his current high post as a judge. He fulfils his duties officiously, enjoying his power and showing cool condescension toward inferiors. His marriage is mostly unhappy. He lives beyond his means. He sometimes feels that he doesn't get the respect (or the salary) he deserves or that he is being eclipsed by younger, inferior men. But his life on the whole is leisurely, decorous, and easy. He believes that he lives properly. He is entirely oriented by the norms of his culture and class: Appearance, dress, home décor, rank in the hierarchy of social status, appropriate emotions toward family, friends, and officialdom – these secure a tolerable, largely pleasant life for him. He lives in a meaningful world. Questioning it would be out of the question. But circumstances force him to do so.

He begins to notice a pain in his side and becomes increasingly concerned about it. His wife, unsympathetic and resentful, blames him for his pain. He seeks out doctors. They disagree with one another and treat him with the same condescension that he has shown to the litigants who stood before his bench. His friends, with whom he plays bridge, are bothered by him; he is no longer right, no longer good company. The relations he has had with others over the years fray, showing their shallowness and falsity. While he is in pain, both physically and emotionally, the others retreat. His pain causes them discomfort. It upsets their stable, pleasant equilibrium. They blame him for upsetting them.

As Ivan Ilych's condition worsens, it begins to dawn on him that he is dying. The doctors cannot, given the medicine of their day, correctly diagnose him. Some of their diagnoses (such as "a floating kidney") gave him grounds for hope. The problem is trivial and can correct itself! But he soon sees that his hope was deceitful. So too is the empty solicitude of his wife and friends. He is consumed by anguish and rage. He withdraws from everyone, as they withdraw from him. He is sickened by their lies. Every time his wife or a doctor asks whether he has taken his medicine, he sees it as an evasion of reality: He is dying, but they pretend that the world can be made right again by proper emotions and prudent actions. They are living in the conventional reality that he has lost. That is not just callous, from his point of view, but mendacious. Life has been a lie, an absurdity.

At the end of the novella, Ivan Ilych, Job-like, hurls accusatory questions at God (notwithstanding that he doesn't quite believe in Him). He wants to know why this has happened to *him*. That disease and death happen to human beings in their generality everyone knows, but why has this happened to Ivan Ilych Golovin? He has lived his life properly; he has done everything right. Had he lived his life wrongly, he could understand his fate. It would have been a kind of punishment for having broken the rules. But he broke no rules. The disproportion between the presumed propriety of his bourgeois life and the horror of his encroaching death torments him. Indeed, his anguish prevents him from dying. He needs a meaningful answer to his question. Without an answer, he cannot die. Release – and death – come when Ivan Ilych's young son enters the room. His mind clears briefly from its delirium and he sees his son crying by his bedside. He tries to put his hand on his son's head, as his heart fills with pity for him. He even begins to pity his wife, who has entered the room, freeing himself from years of anger and resentment toward her. He tries to say the words "forgive me" but is too weak to enunciate them. It is at this moment, when he reaches beyond the narrow bounds of morbid self-concern and rises to compassion, indeed to selfless love for the people he is leaving behind that he experiences an epiphany. He accepts his pain. But as to death …

> And death? Where is it?
> He searched for his old habitual fear of death and didn't find it. Where was death? What death? There was no fear because there was no death.

> Instead of death there was light.
>
> "So that's it!" he suddenly said aloud. "Such joy!" …
>
> "It is finished!" someone said above him.
>
> He heard these words and repeated them in his heart. "Death is finished," he said to himself. "It is no more!"
>
> He breathed in, stopped halfway, stretched himself, and died.[5]

In this story, Ivan Ilych's experience of meaninglessness comes about as a result of a deadly disease. The mysterious illness has laid bare how fragile the interrelated structures of social and personal reality are. The structures present a coherent, intelligible world marked by meaningful values, such as dedication to family, work, cultivating pleasurable friendships and activities. Ivan Ilych has constant intimations that things are far from perfect, but he doesn't question the basic structures until the illness dislodges him from them. This is not primarily a philosophical crisis, such as Tolstoy relates of his own struggle with nihilism in his *Confession*. Nor is it Camus's portrayal of the invasion of absurdity into daily life by "beginning to think." ("Beginning to think is beginning to be undermined."[6]) Ivan Ilych would have had nothing to do with philosophical nihilism, nor with thought – he was a calculating, not a thoughtful man – had his life not been hijacked by illness. There are many ways the familiar can become foreign, the onrushing presence of death, one's own or that of a loved one, is surely one of them. It is likely not the most common one, however. We are capable of discomfiture and of a radical reassessment of the value and meaning of our lives *in medias res*, not just *in extremis*.

Ivan Ilych was in extremis. He did not get to rebuild his world. He experienced a kind of repentance, *teshuva*, as Judaism would call it, or *metanoia*, as the New Testament puts it. He got to redeem his life, in Tolstoy's unorthodox but deeply Christian view, by turning from self-centeredness to self-abnegating compassion. Death lost its sting, victory, and dominion. For the rest of us and for Tolstoy himself, however, the challenge remains of how to go on. Ivan Ilych achieved insight into the disjunction between "how it ought to be" and "how it is," as well as into the arbitrariness and contingency of conventional social meaningfulness. But he did not get to reintegrate those insights into a meaningful worldview and ethos. Death relieved him of having to go forward. Just as one must find a way to go on after the death of a loved one, one must figure out how to build up a livable world after a fundamental loss of meaning. A livable world for human beings is one that is held together by meanings, but when all of the meanings are tainted by absurdity, it is difficult to envision how any world could be a home.

But why should we accept the claim that all meanings are tainted by absurdity? Ivan Ilych came to this conclusion due to what we might call ethical considerations. In the first instance, it wasn't existential absurdity as much as mendacity that troubled him. The way people, his former self included, lived was false, cheap, superficial, and duplicitous. He lost confidence in his former way of life not because it was, finally, improper to pursue career, friendship, domesticity, and pleasure but because these were insufficient to attain truth and goodness in an absolute sense. Until his deadly illness, he had no interest in such goals. He had become inured to the inhumanity of daily life and indifferent to a higher humanity of which he was capable. He had not sought for an ultimate significance to human life. He was content with the local, contingent, social meanings provisioned by his culture. But that changed. Faced with his own onrushing demise, he groped toward a truth that could redeem or at least make sense of his life. The perspective of one whose life is ending, a singular event, demands a singular significance to life, an unequivocal end of equivocations. (Whether meaning can bear this strain is an open question. Some philosophers, as we will see, accuse Tolstoy of "perfectionism."[7] His option for an ultimate answer imposes undue stress on meaningfulness, anti-perfectionists claim. Those social meanings that we incorporate as personal meanings just *are* what constitute meaning in life. On this view, while meaning is crucial, its claim to ultimacy must be deflated.)

Put abstractly, Ivan Ilych was searching for an absolute to stop the regress of "why" questions unleashed by his life-threatening experience. He tried to find a justification for the norms, the values, by which he had lived. But no justification was sufficient to withstand the force of another "why?". He was plunged into a regress of questions wherein any stopping point seemed arbitrary, more a matter of exhaustion or willfulness than warrant and reason. Conventional answers became little more than abandoned questions. Therein lay absurdity.[8] A fuller conceptual analysis of absurdity must wait until the next chapter but let us say this much: *The failure to justify the norms by which one lives, coupled with the need to resist abandoning them, is a chief characteristic of absurdity, the root of an absurdist perspective.* This perspective sometimes comes from shattering emotional experiences that have dislodged one from one's accustomed framework.

Another root of absurdity is the taking of an abstract view, in our culture, typically, a scientific view, from which all of human life, all of human striving looks meaningless and futile. From the perspective, as it were, of the universe, human existence looks insignificant, unimportant; what we care about loses its worth. That view, call it, following Thomas Nagel, the "view from nowhere," also leads to a regress of why-questions, which is equally problematic for justification. We come to think that the universe is valueless and indifferent; our values and meanings are only projections, the flotsam and jetsam of our outsized brains. Why should anything matter? *Ivan Ilych* exemplifies the first root; Tolstoy's *Confession* the second.

Ivan Ilych fictionalizes Tolstoy's own story albeit with the added drama of illness and death. Tolstoy's autobiographical *Confession* relates a reflective, philosophical divorce from the social meaningfulness of his aristocratic culture. Although there is no gross crisis, such as a deadly illness that drives him into profound despair and loss of meaning, he depicts his condition as illness-like. At first, he ignores his doubts and questions, but they gradually overcome him. Like Ivan Ilych, Tolstoy becomes disgusted with his peers, especially with their shabby morality. The early death of his brother from an implacable illness haunts him with the thought that there is no justice in the world. Having observed an execution, by guillotine, in Paris undermines the conceit that modernity is a time of ethical progress. Tolstoy cannot help doubting the worth of his fame, literary achievements, wealth, and roles as father, husband, landowner, and so on. Initially, he ignores his doubts, carrying on as before. But they swell and come to dominate and poison his mind. Soon the crisis of meaning takes on a life of its own, fueled by relentless questioning, which he derides as childlike – the child's endless "but why?" – but which seems ever more valid, if maddening, to him. He falls into a ruminative loop from which he cannot extricate himself:

> My question, which at the age of fifty brought me to the point of suicide was the very simple question that lies in the soul of every human being, from a silly child to the wisest of sage – the question without which life is impossible as I experienced in actual fact. The question is this: What will come from what I do and from what I will do tomorrow – what will come from my whole life? Expressed differently, the question would be this: Why should I live, why should I wish for anything, why should I do anything? One can put the question differently again: Is there any meaning in my life that wouldn't be destroyed by the death that inevitably awaits me?[9]

If Ivan Ilych echoes the *Book of Job*, Tolstoy's *Confession* echoes *Ecclesiastes.* Ecclesiastes presents the jaded reflections of a wise king who comes to believe that his wealth, fame, knowledge, and power are meaningless, a futile effort to chase the wind. Just as King Solomon, the putative author of Ecclesiastes, searches out the wisdom of his time (Ecclesiastes 1:13), Tolstoy tells us that he read voraciously in both the sciences and philosophy, trying to find answers in these rational approaches to reality. The sciences, however, offered nothing but materialistic, reductionist answers; the universe is the sum total of meaningless, albeit law-abiding, physical contingencies.

("You are an ephemeral, casual connection of particles. The interaction, the change of these particles produces in you what you call your life. The connection will last some time; then the interaction of these particles will stop – and what you call your life will stop and all your questions will stop too."[10]) Most philosophy, for its part, only disciplines and reformulates the questions; its ultimate answer is refined perplexity. And for those few philosophers – Tolstoy singles out Socrates, Solomon, Buddha, and Schopenhauer – who boldly engage with the questions, the answers are shatteringly negative. Tolstoy sees this as the final deliverance of reason: "All is vanity. Happy is he who was not born; death is better than life; one needs to be rid of life."[11]

Tolstoy's way out of the dead end to which his reason has led him is to question his own presumptive rationality. His reason has emptied life of meaning; the only honest response is suicide. But he resists suicide – not because he is cowardly; he is not. He resists it because it seems an evasion, not entirely distinct from the common forms of evasion practiced by others in his class (such as hedonism). The mass of humanity, especially the Russian peasantry, despite their hard lives, are much more at peace with life than the aristocracy. They are at home in life; they have a meaningful, and so a livable world. The rationalizations that frame the Russian caste system – namely, that Tolstoy and his class are fully human while the peasantry are hardly more than animals – now appear to him as pernicious biases. They are part of the conventional social meaningfulness that the crisis of meaning has exposed. Is there a more illuminating way to interpret the fact that the peasants' lives are more vital, more life-affirming than the aristocrats' lives that doesn't invoke the tired trope of the peasants being ignorant and simplistic? Could it be that the peasants *know* something about life that Tolstoy doesn't?

> It proved to be the case that the whole of mankind had knowledge of the meaning of life, unrecognized and scorned by me. It turned out that rational knowledge does not give the meaning of life, it

> excludes life; the meaning is given to life by millions of people, the whole of mankind, is founded on some kind of despised false knowledge. Rational knowledge in the person of scholars and wise men denies the meaning of life but the great mass of people, the whole of mankind, recognizes that meaning in irrational knowledge. And that irrational knowledge is faith, the very thing I had to reject.[12]

Tolstoy is thus led to the gate of a radical, renewed Christian faith, categorically different from the casual, cultural one in which he was raised and later abandoned. He describes how he both thought that faith is the only answer to the suicidal bent of reason and, at the same time, repugnant: "My situation was terrible. I knew that I would find nothing on the path of rational knowledge but the denial of life, but there, in faith, nothing but the denial of reason, which was even more impossible than the denial of life."[13]

The ultimate meaningfulness that Tolstoy sought involved a drastic change of life. Faith was not just an intellectual orientation – taking on previously rejected and implausible beliefs, for example – but a deeply committed way of living. His "straying" into nihilistic conclusions about the meaning of life had come about:

> not so much because I thought wrongly as because I lived badly. I understood that the truth was hiding from me not so much by the error of my thinking as by my life in the exclusive conditions of Epicureanism and of satisfying my lusts in which I spent it. I understood that my question of what is my life and the answer, [an] evil, were quite right. What was wrong was just that the answer that only applied to me I applied to life in general.[14]

His assuming the perspective of a "view from nowhere" – "you are an ephemeral, casual connection of particles" – was double-edged. It both undermined his conventional meanings and their justifications, precipitating a crisis, *and* gave him a stance from which to globally critique his dilemma-generating framework. The dead end to which asking why questions led him now appeared to him as an unnecessary trap. A radical shift in his worldview and ethos could spring him from the trap and expose the chimera of its ineluctability.

In both *Ivan Ilych* and the *Confession*, Tolstoy subjects the familiar world of meaning to radical questioning. For Ivan Ilych the motivation is the exposure of a false way of living, a deeply felt sense of personal injustice, and a disproportion between expectations and deserts. For Tolstoy himself, although dreadful experiences shake him to his core, the crisis manifests itself most fully through abstracting from the familiar world to a presumed ultimate perspective: What will all of this mean in the end? Reason itself seemed to drive a depersonalized inquiry into the significance (or lack thereof) of life. The high manifestations of rationality – philosophy and physical science – pronounced human life meaningless. These are the deliverances of a stance fundamentally at odds with a stance embedded in the immediacy of life, a "view from here," to use Nagel's antipode. Absurdity, a gnawing conviction of the meaninglessness of human life, enters through the tear between the two.

The challenge of transcending absurdity and of finding more stable meaning is twofold. It is to reintegrate the insights of the abstract view with the truths of the personal one. It is also to find a way of stopping the regress of insistent why questions that allows one to have good reasons for justifying one's norms, beliefs, and values. The abstract view can yield truth, as well as quicken a sense of the absurd. Tolstoy converted the experience of reason going beyond life, so to speak, into a commitment to a new life going beyond the narrowness of an old one. The new life requires that we transcend our self-centeredness – for Tolstoy genuine transcendence is ethical. We have to efface ourselves and serve others. In both the fictional portrayal of Ivan Ilych and in his autobiographical fragment, Tolstoy depicts an epiphany in which an entire life history comes under judgment, followed by a radical reorientation. There is something total, uncompromising, and final about this. There is a break and then a breakthrough.[15]

Tolstoy's representation of how the most exigent search for meaning can be resolved may strike us as too conclusive or perhaps too hopeful, too redemptive. Should the question of the meaning of life receive so definite an answer? Or is the search in its open-endedness partly constitutive of the answer? It is too facile to say that the search is the answer. Even the belief that one has gotten to an absolute should not arrest the question. Our capacity to shuttle between the view from nowhere and the view from here keeps the question alive, hovering above our ongoing efforts to reintegrate the discrepant stances. I find this shuttling, or better, this struggling, to be characteristic of the Jewish tradition. Its "definite answers" received from the presumed God's-eye viewpoint of revelation constantly dissolve in the give and take of dialogue and interpretation. It is fully apparent in the ancient text known as the Book of Ecclesiastes (or *Kohelet*, in Hebrew) as well as in the classical rabbinic reception of the book.

KOHELET AND THE SEARCH FOR MEANING

The ancient thinker presented in Kohelet poses questions comparable to Tolstoy's, albeit without as certain and hopeful a set of answers. Like Ivan Ilych, Kohelet becomes acutely aware of injustice, both personal and social.[16] (Kohelet was not a prophet, burning with outrage at social sin. It is troubling, but this is just how the world is.[17]) Ivan Ilych was stunned by the gap between living in accord with the accepted moral conventions of his society and the desert that he believed should follow from such a life. It was an absurd injustice that death should arrive so soon. Kohelet makes similar claims.

> Then my thoughts turned to all the fortune my hands had built up, to the wealth I had acquired and won – and oh, it was all futile (*hevel*) and a pursuit of wind; there was no real value under the sun! For what will the man be like who will succeed the one who is ruling over what was built up long ago? (Ecclesiastes 2:11–12)

> So … I loathed all the wealth that I was gaining under the sun. For I shall leave it to the man who will succeed me – and who knows whether he will be wise or foolish? – and he will control all the wealth that I gained by toil and wisdom under the sun. That too is futile. And so I came to view with despair all the gains that I had made under the sun. (Ecclesiastes 2:18–20)
>
> Another grave evil is this: He must depart just as he came. As he came out of his mother's womb, so must he depart at last, naked as he came. He can take nothing of his wealth to carry with him. So what is the good of his toiling for the wind? (Ecclesiastes 5:14–15)[18]

Kohelet observes that one can dedicate oneself, as many do, to the acquisition of wealth but there is no guarantee that one will enjoy it. At any point, one can be swept away by death. ("No man has authority over the lifebreath …." Ecclesiastes 8:8.) One's wealth will go to another who might not deserve it, who hasn't worked for it. Where is the justice in that? Kohelet is not counseling us to repudiate hard work or to despair of its rewards. He is asking us to see that the world does not operate according to our moral logic and expectations. Something is wrong with the world. What we would rationally expect is a relation of agency and fulfillment; one works hard and then gets satisfaction from one's work until one eventually passes away at a ripe old age. But for Kohelet, although the above conjunction might be typical, we shouldn't count on it. There is no necessary connection between virtue and desert. What ultimately occurs is out of our hands. The world should be just, especially given divine control, but it is not. There is a permanent gulf between moral expectation and reality. Unable to give up on either, one is left with a vaporous world where a solid one used to be, or so one thought.[19]

This does not mean, however, that the world is chaotic. It is, on the contrary, under divine guidance. But the *rationality* of divine guidance, the mind of God, as it were, is impenetrable. There is a season for everything, a time for every experience (Ecclesiastes 3:1).

A vast plan runs in the background; we can be dimly aware of it but cannot influence or control it. Kohelet is not a man of prayer. God has determined our fate (*mikreh*) and it is, in broad outline at least, without appeal. We should fear God, but we cannot count on Him. We want to hope for a good outcome in our lives, but our hopes are tinged by anxiety and dread. God Himself has implanted anxiety in us about the future. We cannot free ourselves from it. We must accept both the certainty of our eventual doom and the ongoing constraints of our ignorance about everything else. Under these circumstances, we should seek out the small satisfactions that are available to us.

> I have observed the business that God gave man to be concerned with: He brings everything to pass precisely at its time; He also puts eternity in their mind, but without man ever guessing, from first to last, all the things that God brings to pass. Thus, I realized that the only worthwhile thing there is for them is to enjoy themselves and do whatever is good in their lifetime. (Ecclesiastes 3:10–12)

Kohelet is not a skeptic or a cynic. He doesn't reject the worth of the ethical values that orient daily life in his society. Honest labor is a worthy pursuit. Wisdom, sagacity, discipline, moral uprightness are genuine values. Yet he both affirms them *and* doubts their ultimate efficacy. The values that the Wisdom tradition upholds are not phony. But neither are they secure nor truly vindicated. The world destabilizes them. The world is not so organized that they can prevail. An ultimate negativity – death – shakes the justification of all values.

Although Kohelet affirms that one should be just rather than wicked, the equivalent fate of the just and the wicked threatens the affirmation. It undercuts the justification for righteousness.

> For although I am aware that "It will be well with those who revere God since they revere Him, and it will not be well with the scoundrel, and he will not live long, because he does not revere God – here is a frustration (*hevel*) that occurs in the world:

> Sometimes an upright man is requited according to the conduct of the scoundrel; and sometimes the scoundrel is requited according to the conduct of the upright. I say that all that is frustration (*hevel*). (Ecclesiastes 8:12b–14)[20]

Indeed, not only does death mock value and level any ultimate distinction between the righteous and the wicked, it levels the distinction between human beings and beasts.

> For in respect of the fate of man and the fate of the beast, they have one and the same fate (*mikreh eḥad lahem*): As one dies, so dies the other, and both have the same lifebreath; man has no superiority over the beast, since both amount to nothing (*hevel*). Both came from dust and both return to dust. Who knows if a man's lifebreath does rise upward and if a beast's breath does sink down into the earth? (Ecclesiastes 3:19–21)

It is possible that the beasts are better off than human beings, for humans know what is coming and have to live with the absurdity of that knowledge (Ecclesiastes 9:5). Kohelet goes so far as to claim that it would have been better not to have been (Ecclesiastes 6:3–5).

Kohelet is a sage, a teacher of wisdom. He praises wisdom and believes that the wise are better than the foolish. But unlike the authors of Proverbs or of wisdom psalms, Kohelet envisions the complete breakdown of wisdom.[21] Wisdom (*ḥokhmah*), in the multiple senses of expertise, cannot grant one immunity from moral luck – the arbitrary, but vastly consequential turns that life takes.[22] Whatever benefit wisdom might provide for navigating some of the circumstances of life, it founders on the fact of the final dissolution of life.

> My thoughts also turned to appraising wisdom and madness and folly. I found that wisdom is superior to folly as light is superior to darkness; a wise man has his eyes in his head whereas a fool walks in darkness. But I also realized that the same fate awaits them both. So I reflected: "The fate of the fool is also destined for me; to what advantage, then, have I been wise?" And I came to

> the conclusion that that too was futile (*hevel*), because the wise man, just like the fool, is not remembered forever; for, as the succeeding days roll by, both are forgotten. Alas, the wise man dies, just like the fool. And so I loathed life. For I was distressed by all that goes on under the sun, because everything is futile and pursuit of wind. (Ecclesiastes 2:12b–17)

Kohelet is an absurdist thinker, *avant la lettre*. He is mired in contradictions that he recognizes but cannot resolve; there is no satisfying way out. The justifications for wisdom, confidently tendered by the tradition, are controverted by his own experience as well as by his relentless rational analysis. He has to affirm and deny his way of life, the way of wisdom, simultaneously. He has to break down and reconstruct a meaningful lifeworld with materials that cannot build a secure edifice.

Where does he wind up? Kohelet endorses prudent conduct in the world, moderate piety, and a certain eudaemonism. Holding on to wisdom, he constantly inveighs against rash behavior, against failing to control what little we can control, principally ourselves. The control of our attitudes and our actions (although not, alas, their consequences) is within our grasp: "Better a patient spirit than a haughty spirit. Don't let your spirit be quickly vexed, for vexation abides in the breasts of fools. Don't say, 'How has it happened that former times were better than these?' For it is not wise of you to ask that question" (Ecclesiastes 7:8b–10).

Among the thoughts and actions that we should discipline are those bearing on piety.

> Be not overeager to go to the House of God; more acceptable is obedience than the offering of fools ... (Ecclesiastes 4:17).
>
> When you make a vow to God, do not delay to fulfill it. For He has no pleasure in fools; what you vow, fulfill. It is better not to vow at all than to vow and not fulfill (Ecclesiastes 5:3–4).
>
> In my own brief span of life, I have seen both these things: Sometimes a good man perishes in spite of his goodness, and

> sometimes a wicked one endures in spite of his wickedness. So don't overdo goodness and don't act the wise man to excess, or you may be dumfounded. Don't overdo wickedness and don't be a fool, or you may die before your time. It is best that you grasp the one without letting go of the other, for one who fears God will do his duty by both. (Ecclesiastes 7:15–18)

God has ordained both our portion of wealth and satisfaction in the world, and the hour when we must leave it. Our attitude toward God should mingle gratitude with apprehension. God is more implacable than approachable. We are fundamentally on our own. We must turn to reason and get as much wisdom as we can while also acknowledging that its scope and power are not what we would like them to be.

The goal that should most orient us is joy; we should enjoy the simple satisfactions that God has given us before He takes them (and us) away.

> Go, eat your bread in gladness, and drink your wine in joy; for your action was long ago approved by God. Let your clothes always be freshly washed, and your head never lack ointment. Enjoy happiness with a woman you love all the fleeting days of life (*ḥayei hevelekha*) that have been granted to you under the sun – all your fleeting days. For that alone is what you can get out of life and out of the means you acquire under the sun. Whatever it is in your power to do, do with all your might. For there is no action, no reasoning, no learning, no wisdom in Sheol, where you are going (Ecclesiastes 9:7–10).
>
> How sweet is the light, what a delight for the eyes to behold the sun! Even if a man lives many years, let him enjoy himself in all of them, remembering how many the days of darkness are going to be. The only future is nothingness (*hevel*) (Ecclesiastes 11:9)!
>
> So appreciate your vigor in the days of your youth, before those days of sorrow come and those years of which you will

> say, "I have no pleasure in them"; before sun, and light, and moon and stars grow dark, and the clouds come back again after the rain. (Ecclesiastes 12:1–2)

Kohelet had earlier asked, "What real value (*mah yitron*) is there for a man?" (Ecclesiastes 1:3). *Yitron*, although often given a commercial sense, can mean here: What remains? What is the ultimate answer to life-as-*hevel*? In the judgment of the biblical scholar, Tamara Eskenazi, the above paragraphs are "what remains." His teaching, hard-won in the face of absurdity, is to "take pleasure in the quotidian. Celebrate the gifts. Pay attention. Lower expectations of permanent good or justice but do your part on their behalf. Remember that you will die and live your life with that awareness."[23]

Kohelet has struggled, on this view, to find an affirmation of life that is not defeated by absurdity. The book is a record, as it were, of his experiments in living. The almost nihilistic attitude at the beginning of his quest does not define his conclusion. He had earlier criticized the enjoyment of life. His own experience had taught him the futility of the enjoyment of goods.

> The eye never has enough of seeing, nor the ear of hearing (Ecclesiastes1:8).
>
> A lover of money never has his fill of money, nor a lover of wealth his fill of income. That too is futile (Ecclesiastes 5:9).
>
> All of man's earning is for the sake of his mouth, yet his gullet in not sated. (Ecclesiastes 6:7)

Enjoyment of the present, he thought, was self-defeating. The satisfaction of appetite just sets up the conditions for future appetition. This is as futile as a dog chasing its own tail. Indeed, at one point, Kohelet related how he tried to pursue merriment (*simḥah*) and mirth as ends in themselves but he recoiled at the futility (*hevel*) of doing so, saying "What good is that" (Ecclesiastes 2:2)?[24] Like Tolstoy, pleasure cannot be an end in itself. It has to be made meaningful through successful justification, through answering the no longer childish "why?"

Has he answered it by the end of the book? Kohelet's best answer is to find joy. Enjoy your portion insofar as God has given you one to enjoy. This alone makes meaningful sense of life: "Only this, I have found, is a real good: that one should eat and drink and get pleasure with all the gains he makes under the sun, during the numbered days of his life that God has given him; for that is his portion" (Ecclesiastes 5:17).[25]

How good an answer is this?

In one sense, it is thin gruel. The edifice of meaning built from such materials does not seem secure. It seems extraordinarily vulnerable to fortune and fate (*mikreh*). In another sense, it has the security of living bravely with absurdity. It is a view short on illusion and long on courage. The stress on light and joy anticipates a similar resolution in Camus. Camus, writing of his joy in the landscapes of his native Algeria, couples affirmation with the awareness of absurdity:

> I love this life with abandon and wish to speak of it boldly: it makes me proud of my human condition. Yet people have often told me: there's nothing to be proud of. Yes, there is: this sun, this sea, my heart leaping with youth, the salt taste of my body and this vast landscape in which tenderness and glory merge in blue and yellow. It is to conquer this that I need my strength and resources. Everything here leaves me intact, I surrender nothing of myself, and don no mask: learning patiently and arduously how to live is enough for me, well worth all the arts of living.[26]

Both Kohelet and Camus fall far short of the decisive resolution, the grand narrative coherence sought by Tolstoy. What one wants, ideally, is a definitive end to the regress of why questions as to the value and meaning of life. One wants a transcendent view that doesn't undermine the view from within; a view that is both compatible with affirming the significance of human existence and supportive of it. And one wants this without a deus ex machina, and without illusion. Kohelet has learned to live with less than that. He lives with absurdity. Life, with its moments of surprising joy, has renewed value for him, but absurdity remains undiminished.[27]

To what extent has Judaism sought a decisive, "Tolstoyan" resolution? Or, by contrast, does it allow the aporias and contradictions discovered by Kohelet to stand? To what extent does Judaism let Kohelet's awareness of the putative meaninglessness, futility, and absurdity of human existence leave traces in its thought and life?

THE KOHELET'S JEWISH AFTERLIFE

A preliminary answer to the question of whether the traces of the absurd remain salient is found in the structure of the book itself. Traditional pious readers believed that Kohelet – a title, not a personal name – was Solomon.[28] They thought that Solomon wrote the entire book.[29] However, both the first line of the book and the last five verses are written in another voice; these verses speak about a character with the title Kohelet. The traditional reader thought that Solomon was simply speaking about himself in the third person. The modern reader sees the hand of an editor, framing the words and thought of another figure, real or imagined. What is important here are the last lines. Kohelet's first words proclaim: "Utter futility – said Kohelet – utter futility! All is futile" (Ecclesiastes 1:2). His last words repeat this same formula exactly (Ecclesiastes 12:8), a poignant inclusion. The editor (or epilogist, as scholars call him) does not let the book end on such a bleak note, however. He adds a pious gloss that tries to steer Kohelet's teaching in a more normative direction. He disregards the contradictions and presents Kohelet as an unproblematic teacher of Wisdom. But after having taken away Kohelet's abysmal critique of Wisdom, the epilogist adds his own. Wisdom can be difficult, irritating, and enervating. Better than reliance on human wisdom altogether are simple piety and the observance of God's commandments (*mitzvot* – a term that otherwise does not appear in the book).

> A further word: Because Koheleth was a sage, he continued to instruct the people. He listened to and tested the soundness of many maxims. Koheleth sought to discover useful sayings and recorded genuinely truthful sayings. The sayings of the wise are

> like goads, like nails fixed in prodding sticks. They were given by one Shepherd. A further word: Against them, my son, be warned! The making of books is without limit and much study is a wearying of the flesh. The sum of the matter, when all is said and done: Revere God and observe His commandments (*mitzvotav*)! For this applies to all mankind: that God will call every creature to account for everything unknown, be it good or bad. (Ecclesiastes 12:9–14)

Awareness of absurdity is subordinated to piety – fidelity to Mosaic teaching. Kohelet's words should be understood, from the point of view of the editor, as a contribution to practical wisdom that comports with a life directed to reverence for God and observance of His commandments. Foregrounding Kohelet's practical wisdom effaces his distinctive, absurdist worldview. Eventually, as "wisdom" becomes coextensive with "Torah" for rabbinic Jews, Kohelet is read to advocate conformity with the life of Torah, no more and no less. Kohelet's strong embrace of the absurd leaves but a small trace in the hands of the epilogist, who sets the stage for later Jewish appropriations of the book.

Yet Kohelet's radicalism cannot be entirely suppressed. The ceaseless questioning of wisdom, partly in the name of wisdom, is built into the book. The worries about the meaninglessness of human striving, the groundlessness of human values, and the pall that death casts over life persist. To retain the book is to retain the restlessness of reason that launches it. The Book of Ecclesiastes itself may have emerged from a confrontation, from a clash of perspectives. One interpretation is that the book constitutes an internal dialogue between a conventional proponent of Wisdom and a provocative critic of it, between someone who trusts in a tradition and someone who wants to remain true to his own ragged experience of life. Kohelet stands out as a unique individual, critical of conventions (or at least of the justifications for them) and reliant on his own resources. In addition to his "empiricism," he is aloof from divine revelation. If he knows of it, he brackets its importance or relevance to his own situation.

On this view, the struggle between competing viewpoints is what motivates the book.[30] (A similar case has been made for the *Book of Job*. The "frame story" of Job as a pious man, whom God is provoked to test, motivated the author to protest against such piety and to characterize Job, in the majority of the book, as an uncompromising rebel.[31]) These patterns of acceptance and rejection, reliance and repudiation are known to us from our own experience. Kohelet (and Job) has captured something true to human experience, at least to the experience of people who are moved to question the authorities, conventions, and meanings on which they have relied but also sense the dangers of doing so. "Beginning to think is beginning to be undermined." But not thinking is a stillbirth, a premature death. Kohelet can be tamed, but he cannot be muzzled.

The project of domesticating Kohelet to a less agonistic piety begun by the epilogist is continued by the rabbis. The sages of the Talmud are troubled both by the substance of Kohelet's teaching and by his internal contradictions. Let us first consider objections to the substance, which are recorded not in the Talmud as such but in ancillary rabbinic literature. In *Pesikta d'Rav Kahana*, section 8, we read:

> *What profit hath a man of all his labor wherein he laboreth under the sun?* (Ecclesiastes 1:3). R. Benjamin bar Levi said: The Sages were about to suppress the Book of Ecclesiastes, having found in it ideas which smacked of heresy (*matin l'tzad ha-minut*). They said: Should Solomon have given utterance to such a thought as [that]? This question might imply – might it not? – that Solomon meant to include labor in the study of Torah. But then the Sages decided otherwise, declaring: Had Solomon said *What profit hath a man of all labor* and refrained from being more precise, we might have suspected that he also meant to include labor in the study of Torah. However, by saying *of all* ***his*** *labor*, Solomon implied that there is no profit for a man in laboring for himself, but that there is profit in his laboring at the study of Torah.[32]

On the rabbinic view, championed by Rabbi Akiba, that every word of Scripture, no matter how small, bears tremendous meaning, the sages decide that Kohelet's use of "his" in the phrase "all his labor" makes a crucial difference. Kohelet's dire assessment of the fecklessness of human action might have been thought to include "labor in the Torah." Had Kohelet simply said "all labor" that conclusion would have been inescapable. But specifying "all his labor" limited the category of labor to self-serving action. Labor in the Torah, by contrast is in service to God. It is a commandment, a duty to the Creator, which should be performed selflessly, out of love, and gratitude.

The text goes on to set up an apparent clash between Solomon's ostensibly "heretical" view and the "orthodox" view of Moses:

> R. Samuel bar R. Isaac also said: The Sages were about to suppress the Book of Ecclesiastes, having found in it ideas which smacked of heresy. They asked: Should Solomon have given utterance to advice such as *Rejoice, O young man, in thy youth; and let thy heart cheer thee in the days of thy youth, and walk in the ways of thy heart, and in the sight of thine eyes* (Ecclesiastes 11:9)? For, though Moses had declared, *Go not about after your own heart and your own eyes* (Num. 15:39), Solomon said, *Walk in the ways of thy heart and in the sight of thine eyes*, as though all restraint were removed and there were neither justice nor Judge (*leyt din v'leyt dayan*). Since Solomon went on to say, however, *But know that for all these things God will bring thee into judgment* (Ecclesiastes 11:9) *[the Sages decided that] Solomon had spoken well after all.*[33]

Kohelet's own qualification on his eudaemonism – that God will ultimately call one to account for one's behavior – constrains the possibilities for licentiousness and rescues the text in the view of the sages. Although some modern commentators claim that this verse is an addition, it is not out of keeping with Kohelet's sense of restraint and moderation.[34] The rabbis fully acknowledge the challenge that Kohelet seems to raise. Not only does he conflict directly with Moses, but he invites the unthinkable: that there might be "no justice and no Judge," a view linked to rabbinic Judaism's arch heretic, Elisha ben Abuyah or Aḥer (literally, the "Other").[35]

The rabbis paint a picture of suspicion toward Kohelet. In biblical times, the midrash on *Pirke Avot, Avot d'Rabbi Natan*, reports, King Hezekiah's men studied Kohelet's words closely.[36] Alarmed by what they found, they removed the book from public use. Centuries later, the Men of the Great Assembly found ways to reconcile Kohelet's teaching with Scripture, such as the above interpretation, and brought the book back to acceptability. But there was yet another hurdle to surmount. Even if its teachings were acceptable, they contradicted one another. Doesn't that impugn their credibility? Kohelet's eventual secure place in the canon depended on accepting a view of it as inspired, as divine wisdom. But can divine wisdom contradict itself? (Wouldn't *that* lead to absurd conclusions?) The rabbis needed an interpretive strategy to harmonize the contradictions. The classic discussion in the Gemara (the body of the Talmud) at B. Shabbat 30b begins as follows.[37]

> **Rav Yehuda, son of Rav Shmuel bar Sheilat, said in the name of Rav: The Sages sought to suppress the book of Ecclesiastes** and declare it apocryphal **because its statements contradict each other** and it is liable to confuse its readers. **And why did they not suppress it? Because its beginning** consists of **matters of Torah and its end** consists of **matters of Torah**. The ostensibly contradictory details are secondary to the essence of the book, which is Torah.

The contradictions as much as the content seem to raise suspicions. Rav Yehuda says that the Sages sought to "suppress" (*lignoz*) the book. This might mean that "canonicity" was still a live issue. Or it might mean that the book was considered scripture but the question of its public use remained controversial.[38] Additionally, political considerations bore on the rabbinic debate. Two competing early schools, the House of Hillel and the House of Shammai, had diametrically opposed views on whether the book was sacred. The Hillelites won out. It seems that the risk of confusing the reader was worth taking, given the valuable Torah that the book contained. The challenge then was to normalize its teaching. The rabbis dispelled their concerns by finding normative rabbinic teaching (Torah) both at the beginning and the end of the book. The end, which presumes to sum up and consummate the teaching is the epilogist's conclusion. The beginning is Kohelet's remark, as interpreted by the rabbinic sages[39]:

> The Gemara elaborates: **Its beginning** consists of **matters of Torah, as it is written: "What profit has man of all his labor which he labors under the sun?"** (Ecclesiastes 1:3), **and** the Sages of **the school of Rabbi Yannai said:** By inference: **Under the sun is where** man **has no** profit from his labor; however, **before the sun**, i.e., when engaged in the study of Torah, which preceded the sun, **he does have** profit. **Its ending** consists of **matters of Torah, as it is written: "The end of the matter, all having been heard: Fear God, and keep His mitzvot; for this is the whole man."** (Ecclesiastes 12:13)

As in the prior discussion about the object of labor, the rabbis redeem the text here through making a crucial distinction. Kohelet's signature phrase, "under the sun" (*taḥat ha-shemesh*), which, in context, means something like "where daily life takes place" is taken to mean "in profane matters." The implication is that all of Kohelet's indictments of the absurdity of life *apply only to life without Torah*. The person whose work is directed only to worldly goods is, in fact, leading a futile, meaningless life. The life of Torah, with its holy and transcendent orientation is the only true life. Once again, Kohelet's radicalism is contained; all of his negative judgments *are* true, but they stop, so to speak, at the door of the yeshiva. Torah, which in a famous rabbinic midrash is one of the things that precedes the creation of the universe ("before the sun") is infinitely valuable.[40] It is the proper focus of a meaningful life.

The Aramaic translation/interpretation, called Targum, assumes this view and draws out a further implication. "After one dies, what advantage does he have from all the labor that he performs under the sun in this world, unless he has busied himself with Torah so as to receive a full reward before the Master of the Universe in the hereafter."[41]

For this author, as for many of the rabbis who follow him, the rabbinic conviction of a world to come arrests the sense of absurdity. The opening up of a post-mortem horizon short-circuits Kohelet's troubling questions. If there is a posthumous recompense, Kohelet's judgment of the injustice of it all loses its sting. A meaningful world is restored, albeit at the price of a certain hermeneutic malpractice. One has to impose an alien or, more generously, an additional world of beliefs upon the book. (The rabbis were not, as it were, "originalists.") The Talmud's discussion about the contradictions does just that[42]:

> **And** to the essence of the matter, the Gemara asks: **What is** the meaning of: **Its statements** that **contradict each other? It is written: "Vexation is better than laughter"** (Ecclesiastes 7:3), **and it is written: "I said of laughter: It is praiseworthy"** (Ecclesiastes 2:2), which is understood to mean that laughter is commendable. Likewise in one verse **it is written: "So I commended mirth"** (Ecclesiastes 8:15), **and** in another verse **it is written: "And of mirth: What does it accomplish?."** (Ecclesiastes 2:2)

Rather than see these two contradictory statements about laughter and mirth as inconsistencies in Kohelet's thought, the Gemara refers them to different, morally justified, responses on the part of God.[43]

> The Gemara answers: This is **not difficult**, as the contradiction can be resolved. **Vexation is better than laughter** means: The **vexation** of **the Holy One, Blessed be He, toward the righteous in this world is preferable to the laughter which the Holy One, Blessed be He, laughs with the wicked in this world** by showering them with goodness. **I said of laughter: It is praiseworthy, that is**

> **the laughter which the Holy One, Blessed be He, laughs with the righteous in the World-to-Come.**

Now that the human behaviors of vexation and laughter are referred to God, the Gemara transposes them into the key of theodicy. While the wicked prosper in this world (their unworried enjoyment of their wicked lives implies that God is laughing with them) and the righteous suffer (God is vexed at them, in order to purge them of sin so that they enjoy an eternity of bliss), all of this will be reversed in the *olam ha-ba*, the world to come.

The Gemara's gloss on Kohelet's contradictory treatment of joy (or "mirth," *simḥah*) keeps the emotion in the human sphere but introduces a categorical distinction between the objects of joy.[44]

> Similarly, **"So I commended mirth,"** that **is the joy of a mitzva. "And of mirth: What does it accomplish?" that is joy that is not** the joy **of a mitzva.** The praise of joy mentioned here is **to teach you that the Divine Presence rests** upon an individual **neither from** an atmosphere of **sadness, nor from** an atmosphere of **laziness, nor from** an atmosphere of **laughter, nor from** an atmosphere of **frivolity, nor from** an atmosphere of **idle conversation, nor from** an atmosphere of **idle chatter, but rather from** an atmosphere imbued with **the joy of a mitzva**.

The rabbis distinguish between common or profane joy and *simḥah shel mitzvah*, the "joy of the commandment." Although they certainly don't rule out common joy, they were concerned about how much joy one should allow oneself to feel after the destruction of the Temple and under the conditions of exile. The joy that should accompany the observance of the divine commandments is exempt from those concerns. It is more appropriate to the rabbinic way of life than the "profane" or common joy that human beings feel when life goes well. They take Kohelet's commendation of joy to refer to the joy of the commandment and his doubt about the value of joy to refer to "joy that is not about the commandment." To make this point perfectly clear, they add that God's very presence (Shekinah) rests upon those whose emotions are appropriately formed by their observance of the Torah's commands. One is never simply alone with one's feelings; God is near or far depending on the moral quality of one's emotions.

These thoughts are far from Kohelet's, for whom God is always distant and mostly inscrutable. Furthermore, the common joys that the rabbis marginalize are precisely those at the center of Kohelet's salvage operation. Enjoying natural, "secular" moments of youth, vigor, wealth, food, and drink is basic to a meaningful life. Such moments do not insulate against moral luck nor are they exempt from absurdity, but they are the best we can do. The transcendent register to which the rabbis would relegate joy is unknown to Kohelet.

The rabbinics scholar, Ruth Sandberg, discerns in *Kohelet Rabbah*, an early medieval collection of rabbinic midrashim, four interpretive strategies. The first two interpret the most challenging or offensive passages of Kohelet out of existence. A remark of Kohelet, for example, may be taken as symbolism. Thus, the phrase "the sun rises and the sun sets," since it states a point so obvious as not to be worth stating, is taken to mean, symbolically, the birth and death of the righteous. The symbolic approach has no time for Kohelet's straightforward claims. In the second interpretive mode, what a verse says is overshadowed by what it doesn't say. Thus, the repeated assertion that "all is futile and a pursuit of wind," implies, for the midrash, "except repentance and good deeds." In the third mode, the rabbis acknowledge that some of Kohelet's statements have truth to them, but only in specific situations. "Utter futility. All is futile" is not *the* truth of human existence; it is a partial truth. An existence oriented toward Torah prevents that partial truth from becoming the whole truth. In the fourth mode of interpretation, however, the rabbis accept Kohelet's straightforward meaning as well as the cogency of the context in which it is asserted. They do not try to reinterpret the meaning out of existence or meet it halfway; they accept it as is. Whether this expresses a deep agreement with his absurdist analysis or rather the effect of a methodology that seeks the plain meaning of the text (*peshat*) is open to debate.[45] If we are looking for a place in the rabbinic reception of Kohelet where latitude is given to his absurdist stance, *Kohelet Rabbah* gives us a few.

On "Utter futility!" – said Koheleth – "Utter futility!" "All is futile!" (Ecclesiastes 1:2), the midrash interprets:

> If someone else had said, "Utter futility," I might have said that this person who had never owned two coins in his life belittles the wealth of the world and declares "Utter futility." But it was concerning Solomon that it was written: "And the king made silver to be as plentiful in Jerusalem as stones" (I Kings 10:27) .... Why did he say "Utter futility?" He saw the world and its future at the end.[46]

Solomon, as a wealthy and powerful man, knew of what he spoke. He had the authority to reject the worth of wealth and power. As a wise man, he foresaw the end; he saw the whole sub specie aeternitatis. The rabbis let him offer his negative judgment on existence without correction. The judgment "utter futility" in Kohelet's premonition of the end is allowed to replace the judgment of "good" in God's assessment of the beginning. Whether existence is fundamentally good, as the Creation story would have it, or fundamentally futile and meaningless, as Kohelet would have it is a matter of great import. This is a remarkable – and atypical – moment in rabbinic literature.[47]

Another such moment is found in the midrash's comment to Ecclesiastes 3:9: "What value (*yitron*) then can the man of affairs get from what he earns?" The context of this verse is the characterization of existence as a fateful repetition of cycles. All is determined and comes in in its proper season. If it is determined that one will realize value from striving, then he will; if not, not. (This is similar to the "lazy argument" directed against the Stoics.[48]) Rather than interpolate a confident statement about receiving a reward in the world to come, the midrash just lets the matter stand: "Solomon said: Since there are times for all things, what value has the craftsman in his craft and the righteous man (*kasheira*) in his righteousness (*kashrutay*)?" A related view appears in the Talmud (B. Moed Katan 28a): "Life, sons, and wealth do not depend upon merit (*zekhuta*), but upon luck (*mazala*)." The rabbis bracket their extensive theology of a morally perspicuous divine providence here and cast past and future onto the tides of moral luck. God governs how time, change, and life unfold but God's governance is inscrutable and tantamount to fate.

A final example of *Kohelet Rabbah* letting a problematic view stand is its midrash on Ecclesiastes 5:14: "Just as he came naked from his mother's womb, so must he depart. He can take none of the wealth he earned along with him." The midrash expands on this melancholy truth with a parable:

> This is like a fox that found a vineyard which was fenced in on all sides. There was one hole through which he tried to enter, but he was not able. What did he do? He fasted for three days until he was thin and weak, and he went through the hole. He ate and grew fat. When he wanted to leave, he could not fit through the hole. Again he fasted three more days until he grew thin and weak as he had done before and then left. When he had departed, he turned and looked and said: Vineyard, vineyard! How good you are, and how good are the fruits inside! Everything inside you is wonderful and praiseworthy. But vineyard, what benefit comes from you? Just as one goes inside so does one depart. Thus also is this world.[49]

The world is wonderful. One wants to enter it and will suffer whatever deprivation one has to in order to do so. It is less clear why one has to leave it, but one does, suffering deprivation for that purpose as well. After one has left the world, one looks back appreciatively at its goodness. But the goodness remains fenced in, lingering only in memory. What has been accomplished? What benefit remains, if any? The coming and going brackets a world now lost. The loss overshadows whatever gain once occurred. The episode, which once defined life and made it good, seems splendidly isolated, suspended, and impotent. There is more than melancholy here. There is a retrospective undermining of value.

In general, Jewish interpretation does not let this stand. Consider the classic medieval commentator, Rabbi Shlomo ben Yitzhak, known as Rashi (d. 1105). Rashi's commentaries are informed by the resources of midrash; he continues the approach of harmonizing Kohelet with the perspectives of rabbinic Judaism.

On Kohelet's dour view of the relentlessly cyclical character of nature – "Only that shall happen that has happened, only that occur which has occurred. There is nothing new beneath the sun! (Ecclesiastes 1:9)" – Rashi writes, "in all that one learns that occurs under the circuits of the sun, there is nothing new. There is only what was created during the six days of creation. But the one who contemplates Torah always finds new reasoning in it."[50] Rashi contrasts the endless repetition of nature with the intellectual dynamism of Torah, a work that comes alive in hermeneutic interaction with its devotees. Moreover, since it is divine teaching, it is as if God reserved the freshness of discovery for Torah, leaving nature to tedious predictability. Rashi implies that meaning in a hermeneutic sense can only be found in the word of God, not in probing the acts of God as they were congealed into physical reality.

Kohelet, as we recall, is pained by the injustice of death cavalierly wiping out distinctions between the righteous and the wicked (and the animals). He finds it absurd to have worked so hard to become wise, since death will give him the same fate as a fool. And, "as the succeeding days roll by, both are forgotten" (Ecclesiastes 2:16). Rashi takes Kohelet's judgment on the absurdity of fate and transforms it into a self-indictment or a warning that Kohelet gives himself. "*And I said in my heart,* if I were to think this way [that the remembrance of the righteous and the wicked were equivalent], it would be absurd (*hevel*) for me to do so." Rather than making a grim judgment on our fate in the world, Kohelet is reminding himself, in Rashi's reading, not to be confused about the superior outcome that awaits the righteous.

The same is true for the superiority of humans over animals. At Ecclesiastes 3:19, "For in respect of the fate of man and the fate of beast, they have one and the same fate: as one dies, so dies the other and both have the same lifebreath; man has no superiority over beast since both amount to nothing (*hevel*)," Rashi almost seems to endorse Kohelet's view.

> The Holy One, Blessed be He, gives doom and injury to human beings. There is also doom and injury for the beasts. He gave this to both of them for just as this one dies, so that one dies. And the advantage of humans over beasts is nothing. For the superiority and the success of man do not appear insofar as he dies, and everything becomes nothing (*hevel*) and the dust returns to the earth.

Nonetheless, one can see, reading closely, that Rashi is not saying humans have no superiority over animals whatsoever but only that the superiority which they do have isn't evident in the shared circumstances of their mortality. What then does the superiority consist in? Glossing the next verse, where Kohelet opines that no one can know whether man's "lifebreath" ascends and the beast's descends, Rashi claims:

> Whoever knows and understands, let him attend to the fact that the spirit of man ascends and stands in judgment before the divine throne, while the spirit of the beast descends below into the earth where it does not have to give an account of itself. Therefore, it is necessary for human beings not to behave as beasts, who do not care about their actions.

While Kohelet reduces human distinctiveness to nullity, Rashi fortifies it. He not only distinguishes the human soul from the animating force within animals, he uses this distinction to clinch a moral argument. We are, in the most essential respect, unlike beasts and should not therefore confusedly act as if we were. Kohelet poses no threat. Rashi does not allow Kohelet's courting of absurdity to disturb the meaningfulness of rabbinic Judaism.

To return then to our initial question, does rabbinic Judaism let Kohelet's intuition of absurdity stand or is it anxious to interpret it away? The record is mixed. It is understandable that Kohelet's "heretical" sayings should provoke concern. The rabbis tried to domesticate the book, to bring it into line with their evolving and diverse views. They test the limits of doxastic and ethical acceptability. They struggle with the text and seek its meaning in an irreducible variety of ways. The interpretive pluralism of Judaism is one of its glories. Judaism does not spare its adherents the opportunity for intellectual and moral struggle. Kohelet not only gives rise to struggle; it was itself born of struggle. There is a struggle between the different voices within the book – the voice of confident, traditional wisdom and the voice of a diffident critique of such wisdom. There is a struggle between the contrary voices of the text and its editor, who places the work in an acceptably pious frame. Kohelet struggles with different attempts to solve his problem. Subsequently, there is a struggle among the rabbinic authorities about the status and implications of the book – inspired or secular? Holy or profane? Edifying or dangerous? And there is a struggle over how to read its teachings – in conformity with an overall rabbinic worldview or implacably dissident?

Fixing the book into the canon of scripture did not put these questions to rest. If it was accepted because it was thought to be inspired, with Solomon effectively playing the role of a prophet of God, as the Targum implied, then, bluntly, why would God inspire such sayings as "all is futile"? What kind of divine teaching is *that*? Far from relieving the reader's concerns, the assumption of divine inspiration raised the stakes for reinterpreting such strange, divinely sanctioned words. It sets up a tension, evident in the midrash itself, between interpretations that salve the wounds Kohelet inflicts on conventional opinion and interpretations that keep his straightforward (*peshat*) views alive. Throughout it all, a trace of the absurd remains.

Kohelet and its reception root the question of the meaning of life in an ancient Jewish framework. I have tried to show that questions about the meaning of life are not purely modern, "Death of

God" affairs. Nor are they alien to Judaism. What emerges from Kohelet and its Jewish interpretation are not facile answers but ways of struggling with existential questions. Judaism gives us less a catalogue of presumptive answers than a framework for managing ineliminable perplexity. Rather than provide blanket resolutions to the most troubling doubts about the worth and meaning of it all, Jewish texts preserve and present those doubts, as well as the open-ended struggle to resolve them. Although it is the case that the tradition often tries its best to quell the doubts, the doubts remain. To have accepted Kohelet into the canon is to allow its absurdist elements to continue to provoke.

THE PLAN OF THE BOOK

In Chapter 1, we explore the concept of the meaning of life. The chapter focuses on the historical background and the philosophical issues, as conceptualized by recent (mostly) Anglo-American analytic philosophers. The terms "meaning," "the absurd," and "nihilism" are vague, historically freighted, and contested. The chapter brings greater clarity to these terms, their concepts, and their linguistic and conceptual histories. I assess the problem of the meaning of life as a predominantly modern problem, as well as the status of the meaning question, in contrast to other and older questions about the human good.

In addition to gaining clarity on the state of the question, I argue for a specific understanding of meaning: Meaning arises from our attempts to interpret the values that confront us in our lives. We are constantly about the business of ordering values, resolving conflicts among them, seeking a coherent way of justifying and integrating them into a livable whole. Our construals of meaning are relatively free and open-ended, but not indefinitely so. Value is not arbitrary, nor should our interpretations of its significance be. Value imposes some constraints on how we respond to it. Meaning is not a sheerly subjective matter. There are better and worse construals of meaning, whether the meaning of a text or the meaning of a life.

For Jews, at least, inherited, traditional interpretations of valued aspects of life have scaffolded meaning. Nature has been conceptualized in terms of a story about creation. The grounds of value have been explored through a story about revelation. Finally, the end of it all – where time, history, and humanity are going – has been interpreted in terms of a story of redemption. Chapters 2–4 of the book take up these meaning-structuring Jewish stories.

Thus, Chapter 2, on "Creation," analyzes Jewish thinking about the value and meaning of the natural world and of the human place within it. I take Creation to be a story about value, not first and foremost a story about physical cosmogony. Given this framing of creation, the motivating questions are: Is the world as such good, bad, indifferent, or absurd? Does the world provide us with inherent standards of value such that we can live by them and find life meaningful in accord with them or is something missing? Is nature, so to speak, enough? To address these questions, the chapter contrasts the claim of the goodness of creation (in Genesis, chapter 1) with a counterclaim as to its brokenness. It then puts the internally contested story of creation into dialogue with contemporary philosophical attempts to find meaning in a strictly naturalistic universe. The chapter probes whether naturalistic, science-dominated philosophical construals of the meaning of life are plausible. Can Jewish perspectives offer anything cogent in the face of radically secular responses to the question of the meaning of life? I find elements of absurdity in both sets of responses. Meaning is chastened on both accounts.

Chapter 3, "Revelation," begins with the Jewish intuition that nature is *not* enough. The chapter explores Jewish thinking about the normative dimension of human experience, especially the phenomena of ethics and law. In Jewish theological terms, it enquires into God's role in revealing normative guidance. Given a foundational Jewish belief in revelation, what is its relation to human reason, to human assessments of value? To what extent does revelation depend on human acceptance, participation, and articulation? Is the authority of revelation objective? "What is Divine about Divine Law?"[51]

My approach is to treat revelation less as a putative historical event at Mt. Sinai and more as a story, a genealogy, of normative authority. As such, revelation invites ongoing inquiry into the nature and sources of value, and hence of the possibilities for meaning. This genealogical characterization of revelation is not just a consequence of modern skepticism. Ancient Jewish texts *themselves* problematize both the divine and the human contribution to normativity. Without human receptivity to and incorporation of norms, what would their status be? Without human acceptance, would divine teaching, assuming for the sake of argument that it exists, even matter?

Debates over the grounds and status of normativity in Jewish thought are comparable to the philosophical problem of objectivity versus subjectivity with regard to meaning in life. Both discourses explore the human role in generating and justifying norms. Is there an objective answer to the question of what constitutes a meaningful life or are there indefinitely many subjective answers? Is meaning "out there" to be discovered? Or is it our own projection – something that we can affirm, even *ought* to affirm, in full recognition of its objective groundlessness?

Philosophically, there is debate in the literature between subjectivists and objectivists – and nihilists who view both positions as fatally flawed. The chapter explores these philosophical positions. It then asks whether purely secular accounts of meaningfulness are robust enough to preempt nihilism or is the latter the most honest, even heroic, view? Are Jewish accounts sufficiently plausible to preempt it?

Although these questions must be explored, they cannot receive doubt-resistant answers. Nonetheless, I don't think that the problems with subjectivism and objectivism license nihilism. Oriented toward what John Cottingham calls "the primacy of praxis," I will argue in Chapter 4 that hopeful, courageous human action is the best *practical* response to terminal uncertainty about the grounding of norms and the tenability of meaning. Virtuous human action, I conclude is not just *faute de mieux*; it is the foundation of the most meaningful life for human beings. I argue that moral and intellectual virtues are basically constitutive of meaningful lives on any remotely plausible account of meaning. Emphasis on practical virtues, such as courage, steadfastness, and fidelity have been integral to Jewish reflections on the meaning of life. Nonetheless, without a transcendent dimension the meaning of the practical virtues may be circumscribed.

The last category of the Jewish theological trinity is Redemption. Redemption focuses our thought on the future, albeit not as an exercise in fortune telling. The future that we hope for (or dread) redirects us to the meaning of human action here and now. To what extent does human action, virtuous or otherwise, shape the future? To what extent does the world go its accustomed way? To what extent does a divine plan supervene on human action or subvert it? These large questions inform Jewish imaginations of redemption.

Philosophically, the chapter engages with perhaps the most intellectually compelling contemporary proponent of nihilism, James Tartaglia. Tartaglia maintains that life is (simply, as a matter of fact) meaningless. There is no context in which to ask the question of the meaning *of* life that will produce a substantive answer. Since the question is unanswerable, we are left not just with doubt about an answer but with the need to accept that there is no answer. Being unable to answer the question of the meaning of life does not imply, for Tartaglia, that the question stands, but that the question ends. There is no meaning to life. The chapter offers a Jewish philosophical response to such nihilism.

In the conclusion, I step back and reassess the absurdity generating framework that gives rise to problems of justifying meaning. I question the extent of the authority of the austere view, which diminishes our significance by contextualizing our being into a wide, cosmic context. The "view from nowhere" does have authority, but should we grant it a monopoly on epistemic authority, if only briefly? Or is it, too, answerable to values that are constitutive of human life – of human acting and knowing? The latter should be answered in the affirmative, I believe.

NOTES

1 The phrase is Charles Taylor's. See his *A Secular Age* (Cambridge: Belknap Press, 2007), p. 543.

2 Martin Buber, *Between Man and Man* (New York: Macmillan, 1965), p. 184.

3 See the interview with Patricia Churchland, "The Benefits of Realising You're Just a Brain," *New Scientist*, 27 November 2013, www.newscientist.com/article/mg22029450-200-the-benefits-of-realising-youre-just-a-brain/ (accessed September 6, 2021). See also Alan Mittleman, *Human Nature and Jewish Thought* (Princeton: Princeton University Press, 2015), p. 116.

4 Wilfred Sellars, "Philosophy and the Scientific Image of Man," in *Science, Perception, and Reality* (Atascadero, CA: Ridgeview Publishing Co., 1991), pp. 1–40. For a discussion, see Mittleman, *Human Nature and Jewish Thought*, pp. 25–28.

5 Leo Tolstoy, *The Death of Ivan Ilyich and Confession*, Peter Carson, trans. (New York: Liveright Publishing, 2014), p. 110.

6 Albert Camus, *The Myth of Sisyphus*, Justin O'Brien, trans. (New York: Vintage Books, 2018), p. 4.

7 This is the general approach of Iddo Landau. See Iddo Landau, *Finding Meaning in an Imperfect World* (New York: Oxford University Press, 2017).

8 Thomas Nagel, *Mortal Questions* (Cambridge: Cambridge University Press, 1979), p. 15.

9 Tolstoy, *The Death of Ivan Ilyich and Confession*, pp. 139–140. See also pp. 130–131, where Tolstoy arraigns every one of his accomplishments and future plans before the court of "Why?" and finds each one empty.

10 Tolstoy, *The Death of Ivan Ilyich*, p. 148.

11 Ibid., p. 156.

12 Ibid., pp. 165–166.

13 Ibid., p. 166.

14 Ibid., p. 178.

15 The picture is more complicated when we look at *War and Peace*, where Prince Andrei's and Pierre's epiphanies have more nuanced and inconsistent consequences.

16 In using the name "Kohelet" here, I mean to indicate (a) the character depicted in the text who speaks words of wisdom or (b) the book as a

whole. I do not mean to imply that Kohelet is the actual author of the text. Additionally, some of the translations and books that will be cited transliterate Kohelet as "Qohelet" or "Koheleth." I will use "Kohelet" for the sake of consistency, but when a cited author uses another spelling, I will not alter his or her spelling.

17 See, for example, Ecclesiastes 4:1–3 and 5:7–8.

18 All biblical translations are from the New Jewish Publication Society (NJPS) version, which frequently translates *hevel* as "futile." Michael V. Fox takes *hevel* to mean, often but not always, "absurd." Although "futile," "frustration," "ephemeral," etc. are sometimes apt, Fox writes: "*hevel*" means "senseless" or "absurd," not in the sense of ludicrous but in the sense of counterrational, a violation of reason. Facts or scenarios (which would not naturally be called futile or brief) are judged to be absurd .... In 2:18–26, what is *hevel* is the fact that the wealth Koheleth laboriously accumulated will go to someone else after his death – someone who did not work for it, no less. This violates Koheleth's sense of fairness and reason. Koheleth sees numerous such contradictions in the world, which violate rational expectations and lead him to call everything *hevel*." Michael V. Fox, *The JPS Bible Commentary: Ecclesiastes* (Philadelphia: The Jewish Publication Society, 2004), p. xix. The concept of absurdity in Ecclesiastes is thoroughly worked out by Fox in Michael V. Fox, *A Time to Tear Down and a Time to Build Up: A Rereading of Ecclesiastes* (Grand Rapids: Wm. B. Eerdmans Publishing, 1999).

19 The original meaning of *hevel* is vapor, as in breath – what one sees, for example, on a cold day. It lasts a few seconds and then is gone. The murdered son of Adam and Eve, whose name is fixed in English as Abel, is in the original biblical Hebrew *hevel*.

20 NJPS translates ירא as "revere." Fox remarks that "Hebrew root y-r-'; better, here and throughout Ecclesiastes: 'fear'. Koheleth's unpredictable and aloof deity provokes real fear and consternation, not only pious reverence." Fox, *JPS Bible Commentary*, p. 24.

21 Kohelet is not the first sage in the Wisdom literature to notice that the outcomes we expect from a life lived according to the regnant values often defy our moral expectations. The Wisdom literature sometimes relativizes its values, including that of wisdom. What is unique about Kohelet is his method, his reliance on his own experience rather than on inherited norms and traditions of Wisdom. He is personal and

empirical. His book knows nothing of revelation, of the God of Sinai. (He does know of the sacrificial cult and the Temple.) The book is as close to philosophy as the Hebrew Bible gets. Fox, *A Time to Tear Down and a Time to Build Up*, pp. 80–81, 85–86.

22 Kohelet's tragic wisdom would more resemble Bernard Williams' views than that of Kant. Morality cannot be made immune to luck, nor can it transcend luck. See Bernard Williams, *Moral Luck* (Cambridge: Cambridge University Press, 1999), pp. 38–39.

23 Tamara Eskenazi, personal communication (2020).

24 Tolstoy, in his *Confession*, tells of his attempt to satisfy himself with the pleasures of daily life in order to ward off his worries about life's meaning. But the attempt to equate the meaning of life with the enjoyment of pleasure robbed pleasure of meaning. Meaning requires its own register of reflection. See Tolstoy, *Confession*, pp. 129–132.

25 Perhaps the emphasis should be put on the pleasures of one's portion having been given to one *by God*. The experience of pleasure is not sufficient unto itself; the meaning of pleasure as one's divinely given portion is what imparts meaning to the experience, making it humanly intelligible or appropriable. Alternatively, Lenn Goodman suggests that what Kohelet comes to realize is that the negative dimensions of his experience are only possible because of the positive goods that underlie it. The basic goods of existence remain good – and so available to meaningful appropriation – the distortion and negativity of experience notwithstanding. See Lenn Goodman, "Kohelet and the Search for Meaning," in David Birnbaum and Martin S. Cohen, *Search for Meaning* (New York: New Paradigm Matrix, 2018) p. 237.

26 Cited in Morton Høi Jensen, "Without God or Reason," *Commonweal*, January 2021, www.commonwealmagazine.org/without-god-or-reason (accessed January 3, 2021).

27 The French philosopher Catherine Chalier stresses the surprising nature of joy. The surprise breaks the monotony of the "a time for this, a time for that" pattern and distinguishes joy from mere pleasure, personal communication (2022).

28 The ancient Aramaic translation, the Targum, even interpolates Solomonic authorship into its rendering of the first verse: "The words of prophesy, which Kohelet, who was Solomon the son of David, the King in Jerusalem, prophesied" (Ecclesiastes 1:1). The Targum not only asserts Solomonic authorship, a blanket assumption of all rabbinic

literature, but elevates Solomon's wisdom to the rank of divinely inspired prophesy, signaling to the Aramaic reader that nothing in the text should be suspected of going against divine teaching.

29 The premise of Solomonic authorship was near universal in antiquity. It secured the book's place in the developing canon. Although rabbinic leaders had doubts as to whether the book "defiled the hands" – their counterintuitive phrase for canonicity – even on the view that it was canonical, they questioned whether the book should be withdrawn from public use because of its contradictory teachings. For a discussion, see *Encyclopaedia Judaica*, 2nd edition, vol. 3, s.v. Bible: The Canon (Macmillan Reference, 2007) p. 575. A possible exception to the presumption of Solomonic authorship is B. Bava Batra 15a, which holds that King Hezekiah and his men wrote Kohelet and several other books. Rashi takes the verb to mean "copied."

30 See André Neher, *Notes sur Qohélét* (L'Ecclésiaste) (Paris: Les Éditions de Minuit, 1998). For some concerns about this approach, as exemplified by a contemporary scholar, see Fox, *A Time to Tear Down and a Time to Build Up*, pp. 25; 274–275. Fox's concern is that the Wisdom tradition itself sometimes relativizes its own values. This makes it difficult to set up a strict opposition of wisdom and its critique. Fox sees Kohelet's contradictions as *necessary*. Given the absurd nature of reality, it is appropriate that he contradicts himself with competing assessments and prescriptions.

31 See Bruce Zuckerman, *Job the Silent: A Study in Historical Counterpoint* (New York: Oxford University Press, 1991).

32 William G. Braude, Israel J. Kapstein, and Yehiel Poupko, trans. *Pesikta de-Rab Kahana : R. Kahana's Compilation of Discourses for Sabbaths and Festal Days* (Philadelphia: Jewish Publication Society, 1975), p. 154.

33 Braude, Kaplan, and Poupko, *Pesikta de-Rab Kahana : R. Kahana's Compilation of Discourses for Sabbaths and Festal Days*, p. 154. [The author has transliterated Hebrew for two critical expressions.]

34 See Fox, *A Time to Tear Down*, p. 318.

35 For the main story of Aḥer's turn toward apostasy, see B. Kiddushin 39b.

36 *Avot d'Rabbi Natan*, I:4.

37 The following translation/interpretation is called the William Davidson Talmud and is taken from Sefaria.org, www.sefaria.org/Shabbat.30b .3?lang=bi&with=all&lang2=en. The bold print represents the actual (translated) words of the gemara. The lighter font represents the

translator's bridging remarks. The Talmud is famously abbreviated and concise, typically speaking in a kind of coded technical language. The remarks make its utterances more explicit.

38 There are claims and counterclaims about the status of the book in the Mishna. See M. Yadaim 3:5 and M. Eduyot 5:3. Sages of the House of Shammai did not believe that Ecclesiastes should join the canon; sages of the House of Hillel did. See also Tosefta Yadaim 2:14. In the Talmud, B. Megillah 7a, the disputants question whether Solomon's wisdom was divinely inspired or purely human. The conclusion is that the sayings in Ecclesiastes are a divinely inspired subset of Solomon's prolific recorded human wisdom. An ancient rabbinic chronicle, Seder Olam Rabba (2:15), has it that Solomon composed Ecclesiastes (and the Song of Songs, and Proverbs) when he was close to death. The "holy spirit" rested upon him and inspired him.

39 Taken from Sefaria.org, www.sefaria.org/Shabbat.30b.3?lang=bi&with =all&lang2=en. The bold print represents the actual (translated) words of the gemara. The lighter font represents the translator's bridging remarks.

40 *Bereshit Rabbah* 1:4.

41 Fox, *The JPS Bible Commentary: Ecclesiastes*, p. 4. To be clear, the best rabbinic view is that one should observe the commandments not in expectation of a reward, but for their own sake (*Pirke Avot* 1:3). One should serve God out of love for God, not out of self-love expressed in an anxious concern for one's post-mortem future. Rabbinic Judaism does not understand itself as a species of venal "works righteousness," as Luther charged.

42 Taken from Sefaria.org, www.sefaria.org/Shabbat.30b.3?lang=bi&with =all&lang2=en. The bold print represents the actual (translated) words of the gemara. The lighter font represents the translator's bridging remarks.

43 Ibid.

44 Ibid.

45 Ruth N. Sandberg, *Rabbinic Views of Qohelet*, Vol 57, Edwin Mellen Biblical Press Series (Lewiston, NY: Edwin Mellen Press, 1999), pp. 28–35.

46 Qohelet Rabbah 3:11, quoted from Sandberg, *Rabbinic Views of Qohelet*, p. 52.

47 Sandberg, *Rabbinic Views of Qohelet*, p. 52.

48 The "lazy argument" is an argument directed against the Stoics, who were metaphysical determinists, albeit to a greater extent than Kohelet. If you have an illness and you are fated to recover, then whether you see a doctor or not will make no difference. You will still recover. If you are fated not to recover, then whether you see a doctor or not won't matter either. Therefore, it is futile to see a doctor. The argument tries to show that, on the Stoic account of determinism, human action is absurd. Kohelet doesn't go as far as this in asserting determinism or the absolute futility of human action. If Fox's interpretation is correct, he is claiming (a) that one does need to do (*oseh*) things to survive, (b) but one shouldn't do too much (toil; *amel*). Action is appropriate, but since the times govern what action can accomplish, one shouldn't push too hard. The extra effort might well be in vain. Fox, *The JPS Bible Commentary: Ecclesiastes*, p. 22.

49 Sandberg, *Rabbinic Views of Qohelet*, p. 91.

50 All Rashi citations are ad loc; translations are my own.

51 Christine Hayes, *What's Divine about Divine Law? Early Perspectives* (Princeton: Princeton University Press, 2017).

1 The Question of the Meaning of Life

Questions such as "Does life have a meaning?" or "What is the meaning of life?" or, more narrowly, "Am I living a meaningful life?" are modern questions. Our ancestors did not explicitly link their questions about the purpose, point, goal, significance, worth, importance, comprehensibility, or value of life to the concept of meaning. Kohelet, who certainly questions all of the above, does not use the word "meaning" in his searching inquiry. Indeed, biblical Hebrew does not have a term for "meaning."[1] Ancient sources, whether from the Near East or from Greece, are full of questions about the best way of life, the holy way of life, the life most pleasing to the gods or God, the well-lived, happy, flourishing, or thriving life, the most natural life, and so on. They question whether life is good or evil, open or fated, tragic or just. But they were not focused on "the meaning of life." (What does "the meaning of life" even mean? Is it a well-formed question?) In the various anthologies of texts and interpretive essays available on the meaning of life, the ancient and medieval entries must be brushed against their grain to get the texts to speak of the meaning of life. Why is this?

THE MODERNITY OF THE QUESTION

A widespread view is that the question of the meaning of life requires an "awareness of what is missing," to use Habermas's phrase, to get traction.[2] For premodern people, so the story goes, the prevalence of religious faith and of intact traditional societies preempted the question. Roughly, for premodern people, discrete aspects of life might have been deeply problematic but life as a whole made sense. (Or, if one's current life didn't make sense, it could if one made profound changes and gained true wisdom. Think of Buddha's turning away from ordinary life, and then from his subsequent asceticism, into an ultimate enlightenment.) Religious traditions provided people with comprehensive worldviews, with cosmogonies and cosmologies in which to place their lives, as well as with an ethics in accord with the relevant cosmos. A creation account, such as the Enuma Elish from Babylonia or the Genesis stories of the Bible, gave people not only a presumed etiology of how the world got to be as it is but a value-laden portrayal of what human beings are here for – of what they ought to do. This "sacred canopy," as the sociologist Peter Berger put it, got shredded in modernity. The literary theorist Terry Eagleton draws the contrast between, as he sees it, premodern and modern perplexities:

> [T]alk of dread, anxiety, nausea, absurdity, and the like as characteristic of the human condition is a lot more common among twentieth-century artists and philosophers than it is among twelfth-century ones. What marks modernist thought from one end to another is the belief that human existence is contingent – that it has no ground, goal, direction, or necessity, and that our species might quite easily never have emerged on the planet. This possibility then hollows out our actual presence, casting across it the perpetual shadow of loss and death. Even in our most ecstatic moments, we are dimly aware that the ground is marshy underfoot – that there is no unimpeachable foundation to what we are and what we do. This may make our finest moments even more precious, or it may serve to drastically devalue them. This is not a viewpoint which would have rallied much support among twelfth-century philosophers, for whom there was a solid foundation to human existence known as God.[3]

Eagleton does not cite Kohelet as a possible exception to his rule. He is aware that medieval Christian thought (following Muslim and Jewish thought) contrasted God, as the sole necessary Being, with a world populated by contingent beings – beings that might not have been. The contingency of human life is not a modern discovery. But, by his lights, that medieval contrast didn't reverberate through our ancestors' minds to undermine their taken-for-granted place in the world. The necessary Being led them through the contingencies of the Valley of Death, as it were. In contingent existence, the medieval thinkers found more comfort than dread.

On the widespread view, it is the "Death of God," proclaimed in the nineteenth century by Nietzsche, that sets modern nihilism – a negative reaction to the newly heightened sense of the absurdity of existence – on its course. The question of meaning arises as a searching response to nihilism. (Not coincidentally, as we shall see, the term "nihilism" and the increasingly frequent use of the phrase "the meaning of life" are coeval. They both have late eighteenth-, early nineteenth-century origins.) The modernity of the question of meaning is thus apparent both in the circumstances of its origins and in its character as a response. Insofar as it arose as a way to address the God-shaped hole in modern thought, the question of meaning tends to forswear religion – God-centered religion at any rate – as a resource for its answers. (Philosophical Buddhism, by contrast, seems to be an attractive resource for some philosophers.)[4] Thus, the question of meaning is a largely secular question from the outset.

There is some truth in this view. But it is also a summary judgment. The concept of God does not preempt interrogating the issues that are grouped under the phrase "the meaning of life." Premodern religious worlds contextualized the question of meaning in different ways from modern, self-sufficiently secular ones. Kohelet's world is as "hollowed out" as "under a shadow of loss and death" and as "marshy underfoot" as that of Eagleton. It is not the idea of God as such that chokes off an awareness of absurdity and the threat of nihilism but the character of that idea. Kohelet's God is distant, impenetrable, inscrutable, and perhaps implacable. *That* God is a potent ground for human perplexity and anxiety in the face of fleeting, impermanent life – life that is no more substantial than a breath.

Kohelet's God is at a remove from other portrayals of God in the Hebrew Bible. The tension between these portrayals, seen in the rabbinic wrestling with Kohelet, makes the ground underfoot somewhat marshy even in the ages of stout theism. To paraphrase Kohelet, there is nothing entirely new under the sun. The bright line between the secular and the religious is often more broken than either side imagines. The repressed wants to return.

Nonetheless, it is clear that the question of the meaning of life has a modern history, shape, and salience that it did not have in earlier times. I turn to it in a moment. But it is also reasonable to believe that, historical considerations aside, searching for the meaning of things is a universal propensity of the human mind. It is reasonable because human beings are symbolizing creatures. We take events, objects, words – phenomena both natural and artifactual – as signs; we take signs to symbolize, to *mean* something other than what they immediately are. (You, gentle reader, take these black ink marks on the page before you to be more than black ink marks.) We wonder constantly about what phenomena mean. By asking what they mean, we try to understand them and to fix their import. We see patterns in them and embed them into larger patterns. We tell stories about what they stand for and why they matter. Nor is this an idle habit. Fixing the meaning of things is no less necessary for us than it is for antelopes to take rustling in the grass as a sign of a crouching lion. Meaning-seeking is a universal human trait, which takes quite different forms in our endlessly varied historical contexts. We need to attend to both the universality and the particularity of meaning-seeking. The modernity of the question is real, but the search for meaning is archaic.

There is a difference, however, between the universal propensity to seek meaning, especially, of semantic units – whether sentences or symbols – and, derivatively, of events, and seeking the meaning of *lives*. Words mean in the context of sentences that bear meaning in the context of language use. Visual signs have meaning in the contexts of practical life (e.g., traffic signals), emotional life (e.g., smiles, frowns, and cold stares), art, and so on. So too with natural sounds (such as distant thunder meaning that a storm is approaching) or artifactual, structured sounds in the context of music. Context, and the practices that sustain and support it, is a condition on meaning. A bullet leaving the barrel of a gun and entering a human chest means one thing in the contexts of law and ethics, another in the context of physics, and yet another in the context of physiology. Nonetheless, we might say that all of the things whose meanings we seek occur in the context of life.

But what is the context for life as such? The question is disorienting. We can seek meaning for phenomena within our experience, within our "lifeworld," but can we get out of our lifeworld and seek *its* meaning?[5] Perhaps we can get out of this or that lifeworld – there is alienation, after all – but can we get out of all possible lifeworlds? Isn't it the case that any perspective that we have on our lives is a perspective anchored in or bounded by our lives? The novelty of the question of the meaning of life is the attempt, by modern people, to get out of our lifeworlds altogether – to adopt a "view from nowhere." We want to take a God's eye view in the presumed absence of God. We have come to believe that we have a way of taking the perspective of the universe, as it were. From that perspective, our lives appear to be trivial, insignificant, and absurd. The vastly expanded universe conveyed to us by science has, since the seventeenth century, given human life as such a context that endlessly problematizes its significance. The presumptive authority of the scientifically established context allows the problem of meaning to emerge with force.

The idea of taking the perspective of the universe is coeval with the felt decline of the cogency of God's perspective. Even if, as many believe, it is no longer cogent to talk of a (divine) mind that comprehends the whole, there remains a whole. We assert the reality of a whole that is more than a set of discrete phenomena that nature forces on us. Although we might take the universe as a meaningless, brute-factual whole, we have tacitly assigned it some of the axiological work that the concept of God used to do.[6] God may no longer know and judge human creatures, but we imagine that the universe does. (i.e., that it "judges" us to be insignificant.) Thus, Pascal, alarmed by the "eternal silence of its infinite spaces" writes: "Engulfed in the infinite immensity of spaces whereof I know nothing, and which know nothing of me, I am terrified, and wonder that I am here rather than there, for there is no reason why here rather than there, or now rather than then."[7] He takes the perspective, so to speak, of the universe and judges himself on its behalf. And from that perspective, we don't matter. (But whose perspective is it, really – the universe's or our own, transferred to the universe by philosophical sleight of hand?)

Yet, just as surely, that not-mattering matters to us. We don't like the bind into which our perspectival schizophrenia has put us. We sense and believe that our lives do matter and that they have worth. Fundamentally, the meaning of life is a story that we tell ourselves about that intuition – about our intuition that we have worth. To the extent that we feel our lives don't have worth and are, consequently, meaningless, we feel this as a lack or loss. We feel that something is missing. As the *Talmud* says, "*Mi-klal lav, shomin hen,*" that is, "the negative implies a prior positive." Worthlessness is not a primary intuition; it is a belief we fall into or have to develop. When we learn to occupy a perspective detached from our lifeworld, we can come to the belief that we lack value and that nothing previously meaningful is really meaningful. We no longer know how to justify meaningfulness. Yet something pushes back. When, for example, circumstances conspire to demean us, we reflexively, if we have life left in us, resist. We recoil from harm, abuse, and dehumanization. This is more than some crude reflex of pleasure seeking or pain avoidance; it is the affirmation of our value, of the particular worth of our individual being or of human beings in general against nothingness. Existential-axiological consciousness wants to have veto power over nothingness. This is an insight we will try to develop as the argument proceeds.

Our sense that we matter is not an inference; it is basic.[8] As such, it cannot be, nor does it need to be, justified by something more basic. For what could be more basic? The radical, inherent value that we sense in ourselves as conscious, sentient, agentic, first-personal lives is as basic to our being in the world as *human* beings as it gets. Zooming out to a cosmic perspective, which seems to us an epistemologically permissible even virtuous move in the context of science, does destabilize, *but ought not to displace*, our sense of fundamental worth. What is it about modernity that has led us into this paradoxical, even absurd bind?

THE HISTORY OF THE QUESTION

The actual phrase "the meaning of life" first began to be used in the late eighteenth and early nineteenth centuries. Scholars note that the first true appearance of the phrase occurred in German in the unpublished manuscripts of the Romantic poet Friedrich von Hardenberg, known by his *nom de plume* Novalis. In an essay dating from 1797 to 1798, Novalis wrote that the time in which we live is no longer one "where the spirit of God is understandable. The meaning [*Sinn*] of the world has been lost. We stopped at the letter. We lost that which appears [*das Erscheinende*] for the sake of appearance [*Erscheinung*]." And more precisely: "Only an artist can divine the meaning of life [*Sinn des Lebens*]."[9] For Novalis, the world, despite the prodigious growth of the natural sciences – a phenomenon he endorsed – is less intelligible than it once was. The signs no longer mean what they once did. We are stuck at the surface with the letter, not with the animating, generative spirit – with fragmentary appearances that veil the unifying force behind the signs. The natural world has become mute and opaque. Only a genius, whose spirit is attuned to the hidden spirit of the world, can divine the meaning of the signs and thus the "meaning of life." We need to save nature by elevating its physicality, that is, the manner in which it appears to us, in the realm of the spirit. (As Novalis puts it, human beings are the "messiah" of nature.)[10] Only our spiritual nature, which transcends nature and participates in the ideal, can infuse physical nature with unity and make it fully intelligible.

In bringing our spirit down into nature and helping her achieve her own harmony, we also save ourselves. Our participation in nature advances our own *Bildung*, our self-formation. "To grasp nature as a living, dynamic whole, in other words, nature as productivity rather than as isolated products, one must be as active and productive as nature. Thus, Novalis … turns to the artist, for the artist is, like nature, active and productive … [the artist has] the ability to act in nature's spirit."[11] Acting in nature's spirit amounts to an ethics, on the Romantic view. The artist not only brings out the true meaning of life, encoded in the signs of the world, but also writes the book of his or her own life as a meaningful, spiritual–ethical story. Life is a book or a tale that bears a meaning. Shakespeare, in *Macbeth*, said about life that "It is a tale told by an idiot, full of sound and fury, signifying nothing." But Novalis dissents. The artist can find the significance of the tale and embody it in a meaningful life.[12]

Novalis's friend, the thinker Friedrich Schlegel, adopted the phrase and used it in his 1799 novel, *Lucinde*. Schlegel wrote:

> Now the soul understands the lament of the nightingale and the smile of the newly born babe, understands the deep significance of the mysterious hieroglyphs on flowers and stars, understands the holy *meaning of life* as well as the beautiful language of nature. All things speak to the soul and everywhere the soul sees the loving spirit through the delicate veil.[13]

The English writer, Thomas Carlyle, who was much affected by *Lucinde*, used Schlegel's phrase in his 1836 novel *Sartor Resartus*. From thence, the phrase entered the English vocabulary.

More important than the thumbnail sketch of semantic history is why this particular formulation appealed to early nineteenth-century writers. As the Schlegel quote shows, the Romantic author situates the "holy meaning of life" in a context of natural signs: the "lament" of the nightingale, the smile of a baby, and the messages of flowers and stars. Indeed, the whole of nature speaks a beautiful language to which the soul should be attuned. The passage accomplishes a transition from the linguistic context – in which meaning has its proper conceptual home – to the natural world. Nature tells us something. Behind the "delicate veil," nature reveals itself as pure spirit, and spirit reveals itself as loving or lovely (*den lieblichen Geist*). We see through the letter, the mere appearance, and sense the spirit, which yearns to appear. We have a view of the whole of reality as spirit filled. It is an elevating view, not one that diminishes us or deprives us of worth or purpose. It is an attempt to find meaning in life through passionate identification with nature, as early German romanticism understood it. Historically, it is a reaction to an earlier disenchantment of the world that marked some of the thinkers of the eighteenth-century French Enlightenment.

The idea that "Spirit" (*Geist*) lies behind the veil of nature challenged the strictly material and disenchanted view of nature, which had developed among French Enlightenment thinkers. For Schiller, the great poet who preceded the German Romantics by a generation, nature was despoiled of its divinity (*die entgötteter Natur*) and so became a world no longer conducive to human freedom or joy.[14] Schiller's poem *The Gods of Greece* mourns this tragic outcome but holds out no hope for restoring enchantment. The early Romantics, by contrast, sought to reinvest nature with godlike creative power. Sensing that power, through human feeling rather than solely through abstract, scientific thought would strip away the artificial constraints of the rational–scientific outlook and open humanity up to freedom and sublime significance once again.

Scientific materialism – an outlook that remains prominent today – came to the fore in the French Enlightenment. Modern science and materialist metaphysics overlap, but materialism need not be the proprietary ontology of science. Scientific thinkers, such as Newton, Boyle, and Priestly, worked out theologies compatible with their research into material causation. God was active in their universe, using natural causality for divine, providential purposes.[15]

The French rationalists, such as Helvetius, Holbach, d'Alembert and Condorcet, however, rejected any synthesis with theology. Isaiah Berlin portrays them as

> [F]riends of nature and the sciences, for whom man is subject to the same kind of causal laws as animals and plants and the inanimate world, physical and biological laws, and in the case of men psychological and economic too, established by observation and experiment, measurement and verification. Such notions as the immortal soul, a personal God, freedom of the will, are for them metaphysical fictions and illusions.[16]

The materialist program was meant to help advance the sciences; fight "superstition"; and reform society, politics, and economics through rational analysis and application.

An extreme, almost self-parodying instance of this program is found in the writings of the eighteenth-century French physician La Mettrie. In his tract, *L'Homme Machine* (Man–Machine), La Mettrie tries to explain all human phenomena in strictly material, causal terms. Nothing about humanity is, in principle, any more recondite than what one finds in other animals. Scientific analysis will eventually discover the deterministic, mechanical, causal structure of everything. Language usage, which nonmaterialists take as a sign of human difference, for example, is fundamentally similar to animal learning and expression:

> Words, languages, laws, science and arts came, and through them the rough diamond of our minds was at last polished. Man was drilled like an animal; he was trained into being an author in the same way as a dog, for instance is· trained to carry a pack. A mathematician learned how to conduct the most difficult proofs and calculations, as a monkey learns to don and doff his little hat or ride his trained dog. Everything was done by signs; each species understood what it could understand; and that is how man acquired what our German philosophers call symbolic

> knowledge. You see, nothing is simpler than the mechanism of our education! It all comes down to sounds, to words, which go from x's mouth through y's ears to y's brain, which receives at the same time through y's eyes the shape of the bodies that x's words are the arbitrary signs of.[17]

La Mettrie imagines that with enough training (education), an orang-utan would be able to speak like a child. He thinks that neither its vocal apparatus nor its brain would preclude that possibility. Since everything is physical, matter must be self-organizing and self-motivating. Mechanical explanations cover all phenomena. Such survivals as "soul" merely name a congeries of physical processes. The world is utterly disenchanted. Such is La Mettrie's thoroughgoing scientism, *avant la lettre*.

The German Enlightenment did not take as hard a materialist line as did the French. Against a causally closed, strictly physical universe, German philosophers in the eighteenth century, especially Kant and Fichte, asserted the reality of human freedom. Nature might be a causal system that, within limits, requires a scientific account, but freedom requires a separate account, divined by philosophy. There must be a "causality of freedom."[18] Kant's response was to see nature as essentially deterministic – at least that's the way human understanding grasps the natural world – but at the level below our world-structuring cognition, the fact of the matter cannot be ascertained. Nature remains opaque to us.[19] We don't know whether nature-in-itself is, independent of our cognition of it, absolutely deterministic or not. Our human experience of freedom, which arises in and is essential to our moral life, cannot be integrated into the causal structure of the world, as our understanding grasps it. The centrality of this mysterious freedom to our lives marks us as beings fundamentally different from all others. Our rational apprehension of the "fact" of freedom (the "moral law within") establishes us as beings of infinite worth and dignity; it lends our lives significance and gives us purpose – to live in conformity with the moral law. While we cannot establish the reality of freedom scientifically, we must affirm it in order to accept the authority of the moral law. Forming ourselves in the direction of an ideal, austere, and perfectionist morality is the highest use of our (practical) reason. Kant invites us "to uphold for ourselves the idea or ideal of autonomy or pure self-determination as the highest norm for our conduct."[20] Without rising to conform to that norm, we would just be creatures of nature, like La Mettrie's animal and human machines.

Kant's teaching of a bifurcated reality, in which the world as it is in itself is ultimately unknowable, was too incomplete to be acceptable to his idealist followers. A more radical synthesis of necessity and freedom of the conditions of knowing with the known was needed. His first great Idealist successor, Johann Gottlieb Fichte, tried to make freedom the primordial principle of the whole. As per Kant, freedom cannot be proven but to get to the best account of the world as human subjects experience it, we must assume it. Fichte could have begun his systematic thought with the primitive reality of an objective world – a world of material things. But that, he thought, could never give rise to the subjective reality experienced by the "I." The path leads from the I to the world, not vice versa. Fichte abolishes the independence of a causally determined natural world, locating its origin in pure subjectivity. Fichte's pure subjectivity, characterized as primordial free activity, runs parallel to his Jena students' romantic sensibility; for them, the inner nature of the world is also primordial free activity, that is, creative Spirit.

In Fichte's account, the most fundamental logical principle is the law of identity (symbolized by the expression $A = A$). But to say this assumes that an *A* exists. In order for an *A* to exist in the first place, it must be generated. Beginning as he does with pure subjectivity, the process of generation is carried out by an "absolute I," an infinite creative will. Fichte's absolute I is godlike; it proclaims "I = I" rather like the God of the Torah, who proclaimed "I am that I am" (Exodus 3:14). As Fichte's story progresses, the I, to recognize its self-identity, needs to posit an opposite, a not-I. "For the infinite and undifferentiated activity of the absolute I to recognize itself as I, there must be an other that impels it to reflect upon itself as other than this other and thus as self-same."[21] I and not-I need one another to exist but also threaten to annihilate one another's existence. This leads to the principle of mutual limitation: I and not-I limit one another. Out of this dialectic emerges a world of individual subjectivities (I's) and objective things (not-I's). Thus, at the heart of the world, in which we have our conscious being, is an unstable dialectic issuing from an infinite creative will. Ultimately, both the dialectic and the empirical realities to which it gives rise cannot hold their ground. "In the thought of Fichte, we witness the turn away from coexistence [of freedom, that is, the subjective, and of nature, the objective] toward the assertion of freedom as absolute and the consequent demand that objective nature be annihilated."[22] The endless activity of the absolute I overwhelms the not-I. "The proclamation that the not-I must be eliminated is thus also the proclamation that the empirical I must become the absolute, that man must become an absolutely unconstrained and thus radically free being, must become, in other words, God."[23]

Thoughts like these inspired Fichte's students – the Schlegel brothers, Tieck, Hölderlin – the core group of the early Romantics. They also forced his departure from the University of Jena on suspicion of atheism. His attempt to build a systematic philosophy on a metaphysically ambitious concept of subjectivity inspired the philosophical critic, F. H. Jacobi, in an open letter, to call Fichte a "nihilist." (Jacobi's student Jean Paul used the same term to criticize the Jena Romantics.)[24] Although the term had existed previously, Jacobi launched it on its modern trajectory. In Jacobi's view, Fichte proffered a metaphysics/epistemology in which the self is primitive, and the other is derivative; the other is a "posit" of the self against which the self defines itself. For Jacobi, this is the "nihilism of reason," the obliteration of the given world in which there is "no 'I' without a 'Thou', and [where] the two can recognize and respect one another only in the presence of a transcendent and personal

God."[25] "Nihilism" refers to the annihilation of individual beings, to the annihilation of the world in its givenness, to the annihilation of value.[26] A vastly expanded concept of selfhood filled the whole of reality. What can remain other than the imperative of realizing ever more freedom on the path to becoming an authentic self?[27] The nineteenth-century figure of the political nihilist, contemptuous of all social and cultural norms and refusing to affirm any positive program, such as Turgenev's character, Bazarov, in *Fathers and Sons*, has its origins in this development.

Nature, for Fichte, is no longer, at heart, a causal, deterministic, physical system. It is the expression of an endless, creative, dialectically productive will. Our own experience of subjectivity, especially of the freedom that we sense in ourselves as creators, reveals our true nature and vocation. We are to achieve ever higher levels of freedom and individuality in the knowledge that the activity of doing so is the process, literally, of worldbuilding. Jacobi harshly criticizes Fichte for, on the one hand, elevating the self into God and, on the other, losing real selfhood in the ether of transcendental abstraction. Jacobi is committed to the individual existence of selves and objects, apprehended through an immediate, intuitive grasp of their reality. (He likens this to revelation.) The philosophers, from Spinoza to Fichte, give us rational reconstructions of reality that cannot penetrate to the concrete experience of life. Real selves exist in real relations of "I and Thou," where the Thou is a human other in the presence of a transcendent God. Real rationality is social, reciprocal, and grounded in actual human relations. A philosophy of exclusive, abstract subjectivity is, while not exactly atheism, a world-repudiating "nihilism."

By Jacobi's lights, reason itself leads to nihilism, as rigorously rational system-builders, such as Spinoza and Fichte, exemplify. Each loses the world in a mirror image way: Spinoza swallows the self and its freedom into pure objectivity, the single substance that comprises the whole. Fichte inverts this. The absolute I is a "spiritual" version of Spinoza's substance, which also loses the real objectivity of the world. (These are not naïve errors. They stem from profound and serious attempts to deal with the nature of reason as such.[28]) In Jacobi's usage, nihilism is the reasoned betrayal of the lived reality of the self and the world. Nihilism is not an expression of despair; *it is an irrational consequence of excessive rationality.*

Within this intellectual context, the question of the meaning of life was raised in a new, acute way. Nature had been emptied of meaning, reduced to a causal–physical system by the materialists. Kant and Fichte tried to secure freedom – the condition for a uniquely human being – as a necessary supposition of a worthy human life, with worth defined by the capacity for rational, moral action. Fichte went beyond Kant by hypostasizing the will of an absolute, pure subjectivity as the effective generative principle of reality. In shaping our lives around the expansion of our will, we both gain ever more freedom and bring ourselves into alignment with the innermost nature of the world. The Romantics depress Fichte's idealism and privilege feeling as the connection with the inner nature of the world. They preach a total immersion of oneself, without a map or a guide, into the flux of nature. One is to identify oneself with the turbulent creative will that is found there. In communion with nature as will, one tries to shape the world by values that one creates.

Although nature gives us intelligible signs through which we can discern her secrets, it is upon us to create their meaning. Furthermore, it is upon us to weave that meaning into our lives, to make the world meaningful for ourselves. We must become artists who shape the materials of nature into a significant life. There are neither rules nor reliable traditions. There are feelings; there is the irrational. Earlier justifications for a significant life are all suspect. With no solid floor beneath our feet, with nothing other than nature as the flux of an infinite, creative will, the justifications for what we create are all internal. We value, we choose – our doing so must have its own justification. For critics such as Jacobi, this is no justification at all. It is nihilism. Romantic thinkers, and their intellectual descendants, must argue that it is not and that meaning can be located precisely within this framing of reason, nature, freedom, and the human condition. It is under these conceptual circumstances that the modern question of meaning first arose.

Our situation today is, in some ways, continuous with the post-Romantic one. The emphasis on individual meaning, the deep doubt about traditional religious frameworks, the sense of being accompanied by the specter of nihilism all endure. What is different is an utterly disenchanted view of the universe without any lingering traces of transcendence, "creative will," or hidden normativity to be accessed by feelings. The Romantics, although they put all of the responsibility on free human beings to build meaning from the ground up, gave them a living world of "Spirit" in which to work. We, by contrast, have a sterile positivism. We have gone back to a La Mettrie-like materialism without the concomitant Enlightenment promise of progress, of transcending our present level of knowledge through ever greater scientific achievement, with which will come ever more just and satisfying social arrangements. Deprived of both Enlightenment optimism and Romantic spirituality, the very notion of transcendence became suspect. It has been ethically and epistemologically condemned to the trash heap of supernaturalism. The twists and turns of our intellectual history have depleted our concept of the universe of value and meaning. This is not the discovery of a fact, as much as the result of the vagaries of an intellectual history.

In a fully disenchanted world, transcendence as a source of meaning is dead. The otherwise generous Philip Kitcher writes in one of his briefs for atheism:

> The core of secularist doubt is skepticism about anything "transcendent." Believers may retreat from committing themselves to all-powerful creators with long white beards or to gleaming figures with magnificent wings or to the living physical presence of someone who was previously fully medically dead, but so long as they interpret their doctrines as recording episodes that were connected with something beyond the physical, organic, human world, secular humanists doubt the truth of what is claimed.[29]

Kitcher goes on to claim that even the most ethicized formulations of transcendence remain invidious or otiose. Value does not need an assist from faith, nor do highly abstract expressions of transcendence, such as Tillich's "ultimate concern," become any more plausible for their remoteness from naïve piety.[30]

Contemporary science-allied secularism in pure, philosophical form repudiates transcendence. Meaning, such as it is, is not to be found in an order beyond the "physical, organic, human world" but in one or another version of the immanent frame. The demotion of meaning to immanent, subjectively, or socially variable meaning cannot but disappoint people with an older, more elevated conception of human purpose. Hence, doubt about the question of meaning itself arises.

REJECTING THE QUESTION OF MEANING I

Older versions of seeking the significance of human life continue, of course, to exist. A contemporary conservative, particularly a religious one, might question whether "meaning" is the right rubric under which to pursue the inquiry into the importance, intelligibility, nature, or purpose of humanity. Let us consider one such critic, the Thomist philosopher, Joshua Hochschild. Hochschild, after noting, as I have, the largely nineteenth-century origins of the term "meaning of life," claims that the question arose as a "way of making intelligible, *even if only for the purpose of escaping*, the threat of meaninglessness: The articulation of the question reflects a felt need to overcome a pessimistic or negative view about human life – the kind of answer implied by materialism, positivism, and the scientific critique of religion."[31] The connection between the meaning of life and the threat of nihilism is pertinent, but note the insinuation that the inquiry into meaning is a less than honest counter to the threat; it's a matter of *escaping* it. Hochschild deplores this new formulation.

What the "meaning of life" replaced is a set of venerable questions, reaching back to Plato, Aristotle, and Augustine, about "the *goal*, *good*, or *end* of life .... We may call it the question of human *purpose* – where by 'purpose' we don't mean an individual agent's intention or conscious sense of purpose ... but the intrinsic, essential *why* of the species. What are human beings for? What is the ultimate point of our existence?"[32]

Hochschild claims that the question of the purpose of life is universal, essentialist, and teleological. It alone "presumes that there is such a thing as human *fulfillment*, rooted in human *nature*, which reflects a definite *purpose* or *intention* of its maker."[33] There are objective grounds on which to answer the question of purpose. By contrast, the question of meaning is by design subjective; it emphasizes "interior life, feelings, emotions, awareness, consciousness." It is highly personal. It fails to attain the moral seriousness prompted by the question of our ultimate end and highest good. "The strength, and the weakness, of the question [of meaning] is that it seems to put the weight of responsibility on the one asking it to supply an answer from his or her own private, inarticulate resources."[34]

Presumably, if one followed the teachings of classical and/or Christian teleological doctrines, such as Aristotle's and/or Aquinas's, the threat of meaninglessness would never have arisen. The dodgy strategy of seeking meaning against that threat would have been unnecessary. Hochschild wants us to return to the question of purpose. He is calling us to abandon the meaning question, disown the anxiety that life is meaningless, and work to recover an older wisdom that affirms the objective purposefulness of human life based on an essential, ahistorical human nature and the objective goods that enable it to achieve its fulfillment. Settling for anything less is to be stuck in a vicious circle of idiosyncratic proposals for meaning, none of which will penetrate to the metaphysical and moral core of human life.

Of course, if a compelling account of objective human purpose along Hochschild's lines were persuasive, it would be foolish to reject it. The question of meaning, however, arose in part because the available teleological and divine providential accounts became less compelling, if not implausible. I do not want to reject the possibility of such an account, but I do want to argue that the meaning question has legitimacy and is more than *faute de mieux*.

Hochschild characterizes the meaning question by its contrasts with the presumably deeper and more fruitful question of purpose. It cannot help but look impoverished by comparison. But is the comparison fair? Hochschild assumes that the meaning question fails, by hypothesis, to provide a universal answer, but is the meaning theorist looking for one? Is it clear that any answer short of an objective, universally applicable one is fatally flawed? Is the alternative to authoritative objectivity mere idiosyncratic, personal subjectivity? Hochschild begs the question in favor of the presumed desirability of the universal. Its intuitive appeal notwithstanding, that presumptive desirability should be argued for, not asserted.

The subjectivity versus objectivity of answers to the meaning question is an important topic in the literature. We will explore it in Chapter 3. But to anticipate, not all answers, contra Hochschild, are created equal. Many people would be disposed to say that a life spent loving and helping others was more meaningful than a contemptuous or selfish one; that a life spent creating inspiring art was more meaningful than a life spent, say, watching TV. Are our rough judgments arbitrary, "merely subjective?" Such judgments no doubt fall far short of Hochschild's gold standard of objectively valid evaluations grounded on ahistorical moral and metaphysical truths, but there is something to be said for transsubjective agreement based on broadly held, shared values. A theorist such as Hochschild could point out that widely shared values are not immune to corruption and delusion. (Think, e.g., of a whole society propagandized into acceptance of doctrines about the racial inferiority of certain groups.) Or he could point out that the values by which we roughly evaluate some lives as having been spent more meaningfully than others are residues from the long history of a Christian civilization. And, as that civilization wanes, the values will as well. Our shared sense of what constitutes a meaningful life is parasitic on the answers to an older, wiser question. So, he might say, the secular surrogate for human purpose, meaningfulness, is living on borrowed capital and borrowed time. Without the strong grounding that natural law, a theory of natural goods, and an objective description/endorsement of human fulfillment based on them can provide, no theory of the meaning of life can resist disintegrating into nihilism. This, in fact, is the argument active nihilists, such as James Tartaglia, make.[35] Hochschild's maximalist view, should it not succeed, courts the collapse into nihilism. Modest proposals for the meaning of life, or, even more modestly, for meaning *in* life, may not afford the presumed satisfaction of intellectual completeness, but neither do they invite disaster.

Hochschild's traditional natural law view, with its attendant discourse of objective human purpose, is based, self-evidently, on a view of nature. Nature both provisions us with faculties through which we can seek our perfection and sets the standard for what that perfection (of our physical being, our abilities and talents, our intellectual and moral virtues, etc.) is.[36] There are natural goods, such as knowledge, friendship, and moral virtues, that conduce to human thriving. Our natural reason can recognize them and direct our will to pursue them, to incorporate the pursuit of them into the projects of our lives. Nature can be understood as an ontological domain that, at least potentially, supports the drive of all forms of life to reach the natural end (*telos*, *ultimus finis*) requisite to them. For human beings, that end lies beyond nature. We are to achieve knowledge of nature's Creator or, in a pagan context, likeness to an ultimate logos or *nous*, such as Aristotle's thought thinking itself (*Metaphysics*, Book Lambda, 7, 1072b).

Part of the modern Western outlook has been the rejection of this characterization of nature, of what Roger Scruton called an "encumbered theory of Being," in favor of a "sparse theory of Being."[37] From the latter point of view, Hochschild's stance invests nature with a goodness that thinly veils its presumed origins in the work of a divine, benevolent Creator. Nature is designed so as to guide humans toward the fulfillment of their naturally endowed capacities such that they reach the ends determined for their species.

There is more than a touch of anthropocentricity in this characterization. From the ideal-typical scientific point of view, this is precisely what must be purged. Just as we no longer put the Earth in the center of the universe, so we should no longer bundle human interests into our description of nature. The Oxford physicist David Deutsch writes, "*anti*-anthropocentrism has increasingly been elevated to the status of a universal principle, sometimes called 'The Principle of Mediocrity': *There is nothing significant about humans (in the cosmic scheme of things).*"[38] As the late physicist Stephen Hawking put it, humans are "just a chemical scum on the surface of a typical planet that's in orbit round a typical star on the outskirts of a typical galaxy."[39] The features of human life that we find significant "are themselves anthropocentric: They explain only the behavior of the scum, which is itself insignificant."[40] Science, in so many words, tries to achieve a view from nowhere in which the human presence in the universe is peripheral, rather than central. I do not wish to endorse this view – indeed, I will try later in this chapter to undercut it – but only to underscore, starkly, how different a materialist, scientific characterization of nature is from a portrayal that emphasizes its (presumed) tendency to abet human flourishing. The question remains: Is the latter an illegitimate construal of nature or a legitimate "anthropocentrism?"[41]

REJECTING THE QUESTION OF MEANING II

Hochschild's attack on the meaning question comes out of a venerable framework, that is, natural law theory. It can – but need not – support a deep critique of modern morality and metaphysics. If one of its motivations is that the question of meaning is, in a sense, too modern, an opposite critique holds that the meaning question *is not modern enough.* It is a holdover, in secular guise, from religious yearnings that ought to be exposed as deluded. It's not just that the secular search for meaning is living on borrowed capital, but it's that the capital itself is and always was worthless. Properly modern minds should be asking *neither* the question of purpose *nor* the question of meaning. This view, which acquired traction in the early twentieth century with the Vienna Circle and the philosophical movement known as logical positivism (or logical empiricism[42]), was brought to the English-speaking world by, among others, Sir A. J. Ayer. Ayer's last book was titled, *The Meaning of Life*.[43] In it, he offered reasons for both his early, utter rejection of the question in the 1930s and, despite a somewhat greater indulgence, his continued doubts about its legitimacy up until his death in 1989. It is worth a closer look.

Logical empiricism was born in repudiation of the kind of metaphysics represented not only by natural law but also by German idealism. Even Kant had to be discarded. (Kant's fundamental approach to space and time was shown to be suppositious by non-Euclidean geometry and the theory of general relativity.) Logical empiricism was committed to a self-imposed, limited role for philosophy as a handmaiden of science. Philosophy's principal concern should be the elucidation of scientific procedures, method, and statements. As an American participant in the Vienna Circle, the Harvard logician, W. V. Quine once wrote: "Philosophy of science is philosophy enough."[44] The questions that should orient inquiry included: What does it mean to confirm empirical observations? What licenses inferring lawlike generalizations from observation statements? How does logic work together with empirical observation to support meaningful statements about the world?

The logical empiricists believed that the only meaningful statements were statements that could, in principle, be verified. "Ravens are black" is meaningful – we have an idea of how it can be verified, even though we can't verify it with respect to all ravens (hence, "in principle" verifiability). "All brothers are male" is meaningful – here, logical analysis rather than empirical observation does the work of verification. But "the purpose of human beings is to seek their fulfillment according to nature" is meaningless, on the logical empiricist account, because it cannot be verified either empirically or logically. It sounds like a meaningful statement, but it is not. Having the grammatical form of a conventional sentence is no guarantee of meaning.

If the sentence cannot be analyzed by a procedure that confirms its truth (or falsity), it is, strictly speaking, meaningless. A lot of sentences – of fiction and poetry, of ethics, and most especially of religion and traditional philosophy – get thrown overboard. Their emotional or rhetorical force may remain, but their meaningfulness disappears. Whole fields become nonsense. As many of our most crucial projects and values now seem absurd, how to live with such metaphysical parsimoniousness becomes a problem.

Ayer takes the question of the meaning of life to be typical of traditional philosophy. The traditional philosopher, not content to be a "journeyman," feels called to be a "pontiff." The pontiff seeks and wants to teach wisdom, "not merely scientific knowledge." "Of what use to us," he asks rhetorically, "is the understanding of nature if we do not know the purpose of our existence or how we ought to live? And who is to answer these supremely important questions if not the philosopher?"[45] In a good positivist fashion, however, Ayer decisively rejects this role for the philosopher:

> The reply to this is that there is no true answer to these questions; and since this is so it is no use expecting even the philosopher to provide one. What can be done, however, is to make clear why, and in what sense, these questions are unanswerable; and once this is achieved it will be seen that there is also a sense in which they can be answered. It will be found that the form of answer is not a proposition, which must be either true or false, but the adoption of a rule, which cannot properly be characterized as either true or false but can be judged to be more or less acceptable. And with this the problem is solved, so far as reasoning can solve it. The rest is a matter of personal decision, and ultimately of action.[46]

"What is the meaning of life?" is a pseudo question; it is philosophy's responsibility to point that out. (But doesn't the idea of "philosophy's responsibility" also fall afoul of this strict condition on meaningfulness?) Once philosophical analysis shows that no possible answer can have truth value, then the inappropriateness of the question becomes apparent. It can safely be dismissed; we can get over our need to ask the question and our expectation of receiving a truth-bearing answer.

Matters are not, however, so cut and dried. Ayer recognizes that whole swaths of discourse can't simply be dispatched to logical purgatory. We need to continue to live recognizably human lives while accepting the severe limits imposed by logical empiricism. How to dispel this potential absurdity? Ethical statements may not be true or false, but that doesn't make them less necessary to our conduct. Into the gap come criteria of acceptability that supplant those of verifiability. This is to say that accepted social, cultural conventions (a rule) do the relevant, ethical work. There are no purely logical or empirical criteria that govern whether a rule is "more or less" acceptable. It seems to come down to emotion or to fashion. Values are not based on or justified by facts; they float about in some Humean ether pushed hither and yon by our irrational passions. Ayer sees no way around this. We need, in the end, to act and decide so we must have a "rule" to guide our decision-making.

The distinction between fact and value might be taken to imply that no rule of conduct is better (or worse) than any other. But Ayer rejects this. The judgment that all rules of conduct, or ways of life, are of equal value is also a value judgment; it *too* is unsupported by facts or logic. We are not, therefore, compelled to accept it. This seems to lead to "moral indifference," that is, to complete relativism regarding values. Ayer agrees, but he thinks that relativism is "not easily maintained." Faced with decision-making, we should incline toward principles and values that can be *consistently* carried out. "That these values should be consistent is a necessary condition of their being fully realized; for it is logically impossible to achieve the complete fulfillment of an inconsistent set of ends." So, the best we can do is to affirm those principles and values that we can implement and realize to the maximal degree. The only way to criticize these is to ask, from within the agent's own value system, whether they are conducing, as expected, to the achievement of the agent's aims.

The only real criticism is: Are they instrumentally efficient or rational? Someone outside the agent's value system who wants to make a noninstrumental criticism such as: "Your principles, values, and consequent actions are morally perverse or wrongful" has no justification for doing so. His own freely chosen principles cannot override another's freely chosen principles. "In the last resort, therefore, each individual has the responsibility of choice; and it is a responsibility that is not to be escaped."[47]

Given this hard fact/value dichotomy, Ayer argues against the legitimacy of the question of meaning, which he equates with the question of whether life has a purpose. We know what it means for a person to have a purpose – a person chooses an end toward which to direct her actions. Those actions, as well as the circumstances that enable or impede their success, can now be judged meaningful (or meaningless) by that person, given her intentional adoption of a purpose. If one's purpose were to become a doctor, getting accepted to the medical school of one's choice would be a meaningful event, the outcome of a meaningful assemblage of actions on one's part. Meaningfulness is ordered to purposiveness, with purpose being an object of desire, freely chosen but essentially groundless. This makes some sense in the context of discrete projects in one's life. But Ayer rejects the idea that life *as such* can have a purpose and hence a meaning.

The logic of the discrete project cannot be generalized to life as a whole. All of the events of one's life cannot be understood as meaningful on the model of conducing (or failing to conduce) toward some desired end. Life as a whole is not governed by an intentional plan, our phases of intentional planning notwithstanding. Its end does not reflect the fulfillment of a choice or the realization of a project. But even if one's life were so narrowly focused that this model of meaningfulness was plausible, the question of meaning would still be unanswerable. This is because what one seeks in decoding a pattern of potentially meaningful events is not an explanation but a "justification." Given Ayer's exclusive empiricism, he claims that all we can credibly do is point out *how* one event followed another in a person's life in a brute-factual way; we can't say *why* the events unfolded as they did, as if there were some master plan realizing itself in time. Empiricism trades in answering "how" questions; it rejects in principle "why" questions, at least those why questions that are directed toward impersonal domains, such as nature.[48] We seek a master plan or narrative when we seek the meaning of our lives, *but one does not exist.*

A plan, a grand narrative, would exist if there were some "superior being" who created us and fixed a purpose for us. In that case, the entirety of our lives could be judged as meaningful or meaningless to the extent that we adapted to the divinely intended purpose. But there are no good reasons to believe in a divine being or in a divine plan. Even if there were and we were convinced that the divine being has set a purpose for us to fulfill, that purpose would not be *ours* but that of the deity. Even a firm believer cannot honestly know the divine purpose: "They may indeed claim that it has been mysteriously revealed to them, but how can it be proved that the revelation is genuine?"[49] Even if we assume that it is, Ayer still finds an insuperable problem. If the deity is "sovereign," then everything that happens, including our behavior, is decreed by the deity – our determination to find our purpose in God's purpose is empty, for we could not do otherwise. If the deity is not sovereign and we have choice in the matter of conforming to God's purpose, why should we do so? Any choice to do so would be based on our independent judgment and decision to do so, thus rendering the deity superfluous. If *we* decide to live in conformity with God's supposed will on the basis of *our own* rational assessment, then the divine purpose would be an irrelevancy; it would fail to provide us with the "rule" that it is nonetheless our responsibility or necessity to adopt.[50] The addition of a deity brings more obfuscation than clarification to the search for meaning. The "why?" of life remains bootless, a question not legitimately to be asked.

Ayer revisits this theme forty years later, a year before his death, in a London lecture entitled "The Meaning of Life."[51] He is a bit more indulgent toward the question but no more confident that it can pass logical muster. He entertains the idea that meaning is strictly personal – one's work, hobbies, passions, family attachments, etc. can make for meaningful (i.e., satisfying) life. Thinking that rather shallow, he explores whether the posthumous endurance of one's reputation, or the knowledge of one's deeds as recollected by one's descendants, might contribute to a meaningful life. He admits that the idea that someone could still be reading his books a century after his death pleases him, but it doesn't seem to rise to the kind of answer the meaning-seeker wants. He considers whether the intensity with which a life is lived is an indication of its meaning. He also considers the idea that participating in something larger than oneself is what counts. In the latter case, however, the century was littered with people giving themselves to great causes, some of which were quite wicked. There is, he tells us, no necessary connection between morality and meaningfulness – a provocative insight that he doesn't further develop.[52] So, he comes around again to the question of whether life has a purpose, which would establish its nonsubjective meaningfulness. Absent a God – or even assuming a God – the sheer contingency of the world or, on the latter assumption, the self-defeating character of a divine plan, cannot underwrite meaning. We are left with an infinity of "how" questions insofar as life as a whole does not allow us to cogently raise the question of "why." The best we seem to be able to do is work out private versions of meaningfulness, none of which can really be justified in a noncircular way. Meaning thus founders on absurdity.

Ayer ends with a melancholy reflection on an imaginary saintly figure:

> ... a nun, belonging to a strict order, leading a life of austerity, but serene in the performance of her devotions, confident that she is loved by her deity, and that she is destined for a blissful future in the world to come .... The question is whether it matters that the deity in whose love she rejoices does not exist and that there is no world to come.[53]

In the example, the nun finds great meaning in her life so, in subjective terms, her life is one of satisfaction and worth. She has served God and tried to fulfill his plan for her. But, by Ayer's lights, she is deluded. Should "a strong respect for truth" lead to the view that the nun's life is less worthy than she imagines? "It would indeed be terrible for her to discover that the point of her life was nonexistent. But *ex hypothesi* this is something that she will never know."[54] Her subjective meaningfulness survives her objective (according to Ayer) "ignorance" of the real state of things. But should it? Can one have meaning in defiance of truth? Ayer can't say.[55]

The upshot of the example is that there can be no general answer to the question of what constitutes a meaningful life. It is no longer, as for the logical empiricists, an empty question; it is, rather, a terminally perplexing one. Whether that commends the inquiry or preempts it is unclear. Ayer leaves us with the recommendation of an attitude:

> So far as one can survey the Universe *sub specie aeternitatis* one has to agree with Macbeth. It is 'a tale told by an idiot, full of sound and fury, signifying nothing.' What is wrong with this quotation is its aura of disillusionment. It is not that we are sentenced to deprivation. It is open to us to make our lives as satisfying as our circumstances allow.[56]

No cosmic dread, no debilitating nihilism, no anxiety in the face of freedom for him. No existentialist anxieties darken his bonhomie. This would appear to be more than a quirk of a personal constitution. Believing that life is fundamentally meaningless and learning to live with it in a cheerful way have become a desirable modern stance, the stance of the ironist, who, in the words of a contemporary of the Jena Romantics, "hovers above all and eliminates all."[57]

THE LEGITIMACY OF THE QUESTION OF MEANING

The preceding section was expository. Let us now begin to compose a constructive account. To do so, we must develop some working definitions of "meaning," "absurdity," and "nihilism." To begin, let us consider why the meaning question is left standing.

What is wrong with supplanting the question of meaning by the question of purpose, with purpose constituted along natural law lines as achieving fulfillment through realizing intrinsic goods made evident by right reason? Consider a utopia in which all of its denizens lead thriving lives. It is more like Francis Bacon's *New Atlantis* than Aldous Huxley's *Brave New World*. It is not based on coercion or lies, noble or otherwise. The society is consensual, open, affluent, and, crucially, dedicated to knowledge, in the sense of the advancement of science. It is not, therefore, like a subtropical retirement community with people whiling away their time until the end arrives. Everyone has an estimable pursuit. Many are scientists, pushing the borders of knowledge and serving the common good. This is a society that facilitates real human flourishing – at no else's expense (no slaves, no underclass, etc.). The citizens are happy; their welfare and emotional needs are met. They have achieved the marks of thriving not only as biological creatures (cf. *Brave New World*) but as human beings. Would it still be reasonable for someone in the society to ask: "What is the meaning of all this? Is this all there is? Our lives are sweet, civilized, healthy, and satisfying, but are they meaningful? We have families, raise children, and pursue knowledge so that our children can have families, raise children, and pursue knowledge. What is the point of *that*?"

I think that it would be reasonable, not merely perverse or refractory, to ask these questions.[58] (Wouldn't Kohelet? Wouldn't Tolstoy?) Indeed, I can't imagine a point at which it would be reasonable to arrest such questions, as one arrests a child's persistent "why?" Under utopian conditions, the questions might be even more urgent than they are in our daily dystopia. It is one thing to strive to flourish. It is another to wonder what flourishing is for. The natural law tradition gives us an account of human flourishing, but it hardly precludes skeptical, if impertinent, questions about the presumed ultimacy of eudaimonia.[59] Aristotle considers eudaimonia to be an end in itself in contrast with those instrumental goods that serve it.

(Wealth, e.g., is instrumental to the higher, intrinsic good of happiness/flourishing.) This ordering makes sense in terms of the contrast that he has set up. But is eudaemonia an absolute end without the contrastive context? Nothing prevents us from asking what the end of the eudaemonistic end is.[60]

That we can raise such questions implies that the "absolute end" is less determinate than it once seemed. The justifications for the putative absolute no longer seem as convincing or as firm. They can no longer be asserted and win assent; they need to be backed up by argument. The ground has become "marshy." Human thriving as an ultimate end can look merely contingent or arbitrary. Is there any backstop for eudaemonia? Is there something beyond it that anchors it? Religious traditions that build on the Aristotelian scheme typically consummate the flourishing life in communion with God, an absolute end beyond the eudaemonistic end.[61] That would check the potential arbitrariness. For the contemporary secularist, however, ascribing absoluteness to God, which here means fixing a doubt-resistant justification for the direction the pious give their lives, seems no less arbitrary. It does not stop the regress of why questions. Indeed, doubt about God, the hoped for conceptual backstop, gives the questions renewed motivation.[62]

Flourishing underdetermines meaning. It is possible to live a flourishing life and still wonder what the point or significance of that life is. A good horse, which has achieved the equine virtues requisite to its nature cannot wonder about the point of doing so. A good man or woman cannot help but do so, especially since one of the human virtues is philosophical wisdom.[63] A part of us wants to climb the ladder of questioning for as long as it makes sense to do so or as long as we can hold on. The search for meaning is restless. I don't think that it can be quelled by confident assertions of human purpose, whether emanating from religious views or from natural law ethics, or, most often, from their synthesis. Nonetheless, flourishing is a great human achievement. Its importance should in no way be deprecated. It is simply not an analgesic for the question of meaning.

Meaning is analytically different from flourishing, albeit practically necessary for it. A life of exemplary practical (i.e., moral) and intellectual virtue, although highly desirable, is not its own justification. It must be located within a context that brings out its meaning – its importance and its sense. To flourish, we must interpret the meaning of a flourishing life. But is the requisite interpretive context available? Can we ever really justify, in a noncircular way, the life that we think it is most worthy to lead? Ayer rejected this as futile. All justifications run out somewhere, revealing a trace of absurdity at the end of the justificatory enterprise. Can stable meaning emerge and put the justification for a flourishing life on non-marshy ground? To begin answering these questions, let us look more closely at the terms that are critical to our inquiry: meaning, absurdity, and nihilism.

DEFINING TERMS: MEANING

Meaning is one of the values of the well-lived life, but it is not only a value among values. One's life is made more valuable by being meaningful, as it is by being courageous, generous, just, wise, and so on. But meaning adds value by giving sense to values; meaning fixes the significance of value. What then is meaning, as I am using the term? *Meaning is a response to values that fixes their significance.* Meaning integrates values into intelligible contexts and makes sense of the relations among them. One of its functions is to adjudicate conflicts among values. Say that we have two values: freedom and public health. At the time of this writing – during the pandemic of 2020 – these play an important role in our politics. They sometimes conflict. The maximization of one infringes on the other. We need a framework that brings out their significance and that locates them in a narrative (such as a historical, moral, or political tradition) so that we can get our bearings and decide how to weigh them.[64] This framing allows us to gain perspective on the values, to say why they *matter* to us and how we should *understand* them. There are two strands here: importance and intelligibility. The term "significance" incorporates both of these ideas. Significance implies both why x matters and what x "signifies" or "symbolizes." "Meaning," as I want to use the term, expresses both ideas.[65]

Meaning requires three terms. In the paradigmatic case of linguistic meaning, a locution (a word, a sentence) signifies something to someone. X means y to z.[66] "Help!" (x) means that a speaker is in need or distress (y) to someone (z) who hears the speaker shout. What x means becomes intelligible to z because z relates x to y. The sound "help" means "I am in distress and need assistance!" That latter locution has meaning within a broader context of intentional utterances, speech acts that, if successful, motivate listeners to take relevant actions. If the utterance succeeds, it will not only mean "I need assistance," but it will motivate a listener, who understands what "help" signifies, to assist the speaker.[67] This last step brings out the dimension of importance – of what the point of shouting "help" is. "Help" is not meaningful in and of itself. It is meaningful within a linguistically constituted lifeworld, where vulnerable beings, possessed of the capacity for empathy, can appeal to one another for acts of compassion and solidarity. The speech act, in this example, emerges from and is directed to a dimension of value. Lives, safety, well-being, assistance, mutuality, and solidarity *matter* in this world. A tremendous amount of biological, psychological, linguistic, and moral architecture support the meaningfulness of "help."

If the above is roughly correct, then, as a first approximation, we might say that the question of the meaning of life enquires into the value implicit in one's experiences so as to make their intelligibility and importance discursive and explicit. "Experiences," however, might prematurely limit the inquiry to discrete events – one's first kiss, one's high school graduation, the death of one's mother – and fail to attend to a broader context, such as whole phases of one's life or one's projects and plans. (To want to become a physician will motivate the experiences of going to college, to medical school, etc., but it is not per se an experience.) It also fails to attend to one's unique and particular selfhood, that is, to the subject of one's experiences, that which "accompanies" all experiences, projects, and plans. Better to say then that *the question of the meaning of life enquires into the value implicit in one's very being so as to make explicit its intelligibility and importance.*

Put simply: Meaning is an account we offer about what matters to us. We sense that our lives have value. We sense it both directly and obliquely, that is, through the obfuscation or abuse of that value. In the oblique case, we sense it in the feeling that how we live or what has happened to us *dis*serves the value of our lives. Meaning is a way of articulating the significance of that value – of giving it a voice or form. While meaning is an account we devise to reckon with our own worth as unique individuals, as persons, it is also a story we tell about all of us, about human life per se. Meaning renders this core of perceived value intelligible. It gives the intuition of value, of the worth and goodness of being, a measure. It allows us to evaluate how we are living and, most often, how we are failing to live rightly and well. It gives us a framework within which we evaluate the projects that constitute our lives and serve their underlying value.

Philosophers differ over whether the question of meaning is properly posed in terms of "meaning *in* life" or "meaning *of* life."[68] Those who opt for meaning in life find "meaning of life" wrong-headed. Such meaning aims, they charge, at a one-size-fits-all answer for everyone, thus offending against individuality. It presupposes a grand narrative, such as a divine plan or a rational process of history in which all human beings are assigned a role. Insofar as the meaning of life question assumes a purpose to life, whether divine or historical, many contemporary philosophers find it implausible. They opt for a more restrictive view; the better question is that of meaning *in* life. We should lower our sights and so lower our expectations for meaning. This will mitigate our disappointment with its elusive presence and absence. Ayer's rejection of the "aura of disillusionment" expressed in Macbeth's "tale told by an idiot signifying nothing" is indicative of this stance.

If we switch from the "traditional" question of the meaning of life to the less formidable one of meaning in life, we might pre-empt the threat of nihilism. Given a big question, we will need a big answer, and, lacking a realistic possibility of getting one, we can fall into despair that life is no more than an idiot's tale. If we rule out the big question and train ourselves on smaller ones, we will be content with finding plausible meaningfulness in everyday events, pursuits, projects, and plans.[69] The spiritual agony of a Tolstoy would get no traction. This is part of the motivation for the contemporary revision of the question.

Defining meaning down seems prudent but also premature – what Oakeshott calls "an arrest of thought." How do we know that the "meaning of" question is unanswerable? Aren't the answers to the "meaning in" question too facile? "Everyday" or "social" meaning was easily available to Ivan Illich, but it was also radically inadequate when put to the test. Everyday meaning seems to be compatible with a complete absence of "ultimate meaning." For contemporary philosophers, life as a whole may be meaningless, but that fact should not prevent us from finding adequate meaning in the "everyday." Although that might be the best we can do under our modern circumstances, I am inclined to reject this settlement and not give up on the "meaning of" question.

It may not be a binary choice. Finding legitimacy and exigency in the "of" question does not rob the "in" question of its cogency. The latter has a phenomenological point, not just a methodological one. To illustrate, Metz distinguishes between a "whole life view" of meaning and a "part life view."[70] He asks whether meaning is borne by one's life as a whole or only by stretches of it? Meaning *in* life works well with the partial view. An experience common to most of us supports this: There are times when life has meaningful moments and times when it does not. It's unrealistic, on this view, to think of the whole of one's life as meaningful; some of an ordinary life is mere habit, automaticity, drudgery, and boredom. Meaningful times stand out by virtue of their contrast with the quotidian baseline. If one is lucky to have had many meaningful moments in one's life, then one has had in sum a meaningful life, the "part life" advocate would say.

The whole life view, by contrast, can claim that even "meaningless" stretches of life can be retrospectively integrated into a meaningful pattern. Nothing is truly meaningless when one reflects on the course of one's life. Remembering "meaningless" times implicitly grants them significance.[71] The act of remembering selects and retrieves memories, making them available for interpretation and evaluation. They now matter and become intelligible. Recalling years spent in a dead-end job, soul-killing at the time, can bring one to understand what one learned from that experience. The possibility of retrospective meaning bolsters the whole life view.

The argument against the whole life view often focuses on the implausibility of a master narrative, such as the much-disputed divine plan.[72] Believers in such a plan – what medieval Jewish thinkers called "private providence" (*hashgaḥa pratit*) – can ask at any time, what is God doing here and now? Why is this happening to me? A dimension of meaning is continuously available. But for many in a secular age – not just bygone positivists like Ayer – this seems a fantasy. (Indeed, for some in a religious age, such as Maimonides, an actively intervening, moment-by-moment providence-exercising God was also a fantasy. A medieval naturalist like Maimonides saw God's hand in the regularity of the laws of nature not in the occasions of the moment. The course of a human life within that natural lawfulness and regularity, when devoted to communion with God and intellectual and moral virtue, is what human life on the whole should be about. With some important metaphysical innovations, this is Spinoza's view as well.)

The debate between "meaning in" and "meaning of" advocates with their correlative whole and part life evaluative frameworks brings out a tension between the two criteria that make for meaning: importance and intelligibility. Let us stipulate that life is always important, even if it doesn't feel that way. Life always has value; it always matters. But life is only intermittently intelligible. There are times when we don't understand the meaning of our lives, of what we are living through. It is rationally acceptable to say, when the circumstances of life warrant it, "I am trying to live a life I don't understand."[73] We can and do have crises of meaning, such as Ivan Ilych had. Even though our lives are important, we can fail to grasp some aspects of their significance. We have to work at finding their meaning. Meaning is not simply discovered, as if it were already there; it is construed. Meaning results from an interpretive process. There is no guarantee that we will succeed at this, nor are we continuously engaged in such a process; sometimes we just coast. In this sense, moments or stretches of life can be without meaning. But in none of these moments does life cease to matter. The radical fact of life having value ensures that one aspect of meaningfulness, importance, is continuous even if the intentional construal of meaning is episodic. Meaning-making, being dynamic, can pertain to both the parts and the whole of life. Metz approvingly calls this a "mixed" view.[74]

We can find meaning in the everyday dimension of our lives without preempting a larger, holistic meaning of life. Nonetheless, we have to be alert to the tensions and trade-offs between these levels of meaning. We do well to keep the "meaning of" question open. We should guard against the collapse, without remainder, of that question into the "meaning in" one. On the other side, we also need to guard against the nihilistic conclusion that (a) the "meaning of" question is real, but (b) its most plausible answer is negative – life has no meaning; it is meaningless – and that therefore (c) attempts to substitute "meaning in" answers for the negative "meaning of" answer are evasive and dishonest.[75] What we find meaningful, moment by moment, in our experience finds support in a larger story about the meaning of our lives. The latter is buttressed by occasions of meaning in our lives. One dimension need not undermine or overwhelm the other.

The model that I have proposed is that meaning emerges from a more or less deliberate, interpretive process. But it often feels as if this is not true. We often feel that meaning is found, not made.

That is because we all live, despite our pretensions to independence, in streams of tradition that are partly constituted by how they have interpreted life. Many meanings have been given to us by our normative traditions; we *haven't* devised them ourselves. It feels as if we have discovered them and, in a sense, we have. When one converts from one religious tradition to another, for example, one enters a world of prefabricated meanings, and incorporates them into one's understanding of oneself and one's life. These meanings have a history independent of one's own. But that cuts both ways. Ultimately, they have been construed by someone, by endlessly many past creators of meaning. However natural they might appear, human minds over the ages have drawn them out of the forest of signs, gradually expanding the clearing of the inhabitable, inheritable lifeworld. They have not simply been imposed on us, however. That we inherit them does not preclude our critical scrutiny of them or our personal incorporation of them. We ask what these ostensibly given meanings mean. Should we appropriate them? What would it be like and what does it mean to do so? Both meaning and the practices of creating and appropriating it call out for interpretation. Although meaning is not fully subjective, there is an ineliminable dimension of subjectivity to it.

Meaning is a construal of the value that we find reflected in our experience, indeed, of the value of our very being. But what if a person finds *no* value in being? What if our stipulation – that life is always important; that it always has value – falls flat for such a person? What if a person thinks that life is a cruel joke, that there is nothing worth caring about, nothing that matters? *Mai ikah l'meimar*, as the Talmud asks, what is there to say to such a person? If there is no noticing of value in the first place, there can be no meaning. There would be nothing to interpret or construe. A sense of valuelessness and hence of meaningless insignificance, once ensconced, would have vicious circularity. The conviction of meaninglessness would obscure or obliterate value, further blinding us to its presence. An ontological listlessness or indifference would replace a normal human life of mattering and caring. Perhaps one could come to such a condition through philosophical questioning – through accepting a thoroughgoing skepticism about the worth of life, for example. (Could one be trapped in a view from nowhere and not have to return to a view from here? Would that constitute the ancient ideal of apatheia?) Perhaps an incorrigible belief in reductive physicalism, contingency, chance, or contrariwise, determinism could undermine one's naive feelings about the value of life. Or perhaps the indifference has psychological roots. What to say to such a person depends on how that person came to his or her indifference. Whether the "therapy" is philosophical or psychological or both, it seems right to engage such a person, to enter into a conversation and find out whether one can help. One should care. But perhaps this merely begs the question against the true nihilist. As our inquiry unfolds, I shall argue that it does not.

DEFINING TERMS: ABSURDITY

We have earlier referred to "absurdity" in our discussion of Kohelet. Kohelet's thinking led him to consider human life from a universal, detached, or objective perspective. He didn't like what he saw: A cosmos presided over by a distant, inscrutable God; an implacable, repetitive cycle of nature which mocked human distinctiveness (vis-à-vis the animal world), crushed human achievement, and rendered human action feckless and trivial. From the point of view of the whole, our finitude, transience, and mortality sap the meaning out of life. Life itself and all its manifestations are *hevel*, vaporous. The realization of the transience and insignificance of the vaporous is captured by "absurd," which Michael Fox, a leading scholar of Kohelet, takes as one of the meanings of *hevel*.

In conventional language, "absurd" is equivalent to ludicrous, laughable, illogical, preposterous, or inappropriate. What unites these meanings is the sense that reasoning as such has made itself ridiculous. Reason itself has run into trouble. The sober rational operations of the mind have led to risible, irrational conclusions. Sophistry, which apes reasonableness, can be funny, as in:

This goat is yours.
This goat is a mother.
Therefore, this goat is your mother.[76]

The humor is a response to the unexpected appearance of the unreasonable. Reasoning has led to an absurd conclusion.

Concluding that your mother is a goat is an isolated episode of fallacious reasoning being mistaken for valid inference. That is common enough but also not much to worry about. There is, however, a class of claims that manages to be both reasonable *and* rationally unacceptable. This is the phenomenon of paradox that, unlike common fallacies, motivates us to ask deep questions about language, thought, and even reality as such. Paradoxes have been with us since the dawn of philosophy. The pre-Socratics discovered and labored to solve the paradoxes of time, space, and motion; they "regarded the desire to resolve them as the prime motive of metaphysics ...."[77] Classic paradoxes, such as Zeno's racecourse problem, resist being discarded as mere *nonsense* insofar as they seem to hint at something deeper. That something deeper is intriguing and unsettling. As Scruton puts it with typical elegance: "[Paradox] is a destabilizing force, and also a strange invitation to commitment. There is something in the human psyche which, faced with an unbelievable proposition, rushes forward to embrace it, to say 'yes, it *must* be so!', and to rejoice in the ruin of common sense that follows."[78]

In one of Zeno's examples, in order to complete a race, we must first go halfway over the course. But in order to go halfway, we must go a quarter of the way. In turn, we must go an eighth of the way, a sixteenth of the way, and so on to infinity. Since we can't traverse infinity, we can't finish the race. But, of course, we can. In another version, Achilles races against a tortoise, to whom he has given a head start. Achilles can never catch up because no matter how small a distance the tortoise has traveled, Achilles must travel an infinitely divisible distance to reach the tortoise, who has continued to travel on. Having to traverse an infinity defeats the possibility of closing the gap. But, again, we know from experience that, given the requisite fitness, we can run the course or surpass the tortoise. Yet at the same time, it seems impossible for us or Achilles to do so, at least on the apparently reasonable premise that space is infinitely divisible. We are stuck with two reasonable truths that cannot easily be reconciled. Zeno's conclusion was that our commonsense view of the world – with its seeming reality of continuous motion in traversable space and forward flowing time – has got to go. Fatal self-contradictions are buried in those ideas. (Zeno concluded, therefore, that reality is fundamentally other than how it appears. Change is an illusion; true reality is changeless, as his teacher Parmenides taught. A profound metaphysical shift rather than logical gimmickry was needed to resolve the paradox.) A genuine paradox unsettles because it shows that reason in its deepest deployments fails us. Such self-contradictions are not just unfortunate bugs; they are features of human thought, especially about the most important matters. Paradox reveals reason's propensity to run up against the absurd.

One modern writer, the nineteenth-century Danish philosopher, Søren Kierkegaard, grounds Christianity on the recognition of this condition. Another, the twentieth-century French writer, Albert Camus, accepts its tragic wisdom but rejects, unlike Kierkegaard, the compensations of faith. Kierkegaard puts absurdity at the core of his outlook. For him, reason's inability to dismiss paradox as mere nonsense reveals to reason its own limits and finitude.[79] Self-aware reason, struck by paradoxicality, abandons its naïve claim to infinite scope or confidence. Reason comes to know itself through its limits. Hence, paradox is not an occasional malaise of reason, but of its essence. This has nothing to do with intellectual laziness or languor. Indeed, only the most rigorous and consistent use of reason will reveal its limitations. As Schufreider, interpreting Kierkegaard, puts it: "Only the relentless employment of reason can guarantee [that] its breakdown is genuine, that it occurs in the face of the incomprehensible, of that which cannot be understood, not in the face of that which we have simply not bothered to understand."[80] This is where absurdity enters.

In the absurd condition, the very truths that conflict in paradox defy rational access. For Kierkegaard, it is absurd "that the eternal truth has come into being in time, that God has come into being, has been born, has grown up, and so forth, precisely like any other individual human being, quite indistinguishable from other individuals."[81] The Incarnation is absurd. Its paradoxicality is so deep that its very claims are repellant to reason. For Kierkegaard, the way of genuine faith (i.e., Christianity) is an encounter with the absurd. In the face of the absurdity of central Christian claims what genuine faith requires is total risk, total commitment. This is as it should be, for the highest reality is not rational; objective methods cannot wholly disclose its essence. Kierkegaard doesn't want to sack objectivity and its truths. He does want to demote and relocate them within a rich account of subjectivity. The way to encounter reality as it matters to us is to embrace absurdity in the "extremity of faith."[82]

Camus like Kierkegaard puts absurdity at the center of our relation to the world. He agrees, in his own way, with Kierkegaard's elevation of subjective commitment and resolve. He rejects, of course, Kierkegaard's Christianity. In Camus's *The Myth of Sisyphus*, absurdity is born of a "confrontation between the human need and the unreasonable silence of the world."[83] What is "the human need?" We want to get to the heart of things – to grasp things with certainty. We seek intelligibility and clarity. Above all, we want to know that our lives matter; we want to know the meaning of life. But reason cannot provide these goods; it gives us local truths about how things work, and it gives us truisms about what they mean. But there is always a vast gap between what we need and what the uncooperative, recondite world affords us. "Today people despair of true knowledge."[84] Camus believes that our rational quest for knowledge ends in irrationality. None of us can say, in a significant way, "I know that":

> This heart within me I can feel, and I judge that it exists. This world I can touch, and I likewise judge that it exists. There ends all my knowledge, and the rest is construction. For if I try to seize

> this self of which I feel sure, if I try to define and summarize it, it is nothing but water slipping through my fingers. I can sketch one by one all the aspects it is able to assume ... this upbringing, this origin, this ardor or these silences, this nobility or this vileness. But aspects cannot be added up. This very heart which is mine will forever remain indefinable to me. Between the certainty I have of my existence and the content I try to give to that assurance, the gap will never be filled. Forever I shall be a stranger to myself.[85]

The elusiveness of our own reality is matched by the elusiveness of the external world. The picture of the world given to us by science, painted in descriptions, classifications, statements of law, and ever more reductionist materialistic ontologies, all true in their own ways, becomes akin to poetry. The constructions of science do not, in the end, give us the certainty we seek. They give us models, probabilities, metaphors for how the world is and how it works. Our ultimate ignorance of the world, the science notwithstanding, puts science on the same footing as artistic images and poetic verses – they are "constructions." They don't penetrate to the heart of things about which we yearn to know:

> I realize that if through science I can seize phenomena and enumerate them, I cannot, for all that, apprehend the world. Were I to trace its entire relief with my finger, I should not know any more. And you give me the choice between a description that is sure but that teaches me nothing and hypotheses that claim to teach me but that are not sure. A stranger to myself and to the world, armed solely with a thought that negates itself as soon as it asserts, what is this condition in which I can have peace only by refusing to know .... Hence the intelligence, too, tells me in its way that this world is absurd.[86]

The absurd is thus a relation between humans and the world. We can not give up on our efforts to fully understand the world and neither can we free ourselves from the haunting insight that our efforts inevitably fall short; there is a cleft between yearning and truth, the will to know and what can be known. We are committed in the name of reason to an irrational, because unachievable, project. "I want everything to be explained to me or nothing. And the reason is impotent when it hears this cry from the heart. The mind aroused by this insistence seeks and finds nothing but contradictions and nonsense .... The world itself, whose single meaning I do not understand is but a vast irrational."[87] There is no meaning – *that* is the "meaning" for which we have sought. Living with meaninglessness, accepting the full implications of absurdity – that is our lot. Camus counsels an attitude of courage, responsibility, a heroism in living with the irrational. We are to revolt against illusions and false imputations of meaning, against religions and philosophies that try to relax the tension between humanity and the world that results in absurdity.

It is a troubling vision. There is a permanent structural mismatch between humans and their world such that human beings can never be at home in the world in a meaningful way. ("If I were a tree among trees, a cat among animals, this life would have a meaning, or rather this problem would not arise, for I should belong to this world. I should *be* this world to which I am now opposed by my whole consciousness ...."[88]) All of our rational attempts to secure grounds for the importance and intelligibility of our lives run up against the unreasonableness of the world. We wrest no meaning from it. ("I don't know whether this world has a meaning that transcends it. But I know that I do not know that meaning and that it is impossible for me just now to know it. What can a meaning outside my condition mean to me?"[89]) Absent cosmic meaning, we do not have local or parochial meanings; they cannot hold their own. We have meaninglessness. *But* meaninglessness liberates – life "will be lived all the better if it has no meaning."[90] Camus's charge is to live in constant rebellion against our condition, expressed negatively as a refusal to accept artificial reconciliations and illusory meanings. He rejects nihilism, but his critics might well ascribe that view to him. At any rate, his "nihilism," if such it be, is life-affirming and remarkably humane.[91]

The contemporary analytic philosopher, Thomas Nagel, such as both Kierkegaard and Camus, sees absurdity as an ineliminable feature of the human condition.[92] Nagel, contra Camus, locates it not in the confrontation between human longing and the world but in a confrontation with ourselves.[93] On Nagel's analysis, we routinely shuttle between two distinct stances, namely, an external and an internal view. These are colorfully called "the view from nowhere" and the "view from here." The former is self-transcending. It brackets our individual particularity, our individual importance, our taken-for-granted presumption that the world revolves around our being – that without us there would be no world. Our routine subjectivity (the view from here), the framework in which so much of our lives are lived, can be suspended by another part of us. The taken for grantedness of our personal world, our lifeworld, is put into question by our capacity for objectivity. While Kierkegaard proposes a radical epistemology/ethos that privileges subjective over objective knowing, Nagel wants to remain in a fraught but fertile dialectic between the two.

Perhaps the most structured instantiation of the objective stance is science. But it is far from the only one; we are each involved in objective appraisals without formal training or awareness that we are doing so. In morality, for example, whenever we weigh our own interests against those of others and decide in favor of equality of treatment, we assume a view from nowhere. Morality is a fertile ground for nurturing the objective view. As important as we are to ourselves, we recognize, at least momentarily, that objectivity – bracketing our interests from our assessment of how things are or, in the case of morality, should be – has authority over us as well.

It is important to note that the view from nowhere, the objective stance, does not guarantee access to objective truth.[94] To believe so would be mere cognitive wish fulfillment. The abstract view is a *method*, a way of bracketing our egocentricity, our anthropocentricity. It does not clinch noetic access to the world in itself or any such thing. It is a way of complicating our taken-for-granted beliefs and extricating ourselves from self-interested reasoning. Its results, as to truth, are another matter.

On Nagel's account, absurdity arises because of the tensions between the taken for grantedness of our subjectivity and the pressure put on that standpoint by our capacity to view it as if from afar:

> The subjective view is at the core of everyday life, and the objective develops initially as a form of extended understanding; much of what it reveals can be used instrumentally in the pursuit of subjective aims. But taken far enough, it will undermine those aims; to see myself objectively as a small, contingent, and exceedingly temporary organic bubble in the universal soup produces an attitude approaching indifference .... The same person who is subjectively committed to a personal life in all its rich detail finds himself in another aspect simultaneously detached; this detachment undermines his commitment without destroying it – leaving him divided.[95]

Both the subjective and the objective standpoints are essential parts of us; neither can be suppressed in favor of the other. Absurdity is our awareness of their radically different, but equally ineliminable judgments on our importance and on how we are to understand ourselves.

Nagel has taken the etiology of the absurd and internalized it. It is not the unreasonableness of the external world as a whole, as perceived by the disappointed, outraged, or yearning mind of a Kohelet or a Camus that generates a sense of absurdity. As with Kierkegaard and paradox, its origin lies in the normal operations of thought, as deployed by creatures who have both selves and the ability to bracket and transcend them. Absurdity is a kind of skepticism in which we become aware of the deeply and irreducibly problematic character of our own judgment. Our problem is how to live with absurdity, especially as it undermines our judgments of what is valuable and meaningful in our lives. Given the origins of absurdity in an internal, albeit normal, discord between our epistemic perspectives, securing meaning and integrating those perspectives are related activities. We need to figure out both how to justify the meaningfulness of the lifeworld against the challenge of the view from nowhere and how to keep the view from nowhere and the view from here as integrated as possible.

We can become aware of absurdity and the problem of meaning within the subjectivity of daily life. This was Tolstoy's intimation. In principle, subjectivity has the resources to bring us back to a world of stable meanings. But as with Tolstoy finding all meanings threatened by a godless universe, once the subjective view, with its human lifeworld, accedes to the authority of the objective view, nothing seems to matter. Our greatest, most meaningful activities – such as Tolstoy's writing immortal novels – seem negligible. The justifications for doing what we have been doing seemed valid, given the limited scope of our vision, but from the expanded view from nowhere perspective, they no longer count for much. It is then not just the subjective self whose meaningful world is weakened. Since the objective self – the self as it views the world from nowhere – has to continue to live in this world, too, "the objective self is dragged along by the unavoidable engagement of the whole person in the living of a life whose form it recognizes as arbitrary."[96] Thus, "finding my life objectively insignificant, I am nevertheless unable to extricate myself from an unqualified commitment to it – to my aspirations and ambitions, my wishes for fulfillment, recognition, understanding, and so forth. *The sense of the absurd is the result of this juxtaposition.*"[97]

Nagel sees several possible responses to absurdity as a fact of life. Let us consider two. First, we can deny the claims of the subjective point of view. We could, like some ancient ascetics, attempt to completely transcend and abandon the human world. Nagel is so horrified by this prospect that he admits that "I would rather lead an absurd life engaged in the particular than a seamless transcendental life immersed in the universal."[98]

The second response is the opposite of the first; we can deny the claims of the objective point of view. We could resolve to stay within the familiar world of the subjective self. We could deny the authority (or the reality) of an objective point of view. We could preempt the seeming challenge of objective meaninglessness by asserting that meaningfulness is only available from a point of view *internal* to our lifeworld – and that is all there is. That meaning is unavailable objectively doesn't mean that there is no meaning at all; meaning exists within the lifeworld. Why shouldn't that be enough? A person who is deaf from birth cannot hear music, but she shouldn't conclude from this that music doesn't exist, or that it lacks value, or is meaningless. Looking for meaning in the (alleged) objective order is a category mistake. Justifying values and meanings are internal practices. Saying that justification is unsupported by the external point of view is not a deficiency. Although there is some truth to this, Nagel does not think that it can "harmonize the two standpoints." Our proneness toward adopting an objective view – an essential part of what it is for us to think – will always upset our justificatory practices; they can't be cordoned off or protected from the doubt inspired by the view from nowhere. "Objectivity is not content to remain a servant of the individual perspective and its values. It has a life of its own and an aspiration for transcendence that will not be quieted in response to a call to reassume our true identity."[99] Nagel does not accept a weakening of the reality or of the authority of objectivity. Our true identity always subsists within the uneasy relation between the distinct perspectives that we can assume.

There is more to say about Nagel's strategies for diminishing the tension that gives rise to absurdity. But, for now, we can conclude with his sober – neither resigned (like Schopenhauer) nor rebellious (like Camus) – admission that "the absurd is part of human life. I do not think this can be basically regretted, because it is a consequence of our existence as particular creatures with a capacity for objectivity." Heightening the "civil wars of the self" results in an impoverished life.[100] Better to play the middle against the two ends. Ayer, one imagines, might applaud Nagel's nontragic acceptance of the way it is for us vis-à-vis meaning and absurdity. Kierkegaard might reject his – I would say rather Jewish – insistence on the authority of an objective, rational point of view.

For both Nagel and Camus, the awareness of absurdity emerges from a relation that we have with the world. For Camus, the relation between the mind and the world is as such; for Nagel, it is between discrepant aspects of ourselves in our encounter with the world. Both thinkers see human experience instinct with absurdity. Camus finds this shattering and bracing. Kierkegaard finds it revelatory and transformative. Nagel finds it a problem with which the sober philosopher must cope. It doesn't lead to nihilistic consequences for him but rather to the need for a kind of philosophical therapy. I find Nagel's view appealing and adopt (and adapt) it in what follows. Absurdity is not tragedy; it doesn't negate meaning altogether. If I am correct that Judaism has an ongoing awareness of the absurd and that that awareness does not result in nihilism, Nagel will be helpful in developing my account. First, let us see how nihilism fits into the picture.

DEFINING TERMS: NIHILISM

As mentioned in the previous section, "nihilism" enters the vocabulary of modern European languages with Jacobi's critical description of Fichte's philosophy. Jacobi accused Fichte of the "nihilism of reason."[101] This reminds us that nihilism, in the meaning intended by Jacobi, is not primarily an *attitude*, such as indifference, despair, or contempt, but a flawed way of *thinking*. Jacobi's complaint was that Fichte's philosophy abolished the givenness of the world in which individual humans are constituted by their relations and duties to one another, and by their relationship with God. It is not that Fichte was a cynical or skeptical foe of moral order – far from it. It was that the new epistemological and metaphysical basis on which he proposed to justify it – an ontology developed from radical subjectivity – was wholly inadequate to the task. It undermined what it hoped to secure. *Pace* Jacobi, Fichte (and Kant) had led themselves – and others – astray. Thus, nihilism has to do not with a blind, anarchic assault on normative traditions but on the belief that they can be sustained in an entirely new way.

As the concept of nihilism develops in the nineteenth century, however, it *does* come to signify an attitude of uncompromising negativity toward inherited norms, a commitment to their destruction, and the deliberate lack of a positive program of normative ideals and institutions to replace them. This is the "political nihilism" of mid–nineteenth-century Russian intellectuals, depicted in such novels as Dostoevsky's *Demons* and Turgenev's *Fathers and Sons*. Furthermore, by the end of the nineteenth century, Nietzsche embraced the term "nihilism" to describe both what he was against and what he was for. The term acquires an ambiguity that it has not quite shaken. For Nietzsche, nihilism seems to mean a willful ignorance of the truth that "God is dead," an evasion of this bitter truth, an attempt to keep going with the old morality that was sustained by God, and a blindness toward the real condition of modern humanity, namely, that the old values were devaluing themselves. Nihilism is living in that illusory condition and pretending that things are otherwise.[102] In this sense, Nietzsche presents himself as a prophet, as Zarathustra, an anti-nihilist.[103] On the other hand, Nietzsche portrays nihilism as a *positive* development insofar as it exposes the massive hypocrisy of modern life and clears the path for a new morality, allowing a new post-Christian, spiritual aristocracy (of *Übermenschen*) to emerge.[104] This basic ambiguity complicates how we should take "nihilism." Is it positive or negative, active or passive, political, epistemological, moral, or existential?[105]

It seems to be all of these and therefore highly perspective-dependent. The meaning of "nihilism" as ascribed to a view or a thinker depends on the perspective of the one making the ascription. Socrates seems to be a nihilist, if the anachronism is allowed, in the view of the Athenians; he is condemned to death on the charge of atheism and corrupting youth through his unremitting questioning of all the pieties.[106] In Plato's eyes, however, Socrates is an anti-nihilist. He wants to liberate humanity from its cave of self-imposed ignorance of ultimate truth. Socrates's "nihilism," from Plato's point of view, is heroic, not despicable. The defenders of the existing order are the true nihilists; the radicals who seek to expose its shaky foundations redeem us from our own nihilism. If we keep the perspective-dependence of the usage of the term in mind, it will go some way toward diminishing its ambiguity.

The sense of nihilism that I want to develop here, however, is neither heroic nor positive. I want to stick with the term's history, with, therefore, the negative valence that it has in conventional language. Nihilism, as I will use the term, is a reaction to absurdity. Absurdity, I have suggested, is a longstanding concomitant of our epistemic practices. But it takes on a particular character in modernity; thus, *nihilism is a reaction to modern absurdity.* A sense of the absurd arises when we assume a perspective that minimizes our significance and weakens our confidence that we and all of our works and ways do not, on the whole, matter. Nihilism takes that conclusion to be final. Indeed, nihilism takes it to be original and definitive: We ought to begin with the realization that life is meaningless. Nihilism accepts meaninglessness as a kind of anti-revelation. The truth of nothingness has been revealed. Whether an "aura of disillusionment" accompanies this anti-revelation or a mood of stalwart or even happy resolve, the stance is essentially nihilistic.

Nihilism rejects that there can be a meaning of life (but not necessarily meaning *in* life) in modernity. It is convinced that life is meaningless in an essential way. An ancient sophist could say that "man is the measure of all things," thus asserting a thoroughgoing conventionalism. But there was a backstop. Nature gave us normative guidance as to the best way of life. The sophist was a relativist but not a nihilist. For the ideal-typical modern, there is no backstop. God is dead and nature is mute as to how to live or what to live for. Nature is all fact but no value. Nature is meaningless. The more the universe seems comprehensible, the more it also seems pointless, as Steven Weinberg opined.[107]

Nihilism takes the most important implication of absurdity to be the defeat of meaning. In a defiant mood, it celebrates this as a great truth, a breakthrough to new possibilities for thought and action, a courageous enterprise. It might be. But what justifies our giving up on meaning so quickly and with such finality? Do we know in advance that there is no reason to persevere in the search for meaning, absurdity notwithstanding? Why shouldn't the process of thinking undermine the putative certainties of nihilism as well? Why put a brake on the life of the mind in its properly open-ended practice of interpreting the world? Why should we lose hope? Concerns such as these motivated Hannah Arendt's characterization of nihilism:

> The quest for meaning, which relentlessly dissolves and examines anew all accepted doctrines and rules, can at any moment turn against itself, produce a reversal of the old values, and declare these contraries to be "new values." ... Such negative results of thinking will then be used with the same unthinking routine as before; the moment they are applied to the realm of human affairs, it is as though they had never gone through the thinking process. What we commonly call "nihilism" – and are tempted to date historically, decry politically, and ascribe to thinkers who allegedly dared to think "dangerous thoughts" – is actually a danger inherent in the thinking activity itself. There are no dangerous thoughts; thinking itself is dangerous but nihilism is not its product ... *[Nihilism] does not arise out of the Socratic conviction that an unexamined life is not worth living, but, on the contrary, out of the desire to find results that would make further thinking unnecessary.*[108]

On Arendt's view, nihilism is an artificially imposed arrest, an unwarranted halt on a process of reasoning that ought to go on. It apes the critical function of thought but without the courage of thought. It wants to overturn but is content to remain constrained by that which it has overturned. Perhaps this is not fair to nihilism, at least to Nietzsche's or Tartaglia's nihilism. It does, however, expose the intellectual – and anti-intellectual – root of the matter. Nihilism is the doppelgänger of modern absurdity. But it abandons the path – it announces the end of the path – that absurdity continues to tread.

A MODEL OF MEANING

The question of the meaning of life enquires into the value implicit in one's very being so as to make explicit its intelligibility and importance. Meaning is a construal, an interpretation of value or, more expansively, of phenomena that have value. Something must now be said about both value and interpretation. The questions here have to do with the status of value and of those interpretive practices by which we make sense of it. Are values real features of the world in an objective way or projections of minds onto a valueless world? This is the question of what philosophers call normative (or moral, when ethical values are at issue) realism. It is tied to a more general inquiry into what counts as real; this is the question of metaphysical realism. Can something be objective without being real in the way that physical entities are real? If so, are values objective without being entities? These are vast fields unto themselves; we will have to be content here with some very rough approximations.[109]

As to interpretation, is it a bound variable, an activity responsible to some canons or rules, or is it a free for all? Our reigning prejudice is that it is roughly the latter, a matter of taste or mere subjectivity. Yet this does not seem right. To use Ronald Dworkin's example, a critic who has spent his life working on Hamlet and writes a learned study of the play cannot but feel his interpretation has more truth in it than a tyro's who has just seen the play.[110] Is he wrong to do so? It would be self-impeaching for him to say, "Well, it's only my opinion." Why should we trust his interpretation if it matters so little to him? He would betray the value that motivated his response in the first place. Similarly, if a judge, after interpreting a statute in consequence of which he imposed a severe penalty, said "Well, that's my opinion but yours might be just as good," we would think him unfit to be on the bench. These cases imply that the meanings an interpreter develops in relevant contexts of interpretation gain their authority by being answerable to public standards that govern interpretive practice.

The practices and standards of interpretation in various domains do not seem categorically different from the practices and standards of truth-seeking in the sciences. There, the viability of explanations is bound up with how an explanation takes account of the evidence, whether an explanation conserves or coheres with prior theory, whether it mutilates other bodies of belief, whether it survives falsification, etc. There is nothing about interpretation that condemns it to idiosyncratic subjectivity, while science, by contrast, gets to enjoy the presumption of the objective truth of its claims. Both types of inquiries are embedded in the value-laden practices of human knowing.(Does the view from nowhere forget that condition? Does it not have its own value-laden practices? I shall argue later that it does.) Both interpretation and explanation must be responsive not only to the "facts" that motivate the inquiry but to the norms that govern its conduct. They are dual manifestations of human understanding.[111]

We are disposed to say, given the residuum of positivism that is still with us, that scientific explanations are true or false, while interpretations are good or bad, adequate or inadequate. But is there any practical difference between adequacy and rational acceptability? Without Platonizing truth, is it different from rational acceptability? Whether meaning survives the encounter with absurdity and the negative vote of nihilism depends in part on how we decide how to live with – I won't say "settle" – these questions.

I have claimed that meanings are made, not found. An exception is when we are dealing with "speaker's" or conversational meaning. If we hear a human language that we understand or if we encounter an artifact made by a human being with the aim of communicating, there is meaning implicit in the word or object. We bring it out, collaborating with the speaker or creator.[112] In the case of the meaning of life, or meaning in life, however, it can be a matter of creating meaning that is not antecedent to our reflection. We have a measure of freedom in making sense of ourselves. Nonetheless, it is often the case that traditions of various kinds – which are a pervasive feature of human life – present us with antecedent meaning. We have the experience of finding meaning in and through tradition. Even in this case, however, traditional meanings need to be appropriated through interpretation. Although tradition conveys meaning, we still have to breathe life into it; we have to adapt it to our situation and make it our own. None of this is purely subjective, in the sense of "arbitrary."

What binds meaning with respect to life is its adequacy, more ambitiously, its success as an interpretation of the values with which our lives are constitutively engaged. Getting values right is the job of meaning. Establishing criteria for determining how well meaning does its job, however, is no easy matter. Arriving at workable criteria for the success of interpretations is an ongoing, elenctic process. Prima facie, a plausible view might be that interpretations that have stood the test of time, which have sedimented into traditions and have provided rubrics of meaning for uncountable generations of human beings, have a claim on success. Thus, the interpretation of the departure of Israelite slaves from Egypt as a *liberation*, which in turn is based on the normative value of liberty, which, more deeply, is based on the existential value of human beings as made "in the image of God" is a good candidate for being a successful interpretation. The availability of that complex of meanings in Western culture has funded interpretations of later historical events, such as the struggle to abolish slavery in the United States.[113] The growth of a tradition of meaning over historical time – regardless of the factual status of the events that motivated the interpretation – might speak to the adequacy, even to the success, of those interpretations.[114]

Of course, neither the long duration of a tradition nor its central role in people's lives make it invulnerable to doubt or guarantee its truth (on the assumption that truth pertains to interpretation). It indicates rather that the adherents of the interpretive tradition have found it plausible, even compelling; it has supported the conviction of a meaningful life. This doesn't vindicate the tradition, but it can speak well of its wisdom. That many have found it wise, assuming (as we should if we are generous) that the many are not merely stupid or confused, implies that the meanings are good enough to sustain the lives of the persons who have construed them. Meanings sustain persons, in their joys and sorrows, troubles and triumphs; they are good enough to make sense of vicissitudes and crises. They are able to clarify the complex range of values that all human beings encounter in the course of their lives, bringing out, in a rich way, their intelligibility and importance. Indeed, not only the meanings but the traditions that bear them become meaningful. Tradition as such can be meaningful.

What about the values that underlie interpretation? "Getting the values right" requires much thought about what they are. What is to be gotten right here? At least analytically, values are distinguishable from their meanings. They motivate us to act, judge, deliberate, or desire. They provide us with reasons to think and do. (Wanting to avoid unnecessary reification, some would say that values just *are* reasons simpliciter.) Values also shape our choices, responses, and actions without self-conscious, rational reflection insofar as they have helped form our dispositions. It is not just a matter of rational choice – that might be the least of it. Our character, our very selfhood, comes down to our commitments. What we are is in large measure what we stand for.[115] We constitute ourselves by incorporating the meanings that we construe from the values that guide us. Meaning-making is self-making.

Meaning reflects on values and makes their significance explicit. Values limit the range of possible meanings. If you consistently treat a friend poorly, you lose the right to be considered a friend. Friendship can't mean something wholly idiosyncratic to you such as: Treat friends and enemies indistinguishably. Interpretation, as Dworkin argued, cannot be freewheeling.

Consider a case. You are on a subway and some bigots come up to a woman in a hijab and start saying crude and hateful things to her. You could melt into the crowd and avert your gaze, but you decide to go sit next to her and stare down the bullies. They back off, but even if they hadn't, you resolved to intervene on her behalf. You showed courage. In retrospect, this was a meaningful moment in your life. Reflecting on it, you relate your courage to your strong beliefs about decency, acceptance, respect – about what kind of society you want to live in and about what you think our society fundamentally stands for. These interpretations of courage bring out the meaning – the intelligibility and importance – of your act. What you did then, who you were then, will play an important role in the way you think about yourself and tell others, perhaps your children or grandchildren, about your life. It will clarify the nature of what it is to live well for you. It will establish a benchmark for future actions or omissions. It will be part of your story.

Thinking about your action as courageous is not "merely subjective." There are public, shared criteria to which the description/evaluation "courageous" is answerable. If you behaved in a cowardly way, pretending, say, that the matter didn't concern you and keeping your head down, you could not, without deceit, claim to have been courageous. The value has an objective dimension, not as a "queer" entity in a universe of waves and particles, but as a reason for action that puts pressure on our personal beliefs or inclinations. We don't have to Platonize or reify values and give them some odd ontological standing in a universe that otherwise seems brute factual. (We don't have to be metaphysical realists about value to grasp its objective status.) What we do have to recognize is that we can't be arbitrary in our interpretations and expect to be understood. If we are arbitrary, people will not understand what we mean when we talk about value. Saying that someone is courageous, as well as interpreting what "courageous" means, is governed by linguistic practices that are themselves normative. Interpretation is normative all the way down. We cannot escape the web of norms and still presume to be talking about the world.

From a nihilistic point of view, this is ultimately question begging. The embedding of value in a shared human world of norms does nothing to persuade the nihilist that life per se is meaningful. That the lifeworld is full of meaning is not at issue. The problem, for the nihilist, is that the lifeworld is not firmly rooted in the world as such, that is, the world viewed objectively, the merely (supposedly) brute-factual universe that is indifferent to human beings. But how do we *know*, *pace* Steven Weinberg and endless others, that the world is indifferent (or, more precisely, value-free)? What underwrites our confidence that taking an objective view of nature as a whole gives us a value-free world? I concede that it does not give us a world that aligns with our human values, at least with the ethical ones, but is it value-free for all that? How could we know this? It is analogous to the question of whether beauty is in the eye of the beholder or a property of the independent world to which the beholder responds. Our modern assumption is that beauty is in the eye of beholder, but once we subject our default assumption to critical scrutiny, our reasons for holding it are less cogent than they seemed. This is also true for modality – the status of necessity in the world – and for value as well.[116] Why?

Purging value and value properties from the world is only possible if we can secure a "metaphysically purified" perspective in which brute facts appear without any evaluative accompaniment.[117] But to secure such a perspective, we would need a metaphysical argument to show that the perspective exists. *That* putative argument could not avoid relying on values such as validity, truth, coherence, and reasonableness. The needed "metaphysically purified" perspective would depend on an argument that would be self-impeaching. Relatedly, we would also need a value-free language in which to communicate the deliverances of the metaphysically purified perspective. For that we would have to convince ourselves that *no* evaluative statement about the world beyond our lifeworld (assuming that we could demarcate such a world) is true. The metaphysically purified perspective would need to eliminate all value terms from its language. Is such a reduction even possible? It is hard to see how it could be. Values seem to be indispensable to human cognition and communication. Of course, indispensability is not a proof that the world as it is independently of us has value or value properties. We can't know that either. Our ineluctable skepticism might foster a sense of the absurd. But it shouldn't warrant the dogmatic conclusion of nihilism.

We can despair, if we are so minded, of our epistemic incapacity, but we ought not to despair because of the presumptive valuelessness of the world, for we can't know that that is so. What we can know is that value is ineliminable from our thinking.[118] Thought, belief, and agency are not value-free characterizations of what we are about. We can't think about ourselves as thinkers without value laden concepts. Attempting to eliminate value leads to a performative contradiction:

> A conception of an independent world so austere as not to mention human perceivers or believers or agents at all would not be an adequate conception of the world we live in. It is not a conception of the world that anyone could even have if the world were only as that conception says it is. It leaves no room for anyone's having the thoughts and beliefs we actually have … the very thoughts and beliefs we need to engage in metaphysical reflection on their status.[119]

If the nihilist's conception of the world defeats her ability to make nihilistic claims, it should cast doubt on the nihilist's case.

Our ways of knowing about the world and the descriptions and explanations we give of it, are not value-free. Facts do not exist in austere isolation from values; the vaunted fact/value dichotomy, which nourishes nihilism, seems much less secure than it did when Hume broached the idea. What we pick out as fact in scientific inquiry is typically shaped by theoretical considerations. Putnam writes that "the distinction [between fact and value] is at the very least hopelessly fuzzy because factual statements themselves, and the practices of scientific inquiry upon which we rely to decide what is and what is not a fact, presuppose values." Furthermore, "without the cognitive values of coherence, simplicity, and instrumental efficacy we have no world and no facts."[120] While "cognitive values" are not moral values (or aesthetic values, such as beauty), that is not a fatal objection. To say that we cannot even get to a world of presumptive brute facts without the aid of values weakens the nihilist view. Nor can we segregate "cognitive values" from others so neatly.[121] To say that something – for example, a scientific explanation – is rational is to say that we *ought* to believe it; it is to say that our "cognitive flourishing" depends on having such beliefs. Our cognitive flourishing is part of our overall flourishing, our overall conception of a good and meaningful life. The values on which we build meaning are fundamental to our way of knowing the world. Nor can it be metaphysically ruled out that they are fundamental to the world as such. They are certainly fundamental to how we know ourselves as conscious beings in the world. Any picture of ourselves that eliminates them comes with a built-in problem of plausibility. We know that much.

Camus's claim of absurdity is based, at least in part, on our inability to achieve certainty about the world. Human beings are divorced from the world and yet unable to free themselves from it. Our ineluctable ignorance mocks the possibility of meaning. On the view articulated here, this is a dramatic misreading of our situation. Values are given with our apprehension of the world and meaning is developed in response to them. We cannot reach Camus's desired certainty; we too have to make our peace with some ineliminable trace of absurdity. But we can question the world picture and the corresponding portrayal of the human condition that generates the appetite for certainty and despairs in the wake of its unavailability. We can diminish our appetite for certainty, at least for certainty about an ultimate verdict on the meaning of life, which Camus believed we need. We can remain committed to a quest for a fullness of meaning without a demand that we be able to reach its end.

On the view articulated here, ultimate meaning is neither ruled out nor assured. It is tied to, not undermined by, an ongoing process of interpretation. It is both made and found, objective and subjective, open-textured but bound to values that are shared. That ultimate meaning has an agonistic, unstable quality insofar as it emerges from constant wrestling with absurdity is not a defeater. Both the making and the wrestling are marks of human freedom and of the human role, as Judaism would have it, of being cocreators of the world. We start not with a blank, value-free, indifferent, brute-factual universe but in a world alive with value. Our thriving in this world depends in part on what sense and significance we can find in our sheer existence. Jewish ways of doing so, as well as contemporary philosophical ways, are the focus of Chapter 2.

NOTES

1 There is a biblical Aramaic word, *pesher*, at Ecclesiastes 8:1, in the phrase *pesher davar*, "the meaning of the adage" according to Fox, *JPS Bible Commentary*, p. 53. "Meaning" means "interpretation" of a text. The modern Hebrew words that cover the same semantic range as "meaning" are *muvan* and *mashma'ut*. These are postbiblical. Medieval philosophical Hebrew uses *inyan* (see, e.g., Maimonides, *Guide of the Perplexed*, III:43 in the Samuel ibn Tibbon translation). Biblical Hebrew has a word for "sign" (*'ot*). Famously, after the flood, God puts his sign, the rainbow, in the heavens. Whenever humans see the rainbow, they will remember what happened and be reminded of God's promise never to destroy the earth again. Similarly, God will be reminded of his covenant with Noah that, "Never again shall all flesh be cut off by the waters of a flood (Genesis 9:11)." The sign has symbolic import; it has a "speaker's meaning" ascribed to it by God. Humans can (or should) learn the meaning. In Deut 6:8, where the text commands the Israelites to bind words of Torah upon their hands and foreheads as a "sign," the meaning of the sign has to be taken to heart, taught to the children, and recited twice daily. Saying that the Bible doesn't have an explicit term for, and concept of, meaning (outside of the Aramaic *pesher*) should not be taken to imply that its authors do not use or understand symbolism or were unaware of poetic uses of language. Nothing could be further from the truth. They did not, however, see human existence per se as a "sign" or symbol in the way that moderns intend by the concept of "the meaning of life." For the concept of speaker's meaning, an important but insufficient criterion for meaningfulness in many circumstances, see the classic paper by H. P. Grice, "Meaning," *The Philosophical Review*, 66(3) (1957), pp. 377–388.

2 Jürgen Habermas et al., *An Awareness of What Is Missing* (Cambridge: Polity, 2010), pp. 15–23.

3 Terry Eagleton, *The Meaning of Life: A Very Short Introduction* (Oxford: Oxford University Press, 2007), pp. 13–14.

4 One thinks here of Schopenhauer's "Buddhist" pessimism, his "denial of the will" as the answer to life as suffering. For references to Schopenhauer's argument in *The World as Will and Representation*, see Julian Young, *The Death of God and the Meaning of Life* (New York: Routledge, 2014), pp. 58–60. For a contemporary application of Buddhism, see Owen Flanagan, *The Really Hard Problem: Meaning in a Material World* (Cambridge: MIT Press, 2007).

5 The concept of the "lifeworld" (*Lebenswelt*) was introduced by the German philosopher Edmund Husserl (in a 1936 work, *The Crisis of European Sciences and Transcendental Phenomenology*) to refer to the intersubjective, meaning-laden reality in which our consciousness takes shape. We do not rise into consciousness in a world of bald objects (as in the sense-data of empiricism) but in a culturally and historically constituted world. We have our being within a lifeworld. Later philosophers in the phenomenological tradition, such as Jürgen Habermas, extend the concept to include practices, values, and social realities. I use the term in this book in the latter, more inclusive sense.

6 Or at least our minds synthesize the endless perceptions and events that we experience into a whole, a world. We posit a subject of experience, a self, and an object of experience, an extended, integrated world. The status of the concept of the world is an object of philosophical inquiry. In modern Jewish thought, Franz Rosenzweig's *Star of Redemption* is in part an attempt to understand what we mean by a cosmos or world. For a philosophical view, see Stephen Toulmin, *The Return to Cosmology* (Berkeley: University of California Press, 1985), p. 25. Toulmin shows that the concept of a world has an ineliminable component of metaphysics.

7 Blaise Pascal, *Pensees*, A. J. Krailsheimer, trans. (London : Penguin Books, 1995), I. Cf. 489.

8 Alvin Plantinga, "Religious Belief as Properly Basic," in Brian Davies, ed., *Philosophy of Religion* (New York: Oxford University Press, 2000), pp. 42–94

9 Quoted in Dalia Nassar, *The Romantic Absolute: Being and Knowing in Early German Romantic Philosophy* (Chicago: University of

Chicago Press, 2013), p. 68. Cf. Iddo Landau, "Why Has the Question of the Meaning of Life Arisen in the Last Two and a Half Centuries?" *Philosophy Today*, Summer 1997, pp. 263–269.

10 "Man has always expressed the symbolic philosophy of his nature in his works, in his commissions and omissions. He proclaims himself and his gospel to nature; he is the messiah of nature [*Messias der Natur*]." Novalis, *Heinrich von Ofterdingen und Andere Dichterische Schriften* (Köln: Könnemann Verlag, 1996), p. 224. Translation my own.

11 Nassar, *The Romantic Absolute*, pp. 64–65.

12 Shakespeare, *Macbeth*, act 5, sc. 5. In the early nineteenth century German translation by Jena Romantics Johann Ludwig Tieck and August Schlegel, the last phrase "signifying nothing" is rendered "*das nichts bedeutet*," meaning "that means nothing."

13 Quoted in Stephen Leach and James Tartaglia, eds., *The Meaning of Life and the Great Philosophers* (London: Routledge, 2018), p. 276. This entire discussion of the origins of the phrase follows Leach's and Tartaglia's interpretation (italics added). The original in Lucinde is: *den heiligen Sinn des Lebens wie die schöne Sprache der Natur*; see www.projekt-gutenberg.org/schleglf/lucinde/lucin151.html.

14 Friedrich Schiller, whose "Ode to Joy" memorably provides the chorale text for the last movement of Beethoven's Ninth Symphony, wrote "The Gods of Greece," a lament for a long-gone world of divinized nature. In that world, human experience everywhere revealed divinity; the line between humans and the gods was indistinct. For Schiller, the villain of the piece is not science, French rationalism, or modernity, but monotheism. Max Weber's "disenchantment of the world," the tragic coda of his "Science as a Vocation," was presumably inspired by Schiller's poem.

15 John Hedley Brooke, *Science and Religion* (Cambridge: Cambridge University Press, 2014), pp. 176–189, 240–241.

16 Isaiah Berlin, "The Apotheosis of the Romantic Will," in Henry Hardy and Roger Hausherr, eds., *The Proper Study of Mankind* (New York: Farrar, Strauss, and Giroux, 2000), p. 562.

17 Julien Offray de la Mettrie, *L'Homme Machine*, Jonathan Bennett, trans., 2017 ; see www.earlymoderntexts.com/assets/pdfs/lamettrie1748.pdf.

18 Immanuel Kant, *Critique of Pure Reason*, trans. Norman Kemp Smith (New York: St. Martin's Press, 1965), p. 409 (A 445; B473). Immanuel

Kant, *Groundwork of the Metaphysic of Morals*, trans. H. J. Paton (New York: Harper Torchbooks, 1964), p. 116 (para 101).

19 Kant's teaching on nature is expanded and complicated in the third Critique, the *Critique of Judgment* (Section 77). There, he gives a greater role to what he calls the "intuitive intellect." The latter does not go from part to whole, rationally reconstructing the unity of a phenomenon from its parts, but goes straight to the whole, which it intuits as a living process. This licenses further Romantic developments. See Nassar, *The Romantic Absolute*, pp. 61–62.

20 Karin Nisenbaum, *For Love of Metaphysics* (New York: Oxford University Press, 2018), p. 13.

21 Michael Allen Gillespie, *Nihilism Before Nietzsche* (Chicago: University of Chicago Press, 1995), p. 81.

22 Ibid., p. 86.

23 Ibid. Gillespie's reading tilts in a metaphysical direction, that is, as an account of reality. Other scholars, such as Breazeale, treat his thought in a more phenomenological way, as an account of self-consciousness, with ethical implications. Gillespie's reading is arguably how his students, the early Romantics, understood him. See, Dan Breazeale, "Johann Gottlieb Fichte," in *Stanford Encyclopedia of Philosophy*, February 6, 2018; see https://plato.stanford.edu/entries/johann-fichte/.

24 Gillespie, *Nihilism Before Nietzsche*, p. 106.

25 George di Giovanni and Paolo Livieri, "Friedrich Heinrich Jacobi," in *Stanford Encyclopedia of Philosophy*, December 6, 2018, pp. 1–2, 24–25; see https://plato.stanford.edu/entries/friedrich-jacobi/#:~:text=1743%2C%20d.,Idealism%20of%20the%20late%20Schelling.

26 Nisenbaum, *For Love of Metaphysics*, pp. 35, 39, 43.

27 See Allen Wood on Fichte's Ethics in Sacha Golob and Jens Timmermann, eds., *The Cambridge History of Moral Philosophy* (Cambridge: Cambridge University Press, 2017), p. 419. Wood's focus on Fichte as an ethical thinker for whom self depends on other ("No thou, no I.") provides some resources to counter Jacobi's critique.

28 For the root of these problems in the "conflict of reason" with itself, see Nisenbaum, *For Love of Metaphysics*, especially pp. 1–11.

29 Philip Kitcher, *Life after Faith* (New Haven: Yale University Press, 2014), p. 25.

30 Ibid., p. 72.

31 Joshua P. Hochschild, "Don't Ask about 'the Meaning of Life': An Argument in Five Blog Posts" (emphasis added); see https://thevirtueblog.com/2017/12/13/the-invention-of-the-meaning-of-life/ (accessed November 20, 2020).

32 Ibid.; see https://thevirtueblog.com/2017/12/18/what-the-meaning-of-life-replaced/ (accessed March 20, 2023).

33 Ibid.; see https://thevirtueblog.com/?s=Assessing+the+Difference+between+Meaning+and+Purpose (accessed March 20, 2023).

34 Ibid. John Cottingham ties a meaningful life to one that fulfills our human nature, our deepest and most invariant purpose. For Cottingham, purpose does not replace meaning as the principal category for the evaluation of the worth of life. See, John Cottingham, *On the Meaning of Life* (London: Routledge, 2005), p. 72. For an extensive critique of "purpose theory," including Cottingham's, see Thaddeus Metz, *Meaning in Life* (Oxford: Oxford University Press, 2013), pp. 77–138.

35 See, for example, James Tartaglia, *Philosophy in a Meaningless Life: A System of Nihilism, Consciousness, and Reality* (London: Bloomsbury Academic, 2016). We will take up an analysis of this work in Chapter 4.

36 The classic Jewish account, with heavy reliance on Aristotle, is that of Maimonides; see Moses Maimonides, *The Guide of the Perplexed*, trans. Shlomo Pines (Chicago: University of Chicago Press, 1963), pp. 634–638 (Book III: Chapter 54).

37 Roger Scruton, *Modern Philosophy* (New York: Penguin Books, 1994), p. 143.

38 David Deutsch, *The Beginning of Infinity* (New York: Penguin Books, 2011), pp. 43–44.

39 Ibid., p. 44. Deutsch himself disputes the "principle of mediocrity" and disagrees with Hawking.

40 Deutsch, Ibid., p. 44.

41 A different kind of rejection of anthropocentrism, coordinated with a rejection of the meaning question, comes from the Princeton philosopher, Mark Johnston. Like Hochschild, Johnston is a serious theist. He also sees the meaning question as modern, but its motivation is as old as human sinfulness. For unlike Hochschild, he finds our human expectation of flourishing – and of meaning – idolatrous. "The demand that you live a meaningful life is an inflated form of acquisitive

desire and an ultimate reservation about how far you would go in modeling yourself on the kenotic self-abandonment that is God." See Mark Johnston, *Saving God: Religion After Idolatry* (Princeton: Princeton University Press, 2009), p. 179.

42 See "Logical Empiricism," Stanford Encyclopedia of Philosophy; see https://plato.stanford.edu/entries/logical-empiricism/ (accessed February 12, 2020).

43 A. J. Ayer, *The Meaning of Life* (New York: Charles Scribner's Sons, 1990).

44 "Mr. Strawson on Logical Theory," W. V. Quine, *Mind*, 62(248) (October 1953).

45 Ayer, *The Meaning of Life*, p. 7.

46 Ibid.

47 All citations in this paragraph are from Ibid., p. 13.

48 See Ayer's famous BBC dialogue with Father Copleston, "Logical Positivism: A Debate," much of which turns on whether meta-empirical questions could be cogently asked of nature, such as is there a metaphysical cause (e.g., a Creator) of nature? In Ibid., pp. 18–52. One might compare Ayer with Spinoza, who also claims that the only genuine questions that we can put to nature are "how" questions, not "why" questions. Spinoza rules out final causes and sees nature (qua nature) as a concatenation of endless causes and effects. Other than "nature naturing," there is no sense to the idea of divine causality. See *Ethics*, Part I, Prop. 36, Appendix.

49 Ayer, Ibid., p. 8.

50 Ayer is following the well-trodden path of the Euthyphro dilemma, specifically of those who read the *Euthyphro* to generate a dilemma that is fatal to a divine command ethics. I do not see why an agent's autonomous incorporation of a divine plan vitiates the plan. It may complicate divine authority, but it still leaves the wisdom of the divine plan – which lies beyond the human mind to work out on its own – intact. Ayer conflates the problem of authority with that of plan or purpose. For a view of divine revelation (of a wise plan for life) that *requires* autonomous incorporation, see Samuel Fleischacker, *The Good and the Good Book: Revelation as a Guide to Life* (New York: Oxford University Press, 2017) and Kenneth Seeskin, *Autonomy in Jewish Philosophy* (New York: Cambridge University Press, 2001).

On a weak version of divine command ethics that requires human, agentic incorporation and cooperation, see Daniel Statman and Avi Sagi, "Divine Command Morality and Jewish Tradition," *The Journal of Religious Ethics*, 23(1) (Spring 1995), pp. 39–67.

51 Ayer, *The Meaning of Life*, pp. 178–197.

52 Ibid., p. 194. There is an important germ of an argument here against meaningfulness as a positive value. Can we say that someone who committed great evil, Hitler or Stalin, for example, still had or experienced a meaningful life? To the extent that meaningfulness doesn't exclude this implication, meaningfulness qua value would be problematic. The relationship of meaningfulness to ethics requires further exploration.

53 Ibid., p. 196.

54 Ibid., p. 197.

55 A comparable case is raised by Richard Taylor. Sisyphus, whose life is paradigmatic of meaninglessness – "a repetitious, cyclic activity that never comes to anything" – is given by the very gods who cursed him "a strange and irrational impulse; namely, a compulsive impulse to roll stones." As a result of this divine "gift" his objectively meaningless life becomes subjectively rewarding for him. "His life is now filled with mission and meaning, and he seems to himself to have been given an entry to heaven." For what could be better for a compulsive stone-roller than an eternity of rolling stones? Taylor invites us to question, as Ayer does, the relation between subjective meaningfulness versus putatively objective meaninglessness. How much weight should subjectivity have in the determination of meaning? Richard Taylor, "The Meaning of Life," in E. D. Klemke and Steven Kahn, eds., *The Meaning of Life*, 4th edition (New York: Oxford University Press, 2017), pp. 128–136.

56 Ayer, Ibid., p. 197.

57 Shmuel Hugo Bergman, *Dialogical Philosophy from Kierkegaard to Buber* (Albany: SUNY Press, 1991), p. 16. Bergman quotes the philosopher, K. W. F. Solger. For the modern background to this stance in Montaigne, see Benjamin Storey and Jenna Silber Storey, *Why We Are Restless* (Princeton: Princeton University Press, 2021), pp. 10–49.

58 This claim is inspired by G. E. Moore's "open question method" (see *Principia Ethica*, Chapter 1, para. 13). The idea is that questions about the good are not settled by appeal to any constellation of empirical

conditions or psychological states, such as pleasure. It is appropriate to keep the question open. For Moore, this means that good is a "non-natural" property. In the more religious idiom that I favor, it means that the question has a transcendent dimension.

59 In Aristotle's *Nicomachean Ethics* (NE), the classic of the Western virtue ethics tradition, eudaimonia is the end that is desirable in itself; it is chosen for its own sake and not for the sake of something else (See NE, Book I, Chapter 7, 1097b). Older translations use "happiness" but since "happiness" can be taken conventionally to imply a good mood, which falls very far short of what Aristotle means, recent discussions in the literature use "flourishing."

60 The leading Jewish philosopher of the twentieth century, Hermann Cohen, is highly critical of "flourishing" as the summum bonum of human life. See Hermann Cohen, *The Ethics of Maimonides*, Almut Bruckstein, trans. (Madison: University of Wisconsin Press, 2003), p. 124

61 Bacon, in *The New Atlantis*, does this to an extent. His utopian scientists believe themselves to be Christians, blessed by God with life on a peaceful, isolated island. Their researches are meant as praise.

62 As the late physicist Steven Weinberg, a "cultured despiser of religion" put it: "Either by God you mean something definite or you don't mean something definite. If by God you mean a personality who is concerned about human beings, who did all this out of love for human beings, who watches us and who intervenes, then I would have to say in the first place how do you know, what makes you think so? And in the second place, is that really an explanation? If that's true, what explains that? Why is there such a God? It isn't the end of the chain of whys, it just is another step, and you have to take the step beyond that," https://en.wikiquote.org/wiki/Steven_Weinberg (accessed October 12, 2020).

63 NE, Book VI, Chapter 7, 1141b.

64 Those opposed to mandates for vaccination, for example, point to the salience of personal liberty in the American political-cultural tradition. Others have argued that George Washington required his troops to be inoculated against smallpox. The stakes and nature of the conflict of values are clarified, although not resolved, by putting them in the context of a meaning-laden historical framework. For Washington's order, see www.loc.gov/rr/scitech/GW&smallpoxinoculation.html (accessed October 9, 2021).

65 Landau, noting various senses of "meaning," points to two that pertain to the question of the meaning of life: "importance or relevance" and "understanding." Iddo Landau, "Why Has the Question of the Meaning of Life Arisen in the Last Two and a Half Centuries?" *Philosophy Today*, 41(2) (Summer 1997), p. 263.

66 Following the view of Goldman in Alan H. Goldman, *Life's Values* (New York: Oxford University Press, 2018), p. 125. Cf. Robert Nozick, *The Examined Life* (New York: Simon and Schuster, 1989), p. 166 for a similar, if less formal, distinction.

67 In this case, "help" is a performative utterance, not merely a "constative one." That is, the intention of its speaker is to change the world (by motivating action) rather than to just state a fact about the world. The performative dimension is part of understanding its meaning. Meaning, of course, is not limited to performative utterances.

68 See Goldman, *Life's Values*, pp. 121–125.

69 This is Landau's strategy in Iddo Landau, *Finding Meaning in an Imperfect World*, pp. 31–48. He characterizes his position as "non-perfectionism." It is precisely the evasive strategy roundly condemned by Tartaglia. For him, philosophy loses its raison d'être by shirking its central, constitutive question. See James Tartaglia, *Philosophy in a Meaningless Life* (London: Bloomsbury, 2016).

70 The terminology is Metz's, although he uses the terms in a somewhat different way from my usage. For Metz, the bearer of meaning is the individual who is seeking meaning within her own experience. The question is whether meaning pertains to her life, taken on the whole, or only to parts of it, or whether a mixed view – Metz's option – is possible. The individual focus rules out one side of a prior distinction, "holism" vs. "individualism." "Holism," for Metz, implies asking a cosmic question: what is the meaning of the universe as such? It takes us into metaphysical territory. He brackets this. I would prefer to leave it in, hence my distinction between whole and part overlaps with that of holism and individualism. This is phenomenologically more adequate but analytically messier. See Metz, *Meaning in Life*, pp. 3, 37–58.

71 Charles Taylor, *Sources of the Self* (Cambridge: Harvard University Press, 1989), pp. 50 51.

72 Goldman, *Life's Values*, p. 124. There are, of course, other kinds of master narrative than that of a divine plan. For purely secular construals

of the meaning of life in terms of a whole life master narrative, see Metz, *Meaning in Life*, pp. 52–58.

73 In Jonathan Lear's luminous book, *Radical Hope*, one of the Crow people who survives the nineteenth century dislocation of the tribe from its ancestral lands and way of life says that she doesn't understand the life that she is living. The destruction of the traditional way of life, based on hunting and war-making, undermined all of the traditional values and virtues. "Courage," "purpose," and so on could no longer mean what they timelessly meant. What could they mean under radically new conditions? Initially, nothing. The intelligibility of life collapsed and with it, life ceased to matter. See Jonathan Lear, *Radical Hope* (Cambridge: Harvard University Press, 2008), p. 56.

74 Metz, *Meaning in Life*, p. 51.

75 This is the view of James Tartaglia, cited in note 68. I deal with his work in Chapter 4.

76 Justin E. H. Smith, *Irrationality* (Princeton: Princeton University Press, 2019), p. 33.

77 Roger Scruton, *Modern Philosophy* (New York: Penguin Books, 1994), p. 397.

78 Ibid., p. 398.

79 Gregory Schufreider, "The Logic of the Absurd," *Philosophy and Phenomenological Research*, 44(1) (September 1983), p. 69.

80 Ibid., p. 70.

81 Kierkegaard, *Concluding Unscientific Postscript*, p. 188.

82 Schufreider, "The Logic of the Absurd," p. 77.

83 Albert Camus, *The Myth of Sisyphus*, Justin O'Brien, trans. (New York: Vintage International, 2018 [1955]), p. 28.

84 Camus, *The Myth of Sisyphus*, p. 18.

85 Ibid., p. 19.

86 Ibid., p. 20.

87 Ibid., p. 27. For an analysis of Camus's "existential nihilism" with respect to the meaninglessness of our absurd condition, see Donald A. Crosby, *The Specter of the Absurd* (Albany: SUNY Press, 1988), pp. 33–36.

88 Camus, *The Myth of Sisyphus*, p. 51.

89 Ibid.

90 Ibid., p. 53.

91 See "Camus," Ronald Aronson, *Stanford Encyclopedia of Philosophy*, p. 19. https://plato.stanford.edu/archives/sum2017/entries/camus/ (accessed February 3, 2021).

92 Thomas Nagel, *The View from Nowhere* (New York: Oxford University Press, 1986), pp. 208–231 and Thomas Nagel, *Mortal Questions* (New York: Cambridge University Press, 1979), pp. 11–23.

93 Nagel, *Mortal Questions*, p. 17.

94 Nagel, *The View from Nowhere*, p. 4.

95 Ibid., p. 210. For an analysis of the role of objectivity and subjectivity in Nagel's philosophy, see Alan Thomas, *Thomas Nagel* (Stocksfield, UK: Acumen, 2009), pp. 1–16. The way Nagel uses the distinction, particularly as a way of problematizing the human condition, recalls Wilfred Sellars's famous essay, "Philosophy and the Scientific Image of Man," is found in Wilfred Sellars, *Science, Perception, and Reality* (Atascadero, CA: Ridgeview Publishing Co., 1991).

96 Nagel, *The View from Nowhere*, pp. 216–217. Nagel believes that the Platonic myth of the disembodied soul imprisoned in the body has its origins in this typical human experience.

97 Nagel, Ibid., p. 218 (emphasis added).

98 Ibid., p. 219.

99 Ibid., p. 221.

100 Ibid., p. 223.

101 "Friedrich Heinrich Jacobi," Stanford Encyclopedia of Philosophy, https://plato.stanford.edu/entries/friedrich-jacobi/#OpenLettFich1799 (accessed December 21, 2020). See also Gillespie, *Nihilism Before Nietzsche*, p. 66.

102 Nolen Gertz, *Nihilism* (Cambridge: MIT Press, 2019), pp. 56, 79.

103 Friedrich Nietzsche, *The Genealogy of Morals*, Second Essay, section 24, p. 532 in Walter Kaufmann, ed. and trans., *Basic Writings of Nietzsche* (New York: The Modern Library, 2000).

104 Crosby, *The Specter of the Absurd*, p. 21. See also Camus ("With Nietzsche, nihilism seems to become prophetic… He said of himself that he was the first complete nihilist of Europe.") in Kaufmann, *Basic Writings of Nietzsche*, p. 855.

105 Or is it none of these? One contemporary nihilist, James Tartaglia, claims that it is simply a *fact* – the content of a belief rather than a belief per se.

106 Gertz, *Nihilism*, pp. 14–17.

107 Steven Weinberg, *The First Three Minutes* (New York: Basic Books, 1993), p. 154.

108 Hannah Arendt, *The Life of the Mind*, Vol. I, *Thinking* (New York: Harcourt, 1978), p. 176 (emphasis added).

109 The idea that value is objective has an epistemic version and a metaphysical version. Nagel, Wiggins, Dworkin, and Putnam in quite different ways exemplify the former; Nozick, the latter. The former thinkers proceed by exposing problems in various anti-realist views. For Wiggins, a view of rationality that a priori excludes human interests is a non-starter: "I conclude that there is no such thing as a pure a priori theory of rationality conceived in isolation from what it is for us as we are to have a reason: and that even if there were such a thing, it would always have been irrelevant to the problem of finding a meaning in life, or seeing anything as worthwhile." See, David Wiggins, "Truth, Invention, and the Meaning of Life," in Geoffrey Sayre McCord (ed.), *Essays on Moral Realism* (Ithaca: Cornell University Press, 1988), p. 154. Dworkin's general strategy is to take skepticism about the objective status of norms and to show that skepticism, far from being neutral and austere (that is, non-evaluative and detached), is itself a normative position and so self-impeaching. To be skeptical about norms is not meta-normative but embedded in normative interpretation all the way down. See his "Objectivity and Truth: You'd Better Believe It," in *Philosophy and Public Affairs*, 25(2) (Spring 1996), pp. 87–139. Putnam has a variety of strategies, among which is an argument for truth as rational acceptability. To accept something as true implies that we are justified in doing so if it rises to certain epistemically normative standards. Every factual statement, therefore, is simultaneously a normative statement. It calls for us to accept it, as it were. See Hilary Putnam, *Reason, Truth, and History* (Cambridge: Cambridge University Press, 1992), p. 136; See also Hilary Putnam, *The Collapse of the Fact/ Value Dichotomy* (Cambridge: Harvard University Press, 2002) esp. pp. 28–45. Putnam's Harvard colleague, Robert Nozick took a more metaphysical approach to value, characterizing it as "a degree of organic unity." He sees value implicit in the natural world as such, which he likens to an artwork in which all of the features of the work are integrated in complex relations with one another. This reifies value in a way that goes beyond the epistemic arguments of the others. See Robert

Nozick, *Philosophical Explanations* (Cambridge: Harvard University Press, 1981), p. 612. Although none of these views is fully convincing, they open the possibility of dismantling the fact/value dichotomy on which arguments for meaninglessness and nihilism rest.

110 Ronald Dworkin, *Justice for Hedgehogs* (Cambridge: Harvard University Press, 2011), p. 125.

111 Dworkin, *Justice for Hedgehogs*, p. 123.

112 Ibid., p. 135.

113 For a classic work on the interpretive tradition of the Exodus, see Michael Walzer, *Exodus and Revolution* (New York: Basic Books, 1986).

114 On the normative authority of traditions, see Samuel Scheffler, *Equality and Tradition* (New York: Oxford University Press, 2012), pp. 287–311.

115 Charles Taylor, *Sources of the Self* (Cambridge: Harvard University Press,1989), p. 27.

116 See Barry Stroud, *Engagement and Metaphysical Dissatisfaction: Modality and Value* (New York: Oxford University Press, 2011).

117 Stroud, *Engagement and Metaphysical Dissatisfaction*, p. 96.

118 Ibid., p. 142.

119 Ibid., p. 153.

120 Putnam cited in Lance P. Hickey, *Hilary Putnam* (London: Continuum, 2009), p. 149.

121 Hilary Putnam, *Reason, Truth, and History* (Cambridge: Cambridge University Press, 1992), p. 136.

2 Creation

We start not with a blank, value-free, indifferent, brute factual, material world but in a world alive with value. But what are the values and how far do they take us toward establishing the meaning of life and the best way to live? In this chapter, I claim that on both the Jewish account and on that of contemporary philosophy, the values do not take us far enough. There is something broken and disordered about the world, as Kohelet sensed. This truncates the reach of naturalistic meaning-seeking. Naturalistic inquiries, when they range beyond physical explanation into the territory of value and meaning run into absurdity. This is true also for biblical and Jewish portrayals of creation.

The first creation story in the Bible, Genesis 1, repeatedly affirms that the world is good – indeed, that the ordered whole is "very good." This would seem to give a secure footing to the value of the world and to the worth of our existence within it – at least for those who accept the cogency of the biblical affirmation. It would seem to diminish the possibility of an absurdist interpretation of the human condition. Nonetheless, probing some of the byways of biblical and Jewish thinking on this matter affords a more complicated view. Even within the biblical–Judaic universe of discourse, the putative goodness of being is not as secure as it seems.

Traces of the absurd come to mark Jewish reflection on the human place and role in the world. The very logic that makes for our personhood and dignity – as cocreators with God of an ordered, moral universe – engenders problems with God, creation, personhood, and dignity. In this chapter, we will first consider Jewish religious perspectives that court absurdity. We will then turn to contemporary philosophical accounts that, although dispensing with God and divine creation, nonetheless want to find meaning in life within the limits of naturalistic assumptions. Yet these accounts, the confident tone of the literature notwithstanding, are also infected by absurdity. Absurdity is ineluctable. If our task is to secure meaning in life without repressing absurdity, it is not clear that the naturalistic accounts do a better job than the theistic ones.

CREATION AND VALUE

Ancient creation stories, biblical ones included, may usefully be thought of as genealogies. A genealogy, in Bernard Williams's formulation, "is a narrative that tries to explain a cultural phenomenon by describing a way in which it came about, or could have come about, or might be imagined to have come about."[1] A "cultural phenomenon" is a broad category. The culmination of the first creation narrative in Genesis (at Gen 2:3), which tells us that God rested on the seventh day, is a genealogy of the Sabbath, a culturally salient, ritually demarcated sacred time. Cain's killing of Abel in Genesis, chapter 4, is a genealogy of murder. Genealogies are meaningful interpretations of vivid, significant features of a culture's lifeworld – be they sacred or secular social practices, ethical virtues and vices, traits of human nature, or recurrent problems in human experience. Above all, they try to interpret the value-rich dimensions of a culture's self-understanding. They structure the meaning a culture makes of its life and, through that portal, of life as such.

A genealogy sits somewhere between a myth and a historical account. It has features of both, straddling the broken line between fiction and fact. It is analytically distinct, however, from scientific explanation insofar as its explanandum is value. The famous tale of the Tower of Babel (Gen, chapter 11) is a genealogy of nationhood. It gestures at an actual historical phenomenon – the rise of urban civilization. But it would be a mistake to take it as explanatory in a scientific sense. For ancient Israel, the various creation stories may well have had a science-like function in answering "how" questions, but that couldn't have been their main purpose. (The continued insistence of otherwise profound philosophers that biblical creation stories are just primitive science is embarrassing.[2]) The detached, abstract, purely conceptual interest presupposed by the "science-like function" is atypical of the authors of the Bible. This is not to say that biblical people were incapable of, or disinterested in, abstract reasoning. It is to say that their abstract thought was concerned with making their lifeworld intelligible and with understanding its significance, not with giving ostensibly value-free causal accounts of how things got to be the way they are. One indication of this is that the Genesis, chapter 1 story, simply adopts the basic cosmology of the Ancient Near East; it shares a world picture with the Babylonians. The text has no independent interest in cosmological speculation.[3]

The fact that ancient Israelite thinking, crystallized in Genesis 1, considers the world as a whole from a frankly axiological perspective mitigates absurdity. When the ancient authors ponder the cosmos, they are pondering the human role in the cosmos. The cosmos is portrayed as a "manifest image" that already has room in it for a normative human status; it is not portrayed as a "scientific image" that disembeds humanity.[4] The texts do not set out to deconstruct human personhood or eliminate human uniqueness but rather to ground what human beings ought to be and do. Absurdity does not infect the reasoning of Genesis 1, its view from nowhere similitude notwithstanding. A trace of the absurd, however, creeps into the picture when Genesis 1 is set against a background of earlier mythopoesis. It then enters Jewish thought as elements of that background, *mutatis mutandis*, reemerge. If full blown absurdity is a wholesale breakdown in the justification of values, beliefs, and commitments, a "trace of absurdity" falls short of that. It is, nonetheless, an awareness of the problematic nature of values, beliefs, and commitments with respect to their justification. This can threaten meaningfulness. Although creation accounts in Jewish thought try to support meaning, the traces of the absurd in them destabilize it.

The axiological orientation of Genesis 1 is manifest in the repeated injunctions that the various stages of creation are "good" (Gen 1:10, 18, 21, 25) and that the completed whole is "very good" (Gen 1:31). The world is not a value-neutral conceptual object in need of overarching explanation. It is an exquisitely ordered whole, built on distinctions and contrasts that have been experienced in the life-world, such as light and darkness, heaven (i.e., sky) and earth, wet and dry, plant and animal, animal and human, male and female, and ordinary and sacred. These constitutive elements are in balance with one another. Every piece contributes to the architectonic of the whole, which forms an organic unity, the very exemplar of value.[5] The world is an achievement. It is dynamic. It forms a home, suffused with actual (and potential) goodness, for all its creatures. Yet, as the story unfolds in Gen 2–3, culminating in humanity's expulsion from the primordial, paradisal garden, the world is shown to be a home in which we are not fully at home. It becomes both paradise and purgatory, generous and harsh. The goodness of the world is both radical and elusive. The normative portrayal of humanity's place in the world, as enunciated by the opening chapters of Genesis, is anything *but* primitive science. It is a story expressive of our ambivalence toward a world that we can love but that seldom requites our love. It is a genealogy of our being a part of, while also apart from, the world.

God pronounces the world, in its various stages of emergence, good (*tov*). But what does this mean? Is Being – the mere existence of something rather than nothing – per se good? Or does it take differentiation, individuation, variety, or complexity to be good? Is goodness durable and secure, or is it fragile and defeasible? Is goodness a property that exists by itself or does it require human apprehension, as well as cultivation and protection? How is ontic goodness – the goodness that God (an ideal observer) sees – related to moral goodness, the value instantiated in human character, conduct, and relations?[6] By asking these questions, I want to complicate the bald affirmation that creation is good. Although, ultimately, I believe that the Jewish tradition sustains this affirmation, I think that the honesty of the tradition compels it to consider ways in which creation – being, life, nature – is *not* good. The tradition entertains doubts about the goodness of being. It detects a trace of absurdity in being. How it copes with this – and how it avoids a nihilistic conclusion – tells us much about how the tradition construes the meaning of life in the face of potential meaninglessness.

BIBLICAL BACKSTORIES

Goodness is more contested than it appears in Genesis 1. In the view of biblical scholar Jon Levenson, the serene creation account of Genesis 1, is the result of a long process in ancient Israel of struggling with creation stories derived from the polytheistic cultures of the Ancient Near East. What is unique to Genesis 1 is not that God creates a world from nothing – that is foreign to the text and only fully asserted in the Middle Ages – but that God creates without opposition.[7] In fragments of other creation stories in the Bible, however, God encounters opposition. God wrestles with primordial forces and has to subdue them. (The *tohu va-vohu*, "the waters," and "the deep" of Gen 1:2 is but a dull echo of these once mythological, evil entities.) Thus, Psalm 74:12–14 invokes:

> O, God, my king from of old,
> Who brings deliverance throughout the land;
> It was You who drove back the sea with Your might,
> Who smashed the heads of the monsters in the waters;
> It was You who crushed the heads of Leviathan,
> Who left him as food for the denizens of the desert.

Similarly, Isaiah 51:9–10 calls on God to redeem the Israelites from Babylon in a manner reminiscent of his victory over the forces of primeval chaos:

> Awake, awake, clothe yourself with splendor,
> O arm of the LORD!

Awake as in days of old,
As in former ages!
It was you who hacked Rahab in pieces,
That pierced the Dragon [*tannin*]
It was you that dried up the sea [*yam*]
The waters of the great deep [*tehom*]

In this poem, sea and deep – the same words are used in Genesis 1 – are active, albeit vanquished opponents of God. In Genesis 1, they are but passive elements that God orders in the process of creation. Similarly, in Psalm 104, the deep and the waters flee at the blast of God's voice. God sets bounds for them that they dare not trespass. A parallel text, Job, chapter 38, has God subduing the primordial waters and enclosing them behind "bars and doors" (Job 38:10). In the texts above, Leviathan or the sea monsters or the Dragon – they are interchangeable – have not been created; they preexist the work of creation. In Genesis 1, these beings are created by God on the fifth day (Gen 1:21), a sure sign of their effacement as a source of opposition.[8]

In the accounts that Genesis 1 displaces, evil forces are structural to reality. They sometimes reemerge and wreak havoc. Despite God's having made a habitable world, the threat of immanent (and imminent) evil is real. Evil is God's enemy as much as it is that of humanity. Ancient Israel called upon God to remember his acts of creation and his suppression of chaos, to bestir himself and to perform them once again (see, e.g., Isa 27:1). Significantly, Israel conceived of itself not just as a supplicant, pleading with God for salvation, but as a covenantal partner, *assisting* God in checking cosmic chaos. The scene and instrument of cosmos-stabilizing activity was the Temple and its sacrifices. The account of the creation of the wilderness Tabernacle (Exodus 39–40), a genealogy for the Solomonic Temple (I Kings 8), parallels the creation of the world.[9] The Tabernacle/Temple is a microcosm, a holy, miniature cosmos. Israel, as the builder and custodian of the microcosm, becomes a partner in sustaining and fortifying the forces of cosmic order. As Levenson puts it:

> [T]he creative ordering of the world has become something that humanity can not only witness and celebrate, *but something in which it can also take part*. Among the many messages of Genesis 1:1–2:3 is this: it is through the cult that we are enabled to cope with evil, for it is the cult that builds and maintains order, transforms chaos into creation, ennobles humanity, and realizes the kingship of God who has ordained the cult and commanded that it be guarded and practiced. It is through obedience to the directives of the divine master that his good world comes into existence.[10]

Levenson points not only to the fragility of goodness, to its dependence on the actions of Israel, but to the fragility of God or, more precisely, of God's reign. After the destruction of the Temple, the world – and God Himself, as it were – is sustained by the words of daily prayer. If Israel were not true to God's covenant, God's sovereignty over creation would fade away. The daily enactment of covenantal loyalty and love represented by the declaration of the Shema (Deut 6:4), the core of Jewish daily prayer, keeps God "enthroned upon the praises of Israel." A rabbinic midrash, glossing the words of Isaiah, makes the point with startling clarity: "So you are My witnesses declares the LORD and I am God." That is, if you are My witnesses, I am God, and if you are not my witnesses, I am, as it were, not God.[11]

"God depends, 'as it were,' upon the witness of Israel: without it, his divinity is not realized."[12]

This brings us to a trace of the absurd – an almighty creator God whose power depends on the response of his chosen creatures. A "very good" world whose weak, mortal denizens can return it to welter and waste, unmaking the work of the Creator. God is a contradiction, a model of polarities: sovereign yet dependent on his subjects, victorious but vulnerable to defeat. This dialectical theology only grows in the course of the development of Jewish thought. It undermines the static caricature of "Western theism's" omnipotent, omniscient, and omnibenevolent God, a God who is but a rationalized abstraction from the literary sources of Judaism.

The divine dialectic invites questioning that courts absurdity: Why worship a God as much in need of salvation as he is capable of providing it? Why pray to the Lord of the universe when he is in some ways as much an exile in his world as are his exiled creatures (B. Meg 29a)? There is, of course, the hope that all this will be made right someday; that someday "the Lord will be one, and his name will be one" (Zechariah 14:19). But how can a hope for the future resolve the scandalous absurdity of the present? What is the basis for a well-grounded hope, as opposed to a motivated, wishful one (assuming that this is even a cogent distinction)? Hope seems to be based on trust, which seems itself to be based on the hope that the trust is justified. Does this circularity make hope itself absurd?

Kohelet seems to have denied himself hope, casting doubt on its cogency. Camus positively rejects it.[13] Judaism embraces it.[14] Is that embrace reasonable or irrational, courageous or irresponsible? What is certain is that hope projects the deepest convictions that we hold about the worth of life into the future where we trust they will be fully vindicated. Hope is our stake in the future. What is not certain is that those convictions, our fervor in holding them notwithstanding, are rationally justified. So much the worse for reason, one might say. At that emergent limit of reason, real life begins. It is a life lived, however, in the face of the absurd. To be lived honestly, it must recognize the face that confronts it.

RABBINIC RUMINATIONS

Ruminations on creation in postbiblical Jewish thought speak, in their own way, to these perplexities about justification. Rabbinic midrash wrestles with the meaning of the mysterious *tohu va-vohu*, which, as we have seen, raises fundamental issues about good and evil, nature and value, God's power and its limits. One midrash (Genesis Rabbah 1:5) analogizes God's creation of the world out of preexisting *tohu va-vohu* to a human king who builds a palace:

> If in the ways of the world a king of flesh and blood would build his palace on a place of dung and sewage, all who come to say that the palace is built on a place of dung and sewage do not say anything outrageous. So too, anyone who says the world was built out of chaos and void [*tohu va-vohu*] does not say anything outrageous. Rabbi Huna in the name of R. Kapra says if not written it would be impossible to say that God created heaven and earth from them, from "and the earth was void and chaos."[15]

Analogizing God to a human king is standard in midrash, but the point is typically that God is greater in all ways than a human king. Here, God's "palace" and the human king's palace seem to have the same flaws; God is not above the human king in that respect. In the view of Moshe Halbertal, the midrash expresses unrelieved confusion about the fundaments of the created order and, by implication, about God's role in that order. Halbertal writes: "This [midrash], which includes the expression of outrage itself, alerts us to the difficulty in the idea of creation of the world from chaos and void. The interpretation does not see in this an issue that is worthy of resolution, but rather a problem without resolution."[16] That is, the midrash leaves open the question of the implications of a world with chaos and void at its base.

The phrase "if not written it would be impossible to say" is an important device in rabbinic literature. It often introduces a bold interpretation. Had the text not licensed the interpreter to say such a thing, it could never have been said on the interpreter's own authority. (What the interpreter *does* say, however, is often far from what the text seems reasonably to license.[17]) The boldness of the present interpretation – that there is nothing outrageous about God's world being built on or out of chaos and void – might be in its approximation to Gnosticism. For Gnostics, the world that we inhabit is evil – the product of a demonic rather than a benevolent force. The midrash does not go that far. God, not a demiurge or demonic force, has built an ordered world. Lying at its base, however, is a still potent, immanent disorder that might impugn creation's claim to goodness.

The boldness of the interpretation is not, contra some ancient, medieval, and modern interpreters its refusal to acknowledge *creatio ex nihilo*.[18] The Bible has no straightforward affirmation of creation from nothing; the plain sense of the text indicates that darkness, water, and *tohu va-vohu* already existed when God began to create. Although the doctrine of creation out of nothing does not get fully formulated until the Middle Ages, ancient Jewish sources do gesture in that direction. Their approach is to posit that the primordial elements were themselves created by God before the explicit work of creation, as articulated in Genesis 1, began. This still leaves the question, however, of why God pre-created bad things on or out of which to build the good. The Talmud states that "Ten things were created on the first day of Creation, and they are as follows: Heaven and earth; *tohu* and *vohu*; light and darkness; wind and water; the length of day and the length of night (B. Ḥagigah 12a). The answer then is that the initial components of creation were not purely negative; they were balanced pairs. *Tohu va-vohu* thus loses its negativity and its absolute preexistence. The text breaks up *tohu va-vohu*, treating its two locutions as one equilibrium among others, a biblical yin and yang, as it were.

The subordinate, "orderly" nature of *tohu va-vohu* is expressed in another midrash (Genesis Rabbah 1:9), where a pagan philosopher, in dialogue with a rabbi, praises God for being a good artisan. The rabbi, however, rejects the praise, as it is premised on an offensive assumption:

> A pagan philosopher argued with Rabban Gamliel: "Your God is indeed a great artist (*tzayar*), but surely He found on hand suitable materials which were of help to him." "What are they?" asked Rabban Gamliel. The philosopher replied, "*Tohu*, *bohu*, darkness, water, wind, and the depths." Rabban Gamliel exclaimed, "May the breath of such a man as you be blasted out!"[19]

Rabban Gamliel is offended by the insinuation that God used preexisting materials to form the world. He counterargues by saying that the word "create" (as opposed to "form," or "shape," or "order," etc.) is used for these entities, thereby proving that they have the same originary cause, God, as the rest of creation has. ("Create" in Genesis 1 is expressed by the verb *bara*, which only takes God as its subject. Biblically speaking, human beings don't "create" (*bara*); they combine, form, or shape what already exists.) Of course, in the actual biblical text, God does not *bara* these entities; they are already there. The midrash then has to find other allusions in the Bible to their "creation" and retroject them back into the Genesis text. The allusion for *tohu va-vohu* is especially noteworthy. The midrash cites Isaiah 45:7, "I make (*oseh*) peace and create (*bara*) evil." *Vohu* is identified here with evil that has *also* been created by God.

The idea that God creates evil obviously has troubling implications. This midrash doesn't take them up.[20] The assertion of the subordinate, created aspect of *tohu va-vohu* comes at a cost: God installs evil in the world as one of its fundaments. How can this not destabilize the goodness of being? What is the ground of value if disvalue is as radical to being as value? God is the creator of the ramified world order, but the basis of that order is flawed. To the extent that the world is good, is it good despite its flaws or because of them? Rabbinic thought would seem to take the latter, a rather absurdist stance. When God proclaims the whole of existence to be "very good" (*tov me'od*), the midrash adds that the "very" (*me'od*) is "death" (*mot*).[21] Here there is a sustained effort to affirm the worth of life despite its absurd negation by death.

SHATTERED VESSELS, EXILED GOD

Perhaps the most dramatic account of a flawed creation in Jewish literature is the Lurianic cosmogony of the sixteenth century. Isaac Luria (1534–1572) was a leading mystic in the town of Safed, in the Galilee. He (and his disciples and interpreters) developed a unique kabbalistic system. In the medieval system of Jewish mysticism known as Kabbalah (literally, "tradition"), which Luria inherits and revolutionizes, God emanates the world from himself. The world emerges in stages with the development of God's own being. God is not simple, as in medieval Jewish philosophy. God is complex, expressing his unique being in concentrations of energy known as "sefirot" ("luminosities" is one suggested translation for this ambiguous word). The sefirot are aspects of an evolving, dynamic divine being, but God also transcends the sefirot.[22] The sefirot are immanent forces that are characterized with names such as "wisdom," "beauty," and "kingship" inter alia. They form an interdependent system. The God who is above the sefirot, who emanates them, is called, in kabbalistic language, *ayn sof*, the "infinite" or *ayin*, "nothing." Divine "nothingness" contrasts with the positive descriptions of divine being that the system of sefirot expresses.

Nothingness is already an unfathomable concept; God as nothingness is even more paradoxical. Nothingness is unfathomable because thinking about nothing is equivalent to not thinking. There is thus an inherent contradiction in the notion of nothingness. The philosopher Bede Rundle writes:

> We cannot conceive of there being nothing, but only of nothing being this or that, and this is a use of 'nothing' that presupposes there being something. Intelligible contrasts are within *ways of being* – near or far, long or short, young or old. Existing or not existing fit into the scheme – existing now, not existing then, and, more radically, there being a so and so and there being no so and so – but the contrast is still within how things are ....[23]

For Rundle, our language presupposes being; to imagine nothing is either to cease to imagine at all or to imagine "things lacking where there might have been something: we suppose we can imagine the stars ceasing to exist one by one – like so many lights going out – but we still look to where they were .... To imagine, conceive, or postulate space is not to imagine nothing ... Space is not *nothing*."[24] If Rundle is correct, we cannot truly imagine or conceive of nothing without surreptitiously adding a tincture of something. This seems to me true of the kabbalistic language about divine nothingness.

"Nothing" should be taken not as absolute nonexistence – despite what some medieval philosophers and kabbalists say – but as a contrast term. In comparison with the divine self-manifestation in the sefirot, for example, the *ayn sof* is "nothing." Prior to emanation, there was nothing with which to contrast God, so God may be called "nothing." "Nothing" functions as a technical term to mark a difference, but the difference is contrastive not categorical. In Lurianic thought, divine nothingness is a "space" from which God has withdrawn in order to create a world that is other than himself.

Kabbalah always entails a tension between monotheism and pantheism. God is ontologically connected to/immanent in creation through the sefirot, yet transcendent of it, distinct from it, at the same time. This is a standing problem, dealt with in different ways by different thinkers, none satisfactorily. The paradoxical ontology of divine participation in the world and distinction from it is sometimes called "panentheism," a term that masks the instability of its concept. It is a step short of pantheism, which simply equates the divine and the world. It also reaches toward monotheism, which draws a strong distinction between God and the world. Kabbalah, throughout the course of its development, cannot free itself from the horns of this dilemma. The sefirot, as emanations of God, are self-manifestations of divinity. Even the lower sefirot, which interact with the material world, are divine. On the other hand, the monotheistic impulse wants to preserve the transcendence of divinity. The concept of *ayn sof* tries to accomplish that, but the device of emanation (*atsilut*) undercuts it at the same time. There is an ineluctable, unresolved contradiction in the relationship between God and the world in kabbalah.[25]

In the Zohar, the classic of kabbalah from thirteenth-century Spain, *ayn sof* effuses its being into the sefirot by stages. There is a smooth transmission of divinity from the transcendent to the immanent, from theogony to cosmogony. (The problems come later, when the two sides of the sefirotic system – often portrayed as an array of spheres with pipes connecting them – fall out of balance.

The dominance of the sefirot of the left side, led by judgment (*din* or *gevurah*), causes an imbalance both in God and in the world; this is the source of evil.) In Luria's system, however, the problem goes back to creation itself. Creation per se is catastrophic.

In the biblical texts other than Genesis 1, as we have seen, God has to cope with opposition from refractory, preexisting entities or residual mythic forces. In Lurianic kabbalah, God has to cope with his *own* refractory elements; these form a theosophical analogue to the ancient theomachies. For Luria, *ayn sof*, the divine "nothing" fills all of reality; *ayn sof* is the only reality.[26] In order for a world that has some notional nonidentity with God to emerge, God withdraws into himself (*tzimtzum*), thus making a space no bigger than a point. The first form to gather in this space is a luminous, primordial human (*Adam Kadmon*). God has become a "macro-anthropos."[27] From thence, a line of divine radiance emanates to form the first luminous sphere, the highest *sefirah* (*keter* or "crown"). (Linearity and circularity are the two infinite processes expressive and worthy of divinity.) *Keter* in turn radiates light to two subordinate sefirot. The light is held in bowls or vessels (*kelim*) of "thicker" light. The first three sefirot were able to hold the pure divine light – the very being of God. But then the outflow to the next six vessels was too powerful to be contained. One after another, they shattered and the light, together with the shards of the vessels (*klipot*), cascaded downward in chaos. Although much light flowed back to its source, some remained buried in the materiality that resulted from the breaking of the vessels (*shevirat ha-kelim*). That materiality, in which sparks of divinity are trapped, is our world.

Lurianic Kabbalah takes the old midrashic notion that God's presence accompanied the Jewish people into exile and radically ontologizes it. God has become, as it were, the victim of his own creative process, indeed of his own theogony. For the process described above is not only the story of a cosmos but of the emergence of the fullness of divine being. Something has gone wrong in God as such. God is self-alienated, self-exiled, trapped in the world, awaiting the work of human beings to liberate him from his creation. *Tzimtzum* and *shevirat ha-kelim* are potent symbols of exile. Exile is not only traumatic displacement in history – Lurianic kabbalah developed after the torment of the expulsion from Spain in 1492 – but a cosmic catastrophe. The theogonic/cosmogonic narrative becomes the deepest meaning of Jewish exile. This meaning also licenses a meaningful response to the crisis of exile: Catastrophe contains the promise of redemption. The Jews can raise the scattered sparks of divinity, rescuing God and themselves. This human work of restoring the unity of God is called *tikkun* – a process of divine and cosmic restoration and integration.[28] Tikkun entails performing the commandments with the proper focus and intention (*kavanah*), with "mindfulness" to use today's jargon. The knitting together of one's own being in the mindful act helps to knit God and world together. Just as biblical thinkers believed that the Temple cult kept the world intact, so too the followers of Isaac Luria thought that the purpose of human action was to repair and redeem creation, as well as to restore wholeness to the Creator. This, in turn, would spur redemption. The messianic restoration of the Jewish people was paired with God becoming, once again, "all in all."

Human actions – especially those concerned with the performance of the commandments or, contrariwise, to violations of them – affect the relations among the sefirot and hence the status of divine being. Human sin disrupts the interaction of higher sefirot with the lowest sefirah, *malkhut*, which is conceived as feminine, as the indwelling presence of God (*Shekhinah*), and as the supernal form of the Jewish people. The interruption of flow from above to below strengthens the evil side of the divine/cosmic system. In the Lurianic version, there is a hopeful note. The sparks of divine light caught in the shards are released by human action and return to their source. This is to say that good abides in the midst of evil; evil can be redeemed because it has a hidden point of good within it. Human beings are the transformative factor. Indeed, they can transform themselves. Repentance (*teshuvah*) is part of *tikkun*. This way of thinking about the meaning (as purpose) of human, especially of Jewish, life exerted tremendous influence on Jewish thought for hundreds of years. Jewish modernity, from an internal point of view, is in part the loss of this framework. The collapse of a world-redeeming, cosmic purpose for the Jewish people constitutes a loss of meaning that has yet to be regained.

On the view that creation was catastrophic, the Jews become the saviors of God, as it were. But there were other interpretations of the shattering of the vessels. Rather than a divine plan gone awry, some kabbalists thought that the catastrophe *was* the divine plan.[29] God deliberately created a ruptured world, in which he himself suffered, in order to give human beings a task and a purpose. Although not a kabbalist, a leading twentieth-century thinker Rabbi Joseph B. Soloveitchik had a similar view. God created the *tohu va-vohu*, the imperfection at the heart of creation, in order to give humanity a chance to perfect the world.[30] That is humanity's high vocation, the very purpose of human life. Strategies such as these mitigate absurdity, subordinating it to a divine rationality that we can, to an extent, grasp.

The absurdist reading resists this subordination and refuses to domesticate the rupture that it senses in the way things are. Its meaningfulness derives from its cogency as an interpretation of our experience. The stunning beauty of the world persuades us of its boundless goodness. The abject misery of much of human life and the remorseless indifference of nature to it makes negativity as fundamental. The Lurianic myth supports our ambivalence. With creation comes not only an overflow of the good, but its frustration and dissipation. It would be one thing if this world were strictly natural – this is just the way it is. But to tell this tale with a good God as the main character, the God who in Genesis 1 proclaims the goodness of his creation has a trace of the absurd in it. The story both validates and imperils our construal of value.

Scholem locates the meaning of the Lurianic myth both in its interpretation of exile and in its undergirding of human purpose.

"The tendency," he writes, "to interpret human life and behavior as symbols of a deeper life, the conception of man as a *microcosmos* and of the living God as a *macro-anthropos*, has never been more clearly expressed [in Judaism] and driven to its farthest consequences."[31] The Lurianic formulation may be unique but, in general, the basic pattern is typical of religious and at least premodern philosophical meaning. Before "the death of God," we "discovered" a universal meaning – rather than chose a personal one – in relation to what Julian Young calls a "true world." Whether the true world is Plato's forms or Luria's shattered vessels or Marx's historical dialectic, there is a presumptive objective reality that was believed to orient us. Late modernity, by contrast, has given up on the "true world." "Suppose we acknowledge," Young writes, "that there are no true worlds, that every grand narrative is a fiction, that reality is, in Nietzsche's sense 'chaos'."[32] This is, Young thinks, our situation. It doesn't preclude us from choosing our own meaning, but it does defeat universal, "objectively" grounded meaning. We are supposed to be on our own, living *sans appel*, making it up as we go along, hearing only the voice of cosmic silence. We are not a microcosmos related to a macro-anthropos. We are only so many *klipot*, without the solace of divine light hidden within us. We are flotsam and jetsam elements, effused not by the *ayn sof* but by the stars and destined by entropy to decompose.

If that is the real truth of the world, the situation of human beings seems fully absurd. The views of Young and the nihilists opposed to even his personal, invented, late modern meaningfulness must be given their due. But the full absurdity of our presumptive modern condition is not a monopoly. It doesn't preclude traces of the absurd in the premodern sources. Premodern people wrestled with those traces, too. (Do all moderns? Most moderns? Only a small minority of moderns? One makes sweeping statements about "modernity," but not all of its denizens express its ideal-typical mentality.) Nor does it imply that the meaning that people found in the face of those traces was a "fiction." Fiction expresses meaning; meaning need not be fictitious. There might not be as much of a discrepancy between the situation of the medieval and that of the moderns as the moderns imagine. An exiled, powerless people believing that it can restore wholeness to life through its devotion is not categorically distinct from solitary individuals adrift in the cosmos believing that they can yet salvage personal meanings that make life worth living. Both experience powerlessness, contradictions, the pull of hope and of despair, and the gap between a high sense of the uniqueness of human life and the difficulty of living with the dignity that such life deserves.

A HASIDIC LABOR OF SISYPHUS

The human condition is fraught with ambiguities. Our attitude toward it is often one of ambivalence. Let us consider a final midrash that finds meaning in these ambiguities, as well as its interpretation by a liminal figure, the nineteenth-century Hasidic leader, Rabbi Menachem Mendel of Kotsk. The midrash (Genesis Rabbah 8:5) is about the creation of humanity as such. It picks up, as midrash often does, on a textual oddity in Genesis 1:26. God says, "Let *us* make man in our image, after our likeness." Who is the "us" here? The midrash assumes that it is the heavenly host of angels, God's retinue – a notional consequence of portraying God as a king or a military leader. God then consults his host of retainers. The angels are querulous. They divide themselves into factions and begin to offer God conflicting advice. Their divergence explains a verse from the Psalms: "Faithfulness (*ḥesed*) and truth (*'emet*) meet; justice (*tzedek*) and well-being (*shalom*) kiss" (Psalms 85:11). The angels who advocate for the creation of human beings base their support on the values of faithfulness and justice. The angels in opposition contend for truth and *shalom*. The first group believes that human beings will live with lovingkindness and loyalty. The second group counters that they will spurn truth and will all be liars. Similarly, the first group contends that humans will act justly; the second that they will have a contentious, quarrelsome nature. Exasperated with his dueling advisors,

God "seized truth and threw it to the ground (*natal emet v'hishlikho l'aretz*)." God's impetuous action now makes sense of the verse: "It hurled truth to the ground" (Daniel 8:12). While the angels continued to quarrel, God created human beings.

For the Kotsker rebbe, the creation of human beings means the expulsion of truth from the world.[33] As with other Hasidic thinkers, he takes the theosophy of the kabbalah and gives it an existential – a human psychological/ethical/spiritual – sense. The burying of truth means that the truth of human existence is elusive. The meaning of human life is obscured. Life seems futile and self-defeating. It is as if we were ordered by a master to fill buckets with water, but the buckets are full of holes. Life is a labor of Sisyphus, a protracted experience of meaninglessness and absurdity.[34] Yet, even though we know that we cannot get an answer to our urgent question of "why?" (*far vos*), we ought to believe that there is an answer. It's just that we can never know it – herein lies a trace of the absurd.

There is no truth in human life. We lie to one another and to ourselves. The world appears to be a deception, and we are destined to be its dupes. The Kotsker does not believe that God lies to us, for God is truth. But the evidence does not make the case in God's favor. This is not an abstract matter but a problem of life. The place to begin to work on the problem is to stop lying to ourselves. We must *become* the truth that is otherwise buried in the ground. We must resurrect (*teḥiyat ha-metim*) that truth within ourselves. That means living without self-centeredness, living with absolute integrity, not accepting rationalizations, comforting illusions, and sloppy thinking.[35] The Kotsker rejected the possibility of getting human answers to his gnawing questions about what human life could mean in a world without truth. He could learn nothing more from human beings and so sequestered himself from his family and disciples for 25 years. He had to become free to "disregard self-regard" (*zikh nisht meynen*).[36] This meant a radical honesty with himself and with others – in the latter case, to the point of impolitic bluntness for the sake of truth.

An example: a hasid comes to him and confesses that he has dreadful thoughts (*moyredike machshoves*). The rebbe asks him what they are. The hasid intimates that they are so dreadful that not even hell could help him atone for them. The rebbe pushes him nonetheless to divulge them. The hasid confesses that he sometimes thinks that there is no God, specifically "no judgment and no Judge."[37] The rebbe, completely unperturbed, replies "Why is this distressing to you?" The hasid shrieks: "Why am I distressed? If there is neither judgment nor Judge, what sense does the entire world make?" And, the rebbe answers, why should it bother you if the world has no sense? The distraught hasid answers that if the world is senseless, then Torah has no reason or purpose. The rebbe, continuing to probe, asks why it would be consequential if the Torah were purposeless. "What would my life be, rebbe, if there were no reason for the Torah? If the Torah lacked sense and purpose?" At this point, the rebbe stops the regress of questions and tells his hasid that he has shown himself to be a person of integrity, of radical honesty and depth – and that such a person is allowed to have such thoughts. Such thoughts speak to the nobility of an honest Jew (*ohrentlikher yid*). The Kotsker thus brought the hasid out of his embarrassment and self-regard into an open confrontation with the source of his negativity, freeing him to accept his doubts, fears, and pain. He didn't solve his metaphysical problem – that remains untouched and agonizing – but he did help him take a step toward truth, the truth of a life without pretense or self-deception. The Kotsker affirmed such a life, even though it was lonely, dangerous, and permanently lacking in the "metaphysical satisfaction" of firm answers to the most urgent and troubling questions. *For no answers are available.* One must live bravely, not bitterly, with the questions.[38]

The absurdity of our situation, in the Kotsker's view, is that we must neither abandon our questions and our quest for truth nor expect any resolution of them. The only answer is "existential." It comes in courageous if agonizing living with the dilemma. Of course, unlike a twentieth-century existentialist, and more like Kierkegaard, to whom the great twentieth-century Jewish theologian Abraham Joshua Heschel compares him, the Kotsker is a man of deep faith. His courage to be is grounded in an ultimate trust (*emunah*) in God. This goes far beyond a mere propositional attitude. It is a commitment of the whole being. God is the master who has ordered us to the "*Sisyphus-arbeit*" of drawing water with leaky buckets. For the Kotsker, trust in God is not a surrender, a passive capitulation to some mysterious higher power; it is an act of storming the heavens. The Kotsker believes that the heavens are disordered and that they too need tikkun. The Kotsker doesn't shrink from putting hard questions to God. Although our Sisyphus work in the world is meaningless, God must have an intention. Or does he? God is the one who should be worrying about this. God should worry about our human, all too human suspicion that our lives are meaningless.

The truth and meaning of our lives are buried – but that doesn't mean that truth and meaning are nonexistent, only that they are hidden. We have to raise them up. To do so, we must develop an extraordinary sensitivity to the hints, inklings, and winks (*vunk*) that we receive.[39] All that one gets from heaven is a wink. Neither the senses nor commonsense enable us to receive such hints. The capacity to do so must be cultivated. It is part of the process of learning Torah, learning how to live as a Jew, and learning to disregard one's self-regard. A God whose ways any common person can understand is not a God in whom the Kotsker can trust. There are no available human conclusions to be drawn about God. All we have are questions and occasional, elusive "winks." "He who lives with nothing but questions, must live alone."[40] The answers to those questions will never be forthcoming; thus, in our solitude, we can only endure, trust – and cry out. The most powerful cry, the Kotsker teaches, is silence (*schveigen*).[41]

I make no claim to having sketched an absurdist *tradition* in Jewish thought but only to have shown moments where absurdity appears. The goodness of existence can still be affirmed, but with an ironic, paradoxical, *chutzpah*-like attitude toward the Creator.[42] Gratitude for life is mixed with disgust at its injustice, indeed, at its absurdity. Life as such is not tragic, but anyone who lives attentively experiences tragedy – and has a right to be scandalized by it. One has a right to hold on to the scandal, to refuse the relief of pious submission. Courage is called for, a Jewish "courage to be." The latter is not a given; it is an achievement. The Jew is handed neither meaning nor courage on a platter. The elements out of which meaning can be made likewise threaten to defeat it, hence the need for the courage, hope, and faith to persist.

Let us now turn to some typically modern, atheistic characterizations of the possibilities for meaningfulness developed against the background of a presumed wholly naturalistic world. The contemporary philosophical project of seeking meaningful existence mostly assumes the death of God. If we knew that God existed, we read again and again, the question of meaning would not be as insistent as it is. Our supposed purpose in the world – to do God's will – would be secure, as would our stature in the world as God's chosen creatures, endowed with reason and free will. Such a story about who we are and what we are here to do would be plausible.

The philosophers assume that none of these religious convictions are believable any longer. They then try to work out ways in which human existence still has point, purpose, value, and intelligibility without reliance on the divine. For some, reflexes of the old religious story remain, without its central character. For others, the death of God necessitates a sea change. Humanity loses its stature; it becomes fully naturalized. We are simply another branch on the primate tree. Or, with a different domain of naturalism in the foreground, we are brains working through the possibilities for our survival as organisms. The question posed by this project is: Can inherited human meanings be sustained in the face of a complete naturalization of human existence or do they need, as Nietzsche thought, to be "transvalued?" Few of the naturalists accept Nietzsche's teaching as to the radical consequences of the death of God. (That is, if God is dead, the tradition of biblical values such as that of equal human worth and dignity can no longer be sustained.) Most seem to think that we can keep the most appealing meanings while being relieved of God and "his burden."[43]

The philosophers – and one famous biologist – whom I will next examine are all contemporary contributors to the debate about meaning in life. Their work stands out, in my judgment, for the clarity and vigor with which they press their points, as well as their obliviousness to the absurdity their thought encounters.

MEANING EVOLVES

As philosopher Steve Stewart-Williams sees it, evolutionary biology disallows stipulating a difference in kind rather than degree between humans and other animal species. (Interestingly, biologists themselves can be more permissive and still use the language of human uniqueness.) The title of an essay in the *New York Times*'s "The Stone" column by philosopher Crispin Sartwell conveys the point: "Humans are animals. Let's get over it."[44] The difference between humans and other animals is either no greater than the differences among animals themselves or greater but not sufficient to ground a hierarchy. Our inherited self-image of superiority is both false and pernicious; it has been used to establish morally repugnant hierarchies not just vis-à-vis the biosphere but among human groups as well.

Stewart-Williams writes that "with the corrective lens of evolutionary theory, the view that human life is infinitely valuable seems like a vast and unjustified over-valuation of human life."[45] Stewart-Williams takes the upshot of evolutionary theory to be the dissolution of any sense that human beings are special. Our sense of our own specialness is debunked by a proper reckoning with Darwinian thought, he believes. Truth will vanquish our ancient predilection for species-wide self-aggrandizement. As Darwinism returns us to nature, *Homo sapiens* becomes just another primate group emerging on the African savannah hundreds of thousands of years ago from prior hominins, diverging from a common ancestry with chimpanzees and bonobos, as well as from other by now bygone species.

Yes, we are different in some interesting respects from our primate cousins, but all of us, indeed all of nature's living beings, are more alike than different – a point that would not have scandalized Kohelet. Our likeness consists first in the sheer contingency of our existence: We needn't have come into being. We came into being through random genetic mutation, just like everything else that lives. Furthermore, once launched into life, we, like everything else, seek one thing: to replicate our genes and survive both in the short term as distinct beings and in the long term through our reproductive success. The same Darwinian logic constrains and explains us as it does for all other beings. "Evolution" does not imply progress; we are not "better" than other animals. Evolution simply implies fitness, achieved through adaptation. We have adapted to our environments, no less and no more than beavers or wasps. (Indeed, our ability to shape our environment beyond, say, what beavers do may make us *maladapted* to nature at this point. As our "human niche" is destroying our planetary home, we may be a less successful species than others.) Our ascription of some special importance to ourselves is evolution's cunning trick. The humans who survived in prehistoric times were those who took themselves seriously enough to replicate their genes.[46]

Nonetheless, it would be a mistake to say that the meaning of our existence – our purpose in life – was to replicate our own genes. Evolutionary theory "tells us where we came from, not what to do now that we're here."[47] The language of purpose, x is for y, is teleological. It explains a present x with respect to a future y. Evolutionary explanation, despite the sometimes casual talk of biologists, is strictly speaking nonteleological, Stewart-Williams asserts. The neck of the giraffe did not develop for eating leaves on tall trees. Rather, long-necked giraffes were more successful at surviving and so of passing their genes on to their descendants. Evolution tells of past history but never of future purpose. Consequently, evolution does not give us the meaning (which Stewart-Williams equates with purpose) of human existence. We are here. We evolved. And while it is true, "We all choose little goals for ourselves, and that this can make our lives meaningful in the emotional sense of the term ... there is no reason to suppose that life has any ultimate meaning or purpose."[48] Thus, the deliverance of an austere, Darwinian view from nowhere.

Nonetheless, one must come back to "here." Life has no meaning, but at the subjective, emotional level, Stewart-Williams has us find some point in our "little goals." How to reconcile the tension between the objective lack of meaning or purpose and our investiture of meaning in our little goals? His bridging of the gap between the abstract and the engaged view requires a distinction between the "intellectual" implications of the meaninglessness of life and the "emotional" ones. Our intellectual assertion of meaninglessness does not preclude a cheerful appreciation of the worth of life, that is, of our "enjoyment" of existence. Indeed, the intellectual assertion of ultimate meaninglessness may even be liberating. Emotionally, however, this conclusion may make us gloomy and lead to depression. The challenge then is to let our newfound intellectual liberation affect our emotional response; we ought not to give in to the emotional implications of meaninglessness. We should embrace the truth that "there is no logical contradiction in the idea that life is good but meaningless, and the universe awesome but ultimately pointless."[49] We can and should appreciate the goods of existence and find our own unpretentious subjective meaning in them without seeking to frame them within an objective context. The universe and thus evolution and life as a whole are meaningless, but we can still enjoy the view.

Rather than letting the staunch conviction that life is meaningless undercut the possibility of pleasure in life, Stewart-Williams's strategy is to quarantine unsettling "emotional" aspects from dispositive "intellectual" ones. He introduces a binary as severe as Nagel's without, however, any appreciation of the problematic, let alone absurd nature of the situation into which it relegates us. Stewart-Williams's hedonic emotional creatures who bracket their belief in the meaninglessness of life in order to remain untroubled lack the honesty, depth, and pathos of human beings in Nagel's picture. While Nagel sees the clash of perspectives as giving rise to absurdity, Stewart-Williams uses his binary to deny absurdity. He contents himself, like Montaigne, with worldly satisfactions, with bracketing the problematic implication of his positivist metaphysics. In this, he is unlike James Tartaglia, our marquee nihilist, whom we shall encounter in Chapter 4. Tartaglia also wants the meaninglessness of our lives as natural/physical beings to condition our socially available invented meanings. But he draws a starker lesson from that move: Nihilism is the most basic fact of life. Tartaglia would see Stewart-Williams as not going far enough.

The late Harvard biologist, E. O. Wilson, endorses evolution-shaped views methodologically but also wants to hold on to something akin to Kateb's special-status claim. He would reject Stewart-Williams's radically reductionistic proposal. Like Kateb, a sense of what is unique in humanity, albeit within the framework of an evolutionary account, coupled with a dignity conferring purpose orient Wilson. In his grandly titled book, *The Meaning of Human Existence*, Wilson proposes to use our evolutionary, biological history to decipher the "the riddle of the human species." The riddle is, on the one hand, our conformity, as highly social, intelligent primates, to the general principles of natural selection, coupled with, on the other, our *unique* human capacity to be "self-made, independent, alone, and fragile."[50] How does one square our presumed exhaustive similarity to other living things with our felt uniqueness? Wilson claims that the humanities, by which he means both creative arts of all kinds and the study of those arts, as well as philosophy, excel at giving us textured portrayals of our felt uniqueness. We need the arts and humanities; they give human beings their "soul." However, they do not penetrate to a genuine explanation of our human condition. For that, one must turn to evolutionary biology. (Hence, his longstanding claim that the humanities must align themselves with science as something of a junior partner in the enterprise of explaining human lives.) Evolutionary biology, with additional "insider" perspective provided by the humanities, can solve the riddle, which may not, after all, be as puzzling as we think.

The riddle is solved by a consideration of our kind of sociality. We, and only nineteen other known species, practice "eusociality":

> By definition, the members of eusocial groups cooperatively rear the young across multiple generations. They also divide labor through the surrender by some members of at least part of their personal reproduction in a way that increases the 'reproductive success' (lifetime reproduction) of other members .... Once attained, advanced social behavior at the eusocial grade found a major ecological success.[51]

Eusociality abetted the growth of immense social and general intelligence in our ancestors. Cooperation led to the division of labor between hunters and those who remained at the campsites and cared for the young the hunters had to leave behind. We had to understand one another well within this social world in order for the trust necessary for cooperation, as well as the suspicion necessary for survival, to arise. "The mind is a kaleidoscopically shifting map of others inside the group and a few outside, each of whom is evaluated emotionally in shades of trust, love, hatred, suspicion, admiration, envy, and sociability."[52] The competitive advantage of eusociality vis-à-vis other social forms correlated with an increase in the size of the brains of the predecessors of modern humans in contrast to our genetic cousins, the other great apes. Large brains facilitated enhanced social intelligence.

To come to the most distinctive feature of human beings, our form of sociality produced a high degree of uniquely human inner conflict. We humans are both devoted to our groups, without which our ancestors could not have survived, and in competition with some members of them, as well as with groups other than our own. We have sharply conflicting selfish and altruistic tendencies, which are rooted in our evolutionary history. Our inner conflict is of our essence, our uniqueness:

> So it came to pass that humans are forever conflicted by their prehistory ... They are suspended in unstable and constantly changing positions between the two extreme forces that created us. We are unlikely to yield completely to either force as the ideal solution to our social and political turmoil. To give in completely to the instinctual urgings born from individual selection would be to dissolve society. At the opposite extreme, to surrender to the urgings from group selection would turn us into angelic robots – the outsized equivalent of ants. The eternal conflict is not God's test of humanity. It is not a machination of Satan. It is just the way things worked out. The conflict might be the only way in the entire Universe that human-level intelligence and social organization can evolve. We will find a way eventually to live with our inborn turmoil, and perhaps find pleasure in viewing it as the primary source of our creativity.[53]

Wilson emphasizes the significant, distinctive features of human beings vis-à-vis other eusocial animals, most especially their "human-level intelligence." His Kateb-like moment is an almost ecstatic confession: "Exalted we are, risen to be the mind of the biosphere without a doubt, our spirits uniquely capable of awe and ever more breathtaking leaps of imagination." And yet the counterweight must not be lost: "But we are still part of Earth's fauna and flora, bound to it by emotion, physiology, and, not least, deep history .... Human existence may be simpler than we thought."[54]

Wilson presents human existence as a play of fate and choice. Our sociality shaped our diverging emotional responses to the world, that is, those self-regarding and other-regarding drives. It clinched, as well, our inveterate tribalism, our love for our own, and our fear of outsiders. We are an "innately dysfunctional species."[55] His hope is that now that we have a sound evolutionary biological explanation for why we are dysfunctional, we can do something about it. We can cultivate our better nature and tame our vicious one. Now that we can see the foolishness of religion and tribal political ideology, we can school ourselves to see every conspecific as an equal. Freed of God and supernatural purpose, "We are, it seems, completely alone. And that, in my opinion is a very good thing. It means we are completely free."[56] The meaning of human existence then is to realize possibilities for conceptual clarity and practical social progress unimaginable to our prescientific ancestors. Wilson secularizes providence – the divine guidance of nature and history – into evolutionary progress. Unlike Stewart-Williams, he believes that humans are different in kind from other creatures; we represent real progress in the upward spiral of life "from monad to man."[57] Associating ourselves in a deliberate, conscious way, through culture, with this implicit natural teleology, seeking to preserve biodiversity, being the "mind of the biosphere," will enable human existence to rise to an "infinitely more productive and interesting meaning" than ever before in our history as a species.[58]

Nonetheless, Wilson's view of meaning per se is rather thin. His main point is polemical rather than substantive. It is to build up an evolution shaped-creation story that can definitively supplant that of the Bible, clearing the ground for Darwinism as a robust secular religion that can replace Christianity.[59] Wilson's contribution to meaning is an origin story about the significance and importance of our values, minds, will, and hopes. It is, in its religion-like way, both visionary and strangely naive, as if it were the unironic scriptural revelation of an unenigmatic god.

Far greater philosophical sophistication is brought to Wilson's perspective and program by the historian of Darwinism and philosopher, Michael Ruse. Ruse, agreeing with Wilson on the substance of contemporary evolutionary theory, disagrees on its implications for the meaning of life. Ruse denies that Darwinism can provide an "objective" meaning to life; it cannot function as a secular substitute for religion. Darwinism is indeed, as Daniel Dennett has called it, a "universal acid" that dissolves not only the plausibility of religions but also the need for what they do. Wilson, by Ruse's lights, is trying to get Darwinism to provide the significance and intelligibility – the meaningfulness of human existence – that the Baptist fundamentalism of his Southern youth once provided for him. Ruse is more like Stewart-Williams than Wilson. Darwinism provides no Ultimate Meaning (the self-mocking capital letters are that of Ruse).

Ruse sees only two possibilities for "a meaning to life": one is objective and the other is subjective. The objective version of meaning is provided by traditional religion or, for enthusiasts such as Julian Huxley or E. O. Wilson, by evolution as a story of progress and ascent. But objective meaning cannot succeed. Religion for Ruse has lost its plausibility because Darwinism has taken away one of its main props – teleology or final cause. There is no longer any need to posit a god to explain why the living world is "designed" as it is. Indeed, strictly speaking, there is no design. There is an immanent process of natural selection whereby adaptations allow organisms to better perform relevant functions. Eyes *are* for seeing, but the causality that brought them into being is internal; no outside designer is necessary.[60] Another function of religion is to sustain human value and meaning in the face of moral and natural evil. Here, it is not so much that Darwinism has undermined traditional theodicy as that theodicy itself is too high a price to pay for whatever presumptive intelligibility it brings. If evil is a consequence of humans having been created with free will,

> the free will of Hitler and Himmler and the rest of that sorry crew does not outweigh the deaths of Anne Frank, Sophie Scholl, and Dietrich Bonhoeffer. Nor does it help to look down the road and say God will make it all right in the end. There may be a God. Not the Christian God. Thank goodness. I don't want the Christian God to exist.[61]

Ruse's response is not one of secularist condescension but of deep moral revulsion at the obduracy of theological rationalizations of evil.

Ruse admits that science is a severely limited project; he does not doubt that there are profound questions that science is not well suited to answer. These include why there is something rather than nothing; what, if anything, justifies morality; what is the origin of consciousness (the hard problem); and what, if anything, is the meaning of life.[62] Rejecting Christian answers, he also rejects the belief that evolutionary theory provides answers to these questions. They may well be insoluble. Although evolutionary theory frames the conceptual space in which thinking about the questions of life occurs, it cannot resolve or dissolve them. It shows its limits and so impeaches Darwinism's claim to function as a secular religion. But given that traditional religion can't do the job of giving genuine answers, both fail at providing objective, compelling meanings to life.

Ruse, neither dismissive of deep problems of meaning nor optimistic about scientific answers to them, settles on an agnostic, subjectivist strategy: "We are on our own! We are on our own! God and the soul don't help protect us. Nor does it help to turn nature into a meaning generator. We are on our own! Is this just a counsel of despair?"[63] Calling himself a "Darwinian existentialist," Ruse takes seriously both that we are on our own – meaning is ours to construe and create – and that we do so within a biological context shaped by natural selection. He agrees with Sartre that we are "condemned to freedom" but disagrees over the extent of our freedom; existence does not wholly precede essence. There is an evolved human nature (an "essence") that conditions our freedom. We are, importantly, highly social; we value friendship and family. We are moral creatures. Although biology does not determine morality, morality fits the kind of social beings that we are. Part of our personal experience of morality, say, of the morality of obligation, is that morality does not feel purely subjective; we feel that morality has an objective, imperatival force. This is part of our nature, our essence. So is the "life of the mind," both the sheer reality of consciousness as such and all of the wondrous things that we do with it. Any life worth living is lived in these objective, species-particular domains.

Within this essential, objective framework, meaning equates to *subjective well-being*. Meaning means satisfaction in sociality, family, friendship, ethical life, and the life of the mind. After speaking of his own satisfying experience as a teacher, father, husband, and prodigious scholar, he states:

> I see no reason to expect anything beyond this. From an eternity of oblivion. To an eternity of oblivion. Everlasting dreamless sleep .... Absurd, if you will, although I would not call it this. In the end, though, I am an agnostic. I just don't know whether life has any – time for those capitals – Ultimate Meaning .... There may be something more. There may not. Don't spend your life agonizing about this or letting people manipulate you with false promises .... Life here and now can be fun and rewarding, deeply meaningful .... Live for the real present, not the hoped-for-future. Leave it at that.[64]

Can it be left at that? Ruse's last word, although not radically different from that of Kohelet, seems too blithe. What of all those who have not experienced such well-being in life, whose lives are solitary, nasty, brutish, and short? Is there no redemptive meaning for them? What of those whose futures were tragically cut short through human malice and depravity in camps and gulags? Is there nothing other than to say, "tough luck?" Ruse does not want to call his view absurd because no great contradictions – as in Kohelet – obtain. Life is not of such surpassing value that its diminution or degradation stupefies and offends. There is no great rift at the heart of creation. There is bonhomie, which is not bad, but it hardly seems to be enough.

BRAINS, MINDS, AND MEANING

Allied with the evolutionary approach to secular meaning-seeking is the neuroscientific one. Philosophers Gregg Caruso and Owen Flanigan call ventures in this field "neuroexistentialism."[65] They see neuroexistentialism as a "third wave" of existentialist anxiety. The first wave, represented by Dostoevsky, Kierkegaard, and Nietzsche, reacted to the decline of religious authority and to the credibility of traditional Western theism in nineteenth-century Europe. Its project was to justify norms without taken-for-granted theological foundations. The second wave represented by the likes of Sartre and Camus responded to the failure of Enlightenment-inspired, post-religious humanism to withstand the assault of twentieth-century totalitarianism. It arose in despair over the possibilities for meaningful life in the face of massive and pervasive evil. The third wave is a special development of the centuries-long conflict of science and religion. It comes from taking seriously just how dissolutive of the traditional image of humanity modern evolutionary biology and neuroscience are. "This scientific view results in the same feeling of drift and anchorless search for meaning that is a hallmark of all existentialisms and thereby constitutes the third wave of existentialism."[66] It arises when contemporaries take the full measure of the absence of free will, of the unqualified animality of humans, as well as of the nonexistence of the soul, of the afterlife, of God, and of any transcendent dimension at all. Caruso and Flanagan put it sharply:

> If the soul does not exist, and it does not, then where do we derive our morals, our meaning, and our well-being? This problem is the "really hard problem," the special problem for those of us living in the age of brain science; of making sense of the nature, meaning, and purpose of our lives given that we are material beings living in a material world.[67]

Unlike the blithe proposals of Stewart-Williams and Ruse, neuroexistentialism accepts that the anxiety generated by the exclusively naturalistic picture is legitimate. A proper response to it must show that human flourishing – which presumably solves the "really hard problem" – is possible and sufficient for meaning. The goal is to:

> pursue a kind of descriptive-normative inquiry into the causes and conditions of flourishing for material beings living in a material world whose self-understanding includes the idea that such a world is the only kind of world that there is and thus that the meaning and significance of their lives, if there is any, must be found in such a world.[68]

Presumably, the only spoilers of this eudaemonic quest are those reactionaries who refuse to accept that the world of exhaustive naturalism "is the only kind of world that there is."

This description of the problem and of its presumptive solution well describes the work of the Canadian neuro-philosopher, Paul Thagard. Thagard positions his project as another stage in a revolutionary reconsideration of humanity's place in the world. The first two revolutions were those of Copernicus and Darwin. The first knocked the earth from the center of the cosmos, replacing it with the sun. The subsequent development of scientific astronomy further reduced the centrality, in a metaphorical sense, of our world. The second, Darwinian, revolution located human origins in deep time, in a descent from prior hominins, who themselves shared a common ancestor with the remaining great apes. Far from God's last, most distinguished creation, human beings came about the way every other living thing came about – through lucky accidents of genetic mutation that led to greater fitness for survival within one or another environmental niche. Our origins stretch back not only through the lines of early mammals but to the chance occurrence of self-replicating molecules billions of years ago. These mark a transition from nonlife toward life, no breath of God required.

Thagard's third stage of radical ontological reorientation is the "Brain Revolution."[69] He dubs his approach "neural naturalism."[70] The ramifying new sciences of the brain, even more than those of astronomy and evolutionary biology, touch our essence: We *are* our brains. Mind is brain. Why does Thagard claim this? Mind does not seem at all like brain. The one is extended in space, gray and gelatinous. The other soars above the concrete world, let alone its soft, wet bundles of billions of cells. When we speak of minds, we speak of ideas, beliefs, intentions, experience, and consciousness. When we speak of organs, brains among them, we speak of anatomical structures, specialized cells, DNA, chemistry, and physics. It is far from clear, even at the cutting edge of neuroscience, how an infinitely complex object, the brain, can produce consciousness. How do we experience the way the world lights up for us, and what it is like to have and to be the subject of such experiences? This problem, for some philosophers, is so difficult, so categorically different from explaining discrete brain functions (e.g., sight, smell, and hunger) that it has been called, in the memorable words of David Chalmers, "the hard problem."[71]

Thagard is not one of those philosophers. He rejects the view that consciousness is an uncrackable explanatory nut, orders of magnitude more difficult to understand than anything else that the brain does. He is confident that neuroscience is on a firm path toward the scientific light. Epistemologically, science is the only game in town, and we do well to trust it.

What supports Thagard's confidence is not only steady progress in neuroscience, aided and abetted by the ubiquitous functional magnetic resonance imaging (fMRI) machines that show us which brain areas correlate with which kinds of mental activity, but an austere epistemology. He practices what has been called "evidentialism," a stern faith, articulated by the Victorian mathematician William Clifford, that "it is wrong always, anywhere, and for anyone to believe anything on insufficient evidence."[72] Thagard rejects both religion in all of its varieties *and* traditional philosophy. The former is disreputable for the lack of evidence as to its favorite fictional entities – primarily gods or God and the immortal soul. No mystery or transcendence for Thagard; if there isn't in-principle verifiable evidence for a claim, the claim should not rationally be made. Religion categorically fails that test. But traditional philosophy does, too. Not only is it infected by speculative metaphysics but even at its most strenuous, as in Kant or in modern analytic philosophy, it relies on suppositions. In the case of analytic philosophy, too much weight has been put on thought experiments and the clarification of concepts. The problem here is that our concepts themselves are insufficiently evidence based and highly changeable. Probing and analyzing them will not give us the new knowledge we seek. We need to strap ourselves to the mast of experimental science, with its continuous churn of verification and falsification, in order to gain concepts that have traction to begin with. Only those concepts generated by rigorous scientific inquiry deserve to count in explanations of how the world is. Purging ancient habits from philosophy is as much the mission of the brain revolutionary as consigning religion to the dustbin of history.

The twin dangers are dogmatic authority and – somewhat surprisingly – empiricism. Thagard is not a straightforward empiricist. He is a constructive realist.[73] Evidence isn't a purely empirical matter. The best method of inquiry is inference to the best explanation. The empirical data, in this case of the sciences of the brain, allow us to frame hypotheses, which compete with one another for explanatory adequacy. We judge from, among hypotheses, which one has the most explanatory potential, which one coheres with other plausible hypotheses, theories, and reliable knowledge, and we choose (or our brains do) that one. Arriving at a defensible scientific claim is never a matter of empirical observation alone. Although Thagard thus grants the constructed nature of scientific knowledge, he does not doubt that it is knowledge of real things; it is anchored in an empirical world that checks and constrains it. He has robust confidence in the findings of science, more than in any produced by other forms of inquiry.

All facets of human experience, interior and exterior, are "represented by" neural populations communicating with one another in various parts of the brain. Experience, of whatever kind, *just is* neuronal activity. Of course, neuronal activity takes place not only in the context of the brain and its extended nervous system but within a physicochemical context "below" the level of the brain (the level at which serotonin, oxytocin, dopamine, electrical impulses, etc. do their work) and in a psychological–social milieu "above" the level of the brain. Thagard explicitly rejects reductionism. But implicitly he seems to endorse it insofar as he does not quite let the "higher" levels of social reality and personal psychological reality have causal power equal to the neural and molecular levels. They are part of the feedback loop in which brains do cognitive and emotional work, but most of the arrows of causal explanation still point upward. He does not envision an emergence scenario where "higher" realities, once emerged from the organization of lower ones, have their own causal efficacy.[74] Nor do they have their own independence. All the levels interact, but without the causal activity of the lower level, the upper level would not exist.

How can one link a discourse about values and meaning to all of this brain talk with its inevitable concomitants of physicalism, the denial of free will, and the global debunking of mind as anything other than brain? The answer lies in the emotions. Thagard endorses a view of emotions as cognitive-cum-feeling evaluations of the condition of the organism in the world. Consciousness is fundamentally emotional consciousness, an awareness of how our brains are responding, at the level of feeling, to the world. Emotion attaches an evaluative aspect to the objects of experience ("objects" include thoughts, beliefs, plans, goals, as well as roses, faces, and feces). Value is objective in the sense that objectively existing brain processes assign experiences a positive or negative feeling tone. Value seems to be, in Thagard's ontology, the activity of the nucleus accumbens (the neurons of which are associated with desire, pleasure, and positive emotions) and the amygdala (the neurons of which are associated with fear and other negative emotions). Value (or, more properly, valuing) is part of the "real world" in this sense. Our mental acts of valuing resolve into so much neuronal activity with its basis in lower regions of our brains. Of course, as human beings whose brains process in interconnected and parallel ways, the full suite of our cognitive abilities is engaged alongside our emotional ones. The poet or philosopher's most inspired or insightful thoughts about beauty are "represented by" populations of neurons that are especially active in the nucleus accumbens.

Value enters the world at this level. It seems, like the consciousness that accompanies it, to have an adaptive advantage from an evolutionary point of view.[75] To get to meaning, however, we need a few more steps. Equipped with its powerful, motivating emotional valences, the brain "decides" between courses of action (goals) in furtherance of the needs of the human organism in which it functions. Human beings – universally – have biological needs, but they also have higher order needs for love, work, and play. We are constantly forming goals to satisfy, under the constraints of a world with limited options and resources, these species-wide needs. By a process analogous to the scientific epistemology of inference to the best explanation, the brain infers to the best plan. It considers, imagines, and weighs its competing strategies to reach its subgoals and higher order goals, selecting the most efficient or appealing one. The emotional value that is manifest in these goals makes their satisfaction meaningful.

> The meaning of life is love, work, and play. A more nuanced summary would be better: People's lives have meaning to the extent that love, work, and play provide coherent and valuable goals that they can strive for and at least partially accomplish, yielding brain-based emotional consciousness of satisfaction and happiness.[76]

Suffice it to say that Thagard is generous with what constitutes "love, work, and play." Play, for example, isn't just kids roughhousing in the yard but listening to Beethoven string quartets. Work isn't just making money to buy necessary or desirable things but feeling autonomy, competence, respect from peers, etc. Love, similarly, is trust and friendship, not just oxytocin. Through linking the needs to be satisfied with an expansive range of human values and practices, Thagard seeks to diminish the appearance of crass biologism. Meaning ornaments the model.

Of the innumerable critical remarks that one might make, let's focus on the one most relevant to meaning. Thagard rejects Camus's philosophical diagnosis of the absurdity of life, as well as his fictional depiction of a nihilistic character, Meursault in *The Stranger*, for whom nothing matters. From Thagard's perspective, the overwhelming fact that we have needs, that life is largely oriented to fulfilling them, and that we are often quite successful in doing so – even if we have constantly to revise our needs such that they can be satisfied – means that people can find satisfaction in life. Those who reject this are simply being perverse. Given his brain-based schema, they are likely mentally ill:

> Counting against nihilism is the empirical finding that most people are happy. On average, across many cultures, when people are asked to rate their life satisfaction on a zero-to-ten scale, people rate themselves around 7. Thus, Camus' Meursault … and severe depressives are exceptional in their inability to find aspects of life that matter. Using depressives as the standard for human meaning would be like using schizophrenics as the standard for human knowledge: in both cases neurochemical disturbances seriously diminish brain functioning.[77]

Without justifying the equation, Thagard deflates meaningfulness to the psychological feeling of satisfaction. The meaning of life is to be pleased with how one has been able to fulfill one's needs.

Furthermore, meaning qua personal satisfaction, as for Ivan Ilych, seems to be conventional and conformist. One who steps back and questions the framework of satisfactions, the narrow psychological calculus for gains and losses in the business of need-satisfaction, is defective. Although not an old-style Soviet psychiatrist who ideologized mental illness, Thagard nonetheless does violence to anyone who aspires to be more reflective than a sled dog. The latter, one imagines, also experiences its share of love, work, and play, and if, in addition, its biological needs are met, it must also be satisfied with its life.

One of the liabilities of his model is that it wrenches human beings out of time and place.[78] Camus has just witnessed the horror of a Nazi occupation, of Vichy collaboration, of the utter failure of humanity to be humane. Yet somehow his strong claims, originating in moral outrage, on behalf of the absurdity of human life in such a world amount to no more than a perverse failure to recognize that he can still satisfy his needs under such "constraints." Where, indeed, does the greater absurdity lie – in the honest confrontation with the challenge of justifying value in a world that seems indifferent to it or in defining meaning down to the efficient operation of *l'homme machine*?

Although far from exhaustive, these samplings of the Darwinian and neuroscience inspired meaning of life literature are typical. They apply the confident, can-do attitude of scientific research to "the very hard problem" of meaning. Methodologically, they eschew absurdity as incompatible with the reliable, steady growth of knowledge, whether about the mechanisms of life or about its meaning. Indeed, its optimism and confidence about the availability of meaning set such work apart from both earlier secular versions of existentialism and from strands of Jewish thought. This confident eschewal of absurdity, of limit, of paradox and impenetrable puzzle – the search for meaning as a research program – is shallow and inadequate. How could meaning qua need-satisfaction and subsequent contentment support the moral courage needed to endure humanely in a camp, a ghetto, a gulag? What could one say to those people whose lives, through no fault of their own, have been nasty, brutish, and short? On an account such as Thagard's one would have to conclude that their lives were meaningless.

Biologizing value guts value. This problem is recurrent in the strenuously naturalistic philosophical treatments. The strenuous naturalist, of course, can argue that my criticism comes simply from prejudice. If so, the claim raised in Chapter 1 about the denizens of a Baconian scientific utopia remains apposite. Those well cared for, satisfied, truth seeking people whose lower and higher needs were met and who flourished in a fair and supportive society could nonetheless ask, without churlishness or ingratitude, "is this all there is?" Is the eudaemonic satisfaction of our need for "love, work, and play" and the intellectual satisfaction of our need for good explanations of nature in general and the human in particular sufficient to provide us meaning? Or are there yearnings, perplexities, and quandaries that call for illumination beyond the scope of naturalism? That gets us into the territory of revelation in Western religions, to which we now turn.

NOTES

1 Bernard Williams, *Truth and Truthfulness* (Princeton: Princeton University Press, 2002), p. 20. The paradigm case of a genealogy is the state of nature story in early modern political philosophy.

2 An otherwise impressive philosopher of biology, John Dupré, falls flat when he asserts that "Darwinism undermines the only remotely plausible reason for believing in the existence of God," namely God as the creator of life. Dupré construes religion to be, at heart, a science-like account of origins via divine creation. Since religion is in the world-explaining business, it must now be seen to have been eclipsed by its (literal and metaphorical) Darwinian competitor. Those who, like Stephen Jay Gould or Michael Ruse, would preserve a fallback role for religion – it is about ethics and meaning – also fall short. While religion *is* about ethics and meaning, that becomes a pyrrhic victory. Once religion's fundamental failure as bad science-like explanation is exposed, it needn't be taken seriously with regard to ethics and meaning either. It adds nothing and should be consigned to irrelevance. See John Dupré, *Darwin's Legacy: What Evolution Means Today* (Oxford: Oxford University Press, 2006), pp. 56–57.

3 See Shai Cherry, *Coherent Judaism* (Brookline: Academic Studies Press, 2020), p. 230. I take it as axiomatic that the creation stories are more about "ethics" than about "physics." In this, I follow Hermann Cohen. See, for example, Hermann Cohen, *Religion of Reason Out of the Sources of Judaism*, trans. Simon Kaplan (Atlanta: Scholars Press, 1995), p. 67. See also Marc de Launay, *Une Reconstruction Rationnelle du Judaïsme* (Geneva: Labor et Fides, 2002), p. 47.

4 The philosopher Wilfred Sellars distinguishes between the manifest and scientific images. In the former, "persons" are basic, irreducible constituents of reality; in the latter, humans are analyzed into their constituent parts all the way down to being "bags of particles." See Sellars, *Science, Perception, and Reality*, p. 26.

5 On organic unity as a natural value – and as supportive of a normative realist account of value – see Robert Nozick, *Philosophical Explanations*, pp. 413–428.

6 On these questions, see my essay "The Durability of Goodness," in Jonathan A. Jacobs, ed., *Judaic Sources and Western Thought* (New York: Oxford University Press, 2011), pp. 21–48.

7 Jon D. Levenson, *Creation and the Persistence of Evil* (Princeton: Princeton University Press, 1988), pp. 53, 122.
8 Levenson, *Creation and the Persistence of Evil*, p. 55.
9 Levenson, ibid., pp. 78–99.
10 Ibid., p. 127 (emphasis added).
11 Sifre Deuteronomy 346 on Isa 43:12, cited in Levenson, ibid., p. 139.
12 Ibid.
13 Camus, *The Myth of Sisyphus*, p. 57.
14 The prophet Zechariah describes the Jews as "prisoners of hope" (Zech 9:12), an apt designation. For a comprehensive philosophical study, see Alan L. Mittleman, *Hope in a Democratic Age* (Oxford: Oxford University Press, 2009).
15 Moshe Halbertal, "If the text had not been written, it could not be said," in Deborah A. Green and Laura S. Lieber, eds., *Scriptural Exegesis: The Shapes of Culture and the Religious Imagination, Essays in Honour of Michael Fishbane* (Oxford: Oxford University Press, 2009), p. 149.
16 Halbertal, "If the text had not been written," p. 149.
17 Halbertal, ibid., p. 146.
18 Thus, R. Abraham Steinberg and colleagues, whose commentary appears in their edition of Genesis Rabbah, *Midrash Rabbah Ha-Mevoar* (Jerusalem: Machon Ha-Midrash Ha-Mevoar, 1981) states that nothing pre-existed the world; God created the *tohu va-vohu* from nothing (*ayin*) on the first day. "God forbid!" (*ḥas va-shalom*) that anyone should believe that God created out of pre-existing matter." See p. 11.
19 The midrash is cited in Hayim Nahman Bialik and Yehoshua Hana Ravnitzky, eds., *The Book of Legends (Sefer ha-Aggadah)*, trans. William G. Braude (New York: Schocken Books, 1992), p. 6.
20 The Isaiah verse makes its way into the daily liturgy, where it is recited every morning. Unwilling to accept the idea that God creates evil, the rabbis replaced "evil" with "all." Thus, the prayer book's version of the verse reads: "He makes peace and creates all," a move as elegant as it is evasive.
21 See Bereshit Rabba 9:5. See also midrashim 9:7–11 for other negative meanings for "me'od."
22 Kabbalists differed over the precise relationship between God and the sefirot; is God identical to or different from the sefirot; are they his instruments or himself, as it were? Moshe Hallamish, *An Introduction*

to the Kabbalah*, trans. Ruth Bar-Ilan and Ora Wiskind-Elper (Albany: SUNY Press, 1999), p. 162. The ambiguity as to that relationship finds a parallel in an ambiguity about the polarities between good and evil elements and traits. They are both in the world and in God as such, even though God in some way transcends polarity. In Kabbalah, the cosmogonic and the theogonic merge. For a full discussion of these topics, see the rich study by Moshe Idel, *Primeval Evil in Kabbalah* (Brooklyn: Ktav, 2020).

23 Bede Rundle, *Why There Is Something Rather than Nothing* (Oxford: Clarendon Press, 2004), p. 113.

24 Rundle, *Why There Is Something Rather than Nothing*, p. 111.

25 Hartley Lachter, *Kabbalistic Revolution* (New Brunswick: Rutgers University Press, 2014), pp. 46, 60, 68.

26 For authoritative accounts of the basic Lurianic story, see Gershom Scholem, *Kabbalah* (Jerusalem: Keter, 1974), pp. 128–144 and Gershom Scholem, *Major Trends in Jewish Mysticism* (New York: Schocken Books, 1995 (1946)), pp. 260–275.

27 Scholem, *Major Trends*, p. 269.

28 Scholem, *Kabbalah*, p. 140.

29 Scholem, *Major Trends*, p. 266; Idel, *Primeval Evil*, p. 286.

30 Joseph B. Soloveitchik, *Halakhic Man*, trans. Lawrence Kaplan (Philadelphia: JPS, 1983), p. 102.

31 Scholem, *Major Trends*, p. 269.

32 Julian Young, *The Death of God and the Meaning of Life* (New York: Routledge, 2014), p. 113.

33 For an excellent overview of the Kotsker's thought, as presented in Abraham Joshua Heschel's retelling of his sayings and life, see Annette Aronowicz, "Heschel's Yiddish *Kotsk*: Some Reflections on Inwardness," in Stanislaw Krajewski and Adam Lipszyc, *Abraham Joshua Heschel: Philosophy, Theology, and Interreligious Dialogue* (Wiesbaden: Harrassowitz Verlag, 2009), pp. 112–121.

34 Abraham Joshua Heschel, *Kotsk* (Yiddish), Vol. II (Tel Aviv: Ha-Menorah Varlag, 1973), pp. 614–615.

35 Heschel, *Kotsk*, pp. 545, 616.

36 David Roskies, "My Encounters with Abraham Joshua Heschel," in Krajewski and Lipszyc, *Abraham Joshua Heschel*, p. 25.

37 The phrase *layt din v'layt dayan* – there is no judgment and there is no Judge – is a rabbinic way of describing a chaotic, godless world, an *il y*

a, as it were. Human beings are responsible for nothing and to no one; divine judgment is non-existent. This conclusion might have been what motivated the arch-heretic of rabbinic literature, Elisha ben Abuyah, to renounce his Judaism. R. Akiba raises this possibility and rejects it (there is judgment and there is a judge) in Genesis Rabbah, parashat Bereishit, 26:6. I am indebted to Dr. Benjamin Schvarcz for the reference.

38 The above story is from Heschel, *Kotsk*, pp. 606–607.

39 Heschel, Ibid., p. 617.

40 Ibid.

41 Ibid.

42 For "impudence against heaven," see B. Sanhedrin 105a. For a superb study of this topic in ancient and early medieval rabbinic literature, See Dov Weiss, *Pious Irreverence* (Philadelphia: University of Pennsylvania Press, 2017).

43 George Kateb, *Human Dignity* (Cambridge: Harvard University Press, 2011), p. 25.

44 www.nytimes.com/2021/02/23/opinion/humans-animals-philosophy.html (accessed March 1, 2021).

45 Steve Stewart-Williams, *Darwin, God, and the Meaning of Life* (Cambridge: Cambridge University Press, 2010), p. 266.

46 A sense of our extraordinary difference from the rest of nature as nature's way of motivating us to survive is at the core of evolutionary psychologist Nicholas Humphrey's book on the "internal magic show" of consciousness. See Nicholas Humphrey, *Soul Dust: The Magic of Consciousness* (Princeton: Princeton University Press, 2011).

47 Stewart-Williams, *Darwin, God, and the Meaning of Life*, p. 192.

48 Ibid., p. 194.

49 Ibid., p. 195.

50 E.O. Wilson, *The Meaning of Human Existence* (New York: Liveright Publishing, 2014), p. 26.

51 Wilson, *The Meaning of Human Existence*, pp. 19–20.

52 Ibid., p. 24.

53 Ibid., pp. 33–34.

54 Ibid., pp. 25–26.

55 Ibid., p. 176.

56 Ibid., p. 173.

57 Cf. Michael Ruse, *A Meaning to Life* (New York: Oxford University Press, 2019), p. 111.

58 Wilson quoted in Ruse, *A Meaning to Life*, p. 125.

59 Ruse, ibid., p. 103. Ruse's insight into the true nature of his friend, Wilson's, project explains the stress that Wilson puts on the centrality of creation stories for religion. Wilson, *The Meaning of Human Existence*, pp. 151–152. It also shows that the book is best framed as an *alternative creation story* for the new, secular religion.

60 Ruse, ibid., p. 39.

61 Ibid., p. 78.

62 Ibid., pp. 62–65.

63 Ibid. p. 131.

64 Ibid., pp. 169–170.

65 Owen Flanagan and Gregg Caruso, *Neuroexistentialism: Meaning, Morals, and Purpose in the Age of Neuroscience* (New York: Oxford University Press, 2018).

66 Flanagan and Caruso, *Neuroexistentialism*, p. 5.

67 Flanagan and Caruso, Ibid., p. 9.

68 Ibid., p. 11.

69 Paul Thagard, *The Brain and the Meaning of Life* (Princeton: Princeton University Press, 2010), p. 42.

70 Thagard, *The Brain and the Meaning of Life*, p. 214.

71 David Chalmers, "Facing up to the Problem of Consciousness," *Journal of Consciousness Studies*, 2(3):200–219, 1995.

72 William Clifford, "The Ethics of Belief," *Contemporary Review*, 29 (December 1876–May 1877): 295. For a contemporary analysis and critique see, Chignell, Andrew, "The Ethics of Belief," *The Stanford Encyclopedia of Philosophy* (Spring 2018 Edition), Edward N. Zalta (ed.), https://plato.stanford.edu/archives/spr2018/entries/ethics-belief/.

73 Thagard, *The Brain and the Meaning of Life*, p. 75.

74 Ibid., pp. 111, 220–221.

75 Ibid., p. 212. Thagard steers clear of strong evolutionary psychological claims not because he doubts their basic plausibility but because the evidence does not yet support some of them.

76 Ibid., pp. 166–167.

77 Ibid., p. 145.

78 I thank Annette Aronowicz for this insight.

3 Revelation

Kohelet does not rely on a tradition of divine teaching communicated only to Israel. With the exception of the editorial voice in the last line of the book, there are no substantive references to the covenantal theology of the Mosaic Torah.[1] His medium is an international tradition of wisdom. While there are conventions of that genre, his thoughts about God are precisely *his* thoughts. Kohelet interrogates his own experience against the backdrop of an impersonal natural world to draw lessons about what life means and how to live. He arrives at what has been called "immanent contentment," an acceptance of the moderate joys and shared, social meanings available in his lifeworld.[2] There are no appeals to transcendent knowledge or guidance. One must simply live with the absurdities and provisional meanings that experience tenders. Reason cannot fully resolve the riddle of life, but neither apparently can any normative teaching beyond reason such as the revealed will of God. Kohelet does not seem to put much stock in such a revelation. Should we?

If nature or, on the Jewish story, creation could guide us toward the meaning of life, our experience of the world and our reflection on it would suffice. But nature, even when construed as creation, cannot quite get us to well-grounded meaningfulness. On the religious side, creation, while good, isn't good *enough*. It gives us our chance at life – Lenn Goodman calls this "natural justice" – but it underdetermines what we make of it.[3] Our created condition fills us with perplexity, even despair, at the gap between the value we sense in our lives and the rough (and invariably fatal) treatment that life has in store for us. The indifference of nature to our hopes and sorrows inspires a sense of the absurdity of our situation. Kohelet-like ruminations about our insignificance shadow our wonder at nature's sublimity and our joy in her beauty. Creation, as the darker elements of Jewish thought insinuate, is broken and in need of repair. It is noble for humans to engage in cosmic *tikkun*, but it also seems absurd. Can we really repair the brokenness of creation? Are we to save the God who is supposed to save us?

Can the biblical trope of creation be revised to comprise a universe that may have 10 billion trillion habitable planets, some of them probably sustaining intelligent life?[4] Can anything we do in such a universe matter? What is special or important about us and our highly circumscribed field of action? The incomprehensible scale of the universe suggested by contemporary astronomy deflates us. Our only claim to cosmic recognition is as fledgling knowers, and, at that, the thin film of our knowledge covers an ocean of ignorance. When we retreat from our scientifically chastened perspective (our "view from nowhere") and try to affirm what we find valuable about ourselves, it seems self-serving. Although we find our own minds valuable, the elephant, Steve Stewart-Williams claims, might imagine that its trunk is the most valuable thing in the world.[5] The values on which we build meaning in life seem to reflect our interests rather than objectively valuable features of the world. That they abet our flourishing does not fundamentally justify our demand to flourish. Why do we matter enough to deserve to thrive? That question, absent the intentions of a good God, can only be answered from a point of view internal to human life. That might be the best we can do, but it may well make any argument launched therefrom question-begging. The nihilist notices this (presumed) logical Achilles heel and moves to puncture our pretensions to cosmic self-aggrandizement.

Against the normative and existential inadequacy of nature or creation, revelation – the presumptive disclosure of a higher law, reason, will, or meaning beyond human provenance – beckons. It promises an in-breaking of objective normativity, a prescription for a properly significant life. Judaism has gone this route, affirming that

God has imparted a wisdom and a way otherwise unknown, in its details, to human beings. Unknown, but not unknowable. Jewish thought about revelation is not Gnosticism. It doesn't take the disclosure of divinely communicated truth to be a secret, salvific teaching meant to liberate the chosen few from a dark, false world into an order of light and truth where soul leaves body and real life begins. Judaism is too worldly and life-affirming for that, although one cannot deny that gnostic currents have existed – and continue to exist – in Jewish thought. Revelation may originate in a higher intellect, but it is not impenetrable to our intellects. It speaks to us on many levels, including that of reasonableness. There is a potential paradox here: If revelation were fully reasonable, it would be redundant. But if it were irrational, it would be inscrutable.

The relation of reason and revelation is a topic of ongoing Jewish theological conversation. Reason both facilitates access to revelation and makes its authority problematic. Jewish engagement with and commitment to Torah, both intellectually and practically, are essential to any traditional Jewish view of the meaning of life. On many rehearsals of the story of revelation, however, traditional Jewish obedience to Torah has as much to do with Jewish will as divine will. Roughly, Jews themselves constitute the authority that is "imposed" on them from above. There is no revelation without Jewish participation. God, as it were, agrees to authorize what the Jews decide to do.[6] Is God's own authority legitimated or made irrelevant by this divine deference? In this circularity there inheres a trace of the absurd.

Concepts of revelation, I will argue, run into trouble, but so too does the philosophical analogue of revelation. The project I link to revelation is the inquiry into whether meaning is, very roughly, subjective or objective. Is it sufficient that an individual finds a way of life, a pursuit, project, or a set of values meaningful enough to guide her life or are there meta-individual conditions on individual assent? As I argued in the first chapter, meaning is a construal of value and, as such, open to human discretion to some extent. But to what extent? How open-ended is the process of meaning-seeking and meaning-finding? Certainly, social judgments of value and meaning can qualify purely individual ones. A society may produce a certain number of people who are content to spend their lives reading comic books or playing video games. It may also produce people who accomplish great things in the arts or sciences. The society would be within its rights to find the lives of the latter better spent or more meaningful than the former.[7] But, while this social judgment is shared and so transsubjective, is it *objective* in a robust sense? Is it cogent to think that there are objective meanings that allow an inquirer to sort out whether lives are more or less well spent? There is an axiological question here about the status of value as well as a hermeneutic question about the meaning-seeking interpretation of value.

These questions resemble the theological questions of revelation: Is there an objective, authoritative source that discloses the normative structure of a well-spent life or is this something that we freely devise and enact out of our own personal-cum-social resources? If it seems to us that such a structure is objectively available, how can we, if we can, know this? Can we be wrong about it? These are not solely modern worries. They go back at least as far as Socrates, Plato, and the Sophists. Plato's last dialogue, the *Laws*, discusses whether law is conventional or natural, that is, a product of mere human imagination and ingenuity or expressive of the Ultimate, that is, the idea of the Good, the Platonic placeholder for God. Should we think that there are as many bodies of law as there are political communities, such as cities, or is genuine law only one essentially divine thing? Conventional law at its best would try to approximate real law, which, if it exists, would be eternal, rational, and universal.[8]

Few modern objectivists about value and meaning would endorse such a transcendent view. Correlatively, few, if any, contemporary philosophers would be willing to say that there is *one* objective meaning of life which we should embrace. Such a stringent objectivism about meaning is ill-suited to a democratic age.[9] (There are, however, contemporary philosophers who try to specify a set of values, a basket of basic goods, the appropriate pursuit of which constitute a good life.[10] Disentangling these basic human goods from a metaphysical background story has been dubbed "new natural law." Meaningfulness on this account, if it is raised at all, would have to do with a life of dedication to excellence in the cultivation of such basic goods as knowledge, friendship, practical reasonableness, and religion.)

The debate between the philosophers Harry Frankfurt and Susan Wolf – the former a subjectivist about value and hence about meaning, the latter an objectivist – reiterates some of the conceptual problems of revelation. I analyze their positions below. A third position indicts both subjectivism and objectivism. The philosopher Rivka Weinberg argues that both approaches to meaning categorically fail to find it. For her, neither objective nor subjective construals of the meaning of life as a whole are possible. And that, she says, is "very, very sad." These philosophical moves end in stalemate, although partisans will likely find small but crucial advantages in one view over another. As with most philosophical debates, in the end, one must make a reasoned choice. Are partisans of revelation, who refuse to consent to the exclusive authority of the secular framework irrational? Arguably, neither set of views is more prone to irrationality than the other; neither is immune to ineliminable doubts.

IS REVELATION NECESSARY?

The Holy One, the Talmud states, has no home in this world other than the four cubits of the halakha (Jewish law).[11] God's place in the world, the text assumes, was once the Temple in Jerusalem. God dwelt in the Holy of Holies, an empty room that filled with the divine presence. But after the destruction of the temples at Babylonian and then Roman hands, God no longer has a place in the physical world; God's "place" is the ongoing Jewish acceptance and enactment of the divine Law.[12] God wanders with the Jews in their exile; divine sovereignty is nothing other than Jewish fidelity to God's way. The role of the Jews in God's ontic condition, as it were, is decisive. God's very being, at least as far as this world goes, rests in Jewish hearts and minds.[13]

Jewish hearts and minds, in the classical paradigm, are – or ought to be – shaped by God's Torah, the consummate revelation. The first medieval Jewish philosopher of note, Saadia Gaon (882–942), famously stated that the "nation of the children of Israel is a nation only by virtue of its laws."[14] Without Torah, Israel would have been just another *ethnos*, subject to the growth and decay of the natural world. With Torah, Israel partakes of the Torah's eternity. Yet as transcendent and transformative as God's Torah is, Saadia makes it largely isomorphic with rationality as such.[15] His confidence in the reasonableness of the Torah is so firm that it prompts him to ask why divine revelation was even *necessary*. "Inasmuch as all matters of religious belief, as imparted to us by our Master, can be attained by means of research and correct speculation, what was the reason that prompted [divine] wisdom to transmit them to us ...?"[16]

Saadia finds his answer in the sorry state of humanity. In principle, revelation should *not* have been necessary. Well-disciplined reasoning should have brought us to discern on our own the truths that comprise the Torah. But human creatures inevitably fall short of their potential. Right reasoning takes both time and skill. Generations of human beings would have been without guidance, as they struggled to think through the normative and metaphysical matters condensed in the Torah's laws and narratives. Furthermore,

> many a one of us might never complete the process because of some flaw in his reasoning ... he might not succeed in making use of its [i.e. of reason's] conclusions because he is overcome by worry or overwhelmed by the uncertainties that confuse and befuddle him. That is why God ... afforded us a quick relief from these burdens by sending us His messengers through whom He transmitted messages to us ....[17]

Additionally, the revelation of the Torah took place before the Israelite public, at Mt. Sinai. This vivid spectacle made it a matter not just of rational inference, but of visual and auditory *perception*. The Torah's "authenticity had been proven by the evidence of the senses."[18] Henceforth, reason can take its time studying the Torah and establishing its rational coherence; it need not reach or constitute the Torah on its own.

Saadia does not mean to diminish the uniqueness of revelation, nor does he want to claim that everything in the Torah is rationally perspicuous. He famously discerns two categories of commandments: the rationally transparent ones (*mitzvot sikhliyot*) and the ones "heard" at Sinai and obeyed on the authority of tradition (*mitzvot shimiyot*). In the first category are those commandments that reason reaches easily on its own, such as prohibitions of murder or theft, as well as those that follow from rational principles, such as showing gratitude to a benefactor.[19] Thus, the worship of the Creator, which shows our gratitude to God for the gift of life, is based on a general rational (moral) principle. Even so, revelation provides necessary *detail* – how should we worship? How do we achieve justice in civil and criminal matters, what constitutes proper judicial procedure, evidence, and so on? Revelation helps us operationalize rational moral principles.

More difficult to understand are the reasons for the many laws about the Sabbath and festivals, or the purity and impurity of objects and persons, or which animals can be eaten, and which are prohibited, etc. The particular reasons in such cases are known to God, but our reason can discern general patterns. Designating some days as sacred allows us to relax, to study the Torah, and meet with our peers for more elevated conversation than we would have had in the marketplace. Designating animals as kosher or unkosher diminishes the possibility that we might divinize and worship them – they are our food, not our gods.[20] The traditionally authoritative laws are not irrational – that is a basic principle for medieval Jewish philosophers – although thinkers such as Saadia and Maimonides differ over the manner and extent of their rational perspicuity and justification. While some Talmudic sources speak of the virtue of unquestioning submission, based on radical trust, even that stance does not preclude post hoc inquiry into the reasonableness of the commandments. Only an inquiry that means to undermine them is condemned.[21]

For medieval Jewish philosophers such as Saadia, there are no leaps of faith. The contents of revelation – the divine law – fundamentally make sense to a properly rational mind. It teaches "nothing contrary to reason."[22] He has a robust confidence in reason as a means to get to the truth about what is genuinely valuable and about how to live. Saadia insists on supplementing rational inquiry with traditional teaching as an equal source of truth, for his confidence in tradition is equally robust. Entirely missing is a sense that either of these sources is inherently, as opposed to adventitiously, flawed. There is no sense that reason leads to aporia, paradox, or absurdity. Nor is there a sense that tradition is historical, contingent, and conventional. The threat of nihilism is inconceivable. Saadia is utterly confident that reason leads to proof for metaphysical beliefs, such as the existence of God and the immortality of the soul. From there one can reason on to the objective foundation of the values, laws, and way of life endorsed by God's revealed Torah. This air of confidence can alienate a modern person from Saadia's thought world. (The most thoughtful moderns seem to prefer the tentative to the certain. Even modern theists who write on meaning tack and trim their sails long before they reach Saadia's destination.[23])

The philosopher Samuel Fleischacker offers a contemporary account of the need for revelation that echoes Saadia's but that takes the condition of modern thought (and modern doubt and anxiety) into account. Fleischacker argues that we are prompted to turn to revelation when we discover that fully secular or naturalistic accounts of why our lives are worth living (and loving) fail to provide satisfactory answers.[24] Naturalistic or secular accounts either privilege one activity – for example, finding a great love, producing works of art, taking up a moral or political cause on behalf of a just political order – or a combination of many such activities. Each candidate activity, or the entire basket of them, might have significance. But that significance runs out. It cannot outlast disappointments, doubts, self-subterfuge, and implicit limits. None of the goals seem to provide a compelling telos for life *as a whole*, an overall point to existence. An argument can be found for the insufficiency of any of them, as we saw, mutatis mutandis, in Kohelet. One needs some kind of *faith* that one's activities or projects are worthy, illusion-resistant ends. Given the need for faith in the enduring worth of one's commitments, no secular, naturalistic candidate for a final end is on more solid ground than a candidate based on religious faith.

What Fleischacker is after is a "telic view," the vision of an overall end (*telos*) or point to life. The idea of a telic vision informs his distinction between morality and ethics. He maintains that morality is essentially secular; it is a domain of broad agreement about acceptable and unacceptable ways human beings treat one another. Ethics, by contrast, indicates a vision of a life worth living. Ethics has to do with "telic goods," with those ends that make life as such valuable. Morality provides the consensual social support, in the form of a decently functioning society, for telic visions.[25] Given the claim that the telic visions on offer within a purely naturalistic framework disappoint or undermine themselves, Fleischacker introduces revelation as a religious framing of telic vision. We know enough about the Good to have some idea of what a life that rises to goodness is like, but the Good remains elusive. The Good is obscure to purely naturalistic vision. We cannot dispel its obscurity through empirical investigation, experiments in living, or even ethical and metaphysical theorizing. We need help; we need something from beyond. Faced with such a dilemma about the meaning of life, we "*choose to be guided* to our highest good when we commit ourselves to a revealed religion."[26] (The emphasis on personal choice in response to a crisis of meaning gives the work its distinctively modern cast.)

We have, in our various streams of culture or civilization, wise, challenging, often obscure and elusive traditional texts typically expressed in poetry. (Poetry combines "obscurity with clarity, puzzling us even as it enlightens us."[27]) The texts – and it's important that revelation comes in the form of a text so as to retain its independence over and against our interpretive efforts – need to cohere sufficiently with our morality so as not to repel us.[28] But they need to go beyond it, so as to integrate plausible goods into a telic vision which we could *not* have reached on our own. Indeed, one of the things that a revelation should do is tell us why the ultimate good we seek eludes our best efforts. Faced with such a text and the way of life it supports, we may, within reason, trust it. It is reasonable to rely on revelation as we pursue the ultimate good that it reveals and – to some extent – continues to conceal.

Faith, in the sense of trust in revelation is not blind or discontinuous with our ways of knowing. Trusting reliance is an epistemologically crucial element of all knowing. Nonetheless, Fleischacker does not confuse faith/trust in revelation with *proof* of its divinely revealed status, let alone as proof of the existence of God. (Far from such medieval thinkers as Saadia, he takes divine existence as a warranted "working hypothesis," which can neither be proven nor disproven, but which is woven into our judgments about what makes our lives valuable and so into judgments about what to take as ultimately real.[29]) Further weakening any implication of blind trust, Fleischacker stresses that reliance on revelation entails interpretive interaction with it. We "receive" revelation as a path "by which we can transform the aspects of ourselves that keep us from grasping our highest good," but as we walk the path, as individuals and communities, we must constantly readjust our understanding of the text in light of our deepening ethical awareness.[30]

The norms given in revelation both govern us and depend on human interpretation and practical enactment. Human beings both submit to revelation and interpret its meanings, which change as persons and communities travel through time and history. "We might say: The revelation itself needs continually to be revealed. Or, less paradoxically: The revelatory text, the source of revelation, becomes full revelation only in the endless process of reception."[31] Crisply put: "Revelation is not given until it is received, and its giver, if all-wise, must have known that. It follows that the multifarious human attempts to make sense of sacred texts must themselves be *part* of revelation, not a mere accompaniment to it, let alone a betrayal of it."[32]

This raises the question: To what extent has the presumed divine Giver become indistinguishable from the human receiver? Has such a dialectical view of objectivity, normativity, and authority undermined them?

It is tempting to take Fleischacker's account as an *entirely* modern (or postmodern?) one. It discerns the limits of naturalism without rejecting science. It shows openness to religious wisdom in a gesture of postpositivist epistemological humility. It valorizes human choice and supports creative, hermeneutic interaction with sacred texts. It constitutes authority in a rather liberal democratic way as hinging on human consent. But there are impulses older than modernism, democratic values, and so on at work in this account. In particular, the idea that revelation in its fullness entails human reception and that human beings have been given great latitude to interpret revelation in line with antecedent moral awareness is ancient. Judaism has so emphasized the human construal of the meaning of the revealed Torah that it is hard to draw a line between divine authority and human authority. Revelation, on which we are supposed to rely, relies on us for its cogency, for its very status *as* revelation. This is appealing but, as I have suggested, also implies a trace of the absurd.

WHAT HAPPENED AT MT. SINAI?

The dialectical dynamic of giving if and only if receiving has been intensively theorized by the biblical scholar-theologian, Benjamin Sommer. Sommer has a highly participatory and minimalist account of revelation. By "participatory," he means that human beings participate in the "event" of revelation to the extent that they are essential contributors to its content. By "minimalist," he means that what the Israelites heard at Sinai might have been quite little. It might have been much less than what the canonical text presents, that is, the robust set of laws, beginning with the Decalogue, in Exodus chapters 20–24. (It is important to note that Sommer affirms the historicity of the Sinai event; something revelatory happened there.) A close reading reveals that the text preserves conflicting traditions about what the Israelites heard, when they heard it, and from whom they heard it.[33] The canonical text preserves a host of incoherencies and ambiguities. Biblical critics, such as Sommer, resort to putative source documents to show how these originated.

Sommer makes his case by teasing apart, in classic critical fashion, the presumed independent strands out of which the Torah was developed. The main sources for the account of revelation in Exodus are "E" (for "Elohist," a literary source that favors the use of the divine name, Elohim) and P, the priestly source. (An entirely different account of revelation is given in the *Book of Deuteronomy* (D), which differs from the Exodus account and may be considered an inner-biblical midrash on Exodus.) These sources disagree with one another as to what God communicated (His nonverbal presence? laws articulated in a humanly intelligible language?) and to whom the ambiguous content was communicated (the whole people? Moses alone? Moses, Aaron, and the elders?).

Unlike Fleischacker, who disdains historical, source-critical reconstruction, Sommer celebrates it, not just as an act of intellectual probity but as a theologically fertile commitment.[34] Sommer takes the different sources, rich in mutual contradictions and perspectives, as meaningful: They are fragmentary efforts to capture an event that was singular, incommensurable, overwhelming, and not fully communicable. Inconsistency is not editorial sloppiness; it is deliberate and iconic. The experience of revelation cannot be captured by consistent narration. Its gaps express our gaps in comprehension of a singularity. Given the Torah's analytically distinguishable sources, the revelation narrative of Exodus:

> ... does not want the audience to know whether the lawgiving was direct, mediated, or a mix of the two. The book does, however, encourage the audience to wonder about this issue, to think through its various possibilities, to see their strengths and weaknesses, and perhaps to think about their implications. *Exodus endorses a question, but not an answer; a debate, not a resolution.*[35]

Revelation is so extraordinary that the scriptural accounts of it do not simply narrate an event or record a disclosed, normative content but draw the reader into the mystery of its occurrence. Our perplexity as to what took place, what was given by God, and what was contributed by human beings in response to God is kept alive by the text.

Consider one key ambiguity that Sommer exploits. The word *qol* – God's primary means of communication – has a double meaning: "thunder" or "voice." The repeated use of *qol*, Sommer writes,

> belongs entirely to E: all seven occurrences of this guiding word belong to E, as do the verses that provide for its various meanings. The ambiguities present in E include the paradoxical, or at least arresting, phrasing in 20:18, which suggests visual perception of a sound. Thus, already in E we find a biblical author drawing our attention to the question of Mosaic mediation and the question of whether the legal teachings associated with Moses are heavenly or earthly in origin.[36]

How so? If God's "speech" is heard as thunder, then the unpacking of the meaning of that thunder in the form of normative guidance – the Decalogue plus the law code of Exodus 21–23 – requires a great deal of human participation. Thunder has no semantic content. Moses becomes the author of the law, "translating" divine thunder into humanly intelligible language.[37] But if *qol* means "speech," then the notion of God uttering words that Moses transcribes (rather than supplies) becomes more plausible. Even then, what it means for God to speak, as if God had vocal cords, is difficult. (Maimonides, e.g., rejects such a view; what God communicates to Moses is the deep cognitive structure of reality. Moses develops that intellectual apprehension into a metaphysical/normative project for the perfection of human theoretical and moral virtue, legislating a constitution for an ideal society.[38] Maimonides is, on Sommer's reading, a minimalist with respect to revelation.) E cuts both ways. It could support a "stenographic" account, where Moses hears God's voice and takes dictation or it could support Sommer's preferred participatory view, where Moses authors the law in response to God's thunderous expression.

Although Sommer cannot settle, within E, the question of what was heard and by whom, he discerns a tradition of minimalism beginning in E and running through the Bible, rabbinic midrash, medieval commentary and philosophy, and modern Jewish theology, with Franz Rosenzweig and Abraham Joshua Heschel being the central modern theologians. These two theologians develop revelational minimalism beyond what is implicit in the Bible. They do so, however, in genuine continuity with what E already submitted for our consideration. Rosenzweig wrote that "the primary content of revelation is revelation itself. 'He came down' – this already concludes the revelation; 'He spoke' is the beginning of interpretation."[39] Similarly Heschel writes "as a report about revelation the Bible itself is a midrash."[40] Both Rosenzweig and Heschel cite an early Hasidic master Menachem Mendel of Rymanov (d. 1815), who is quoted by his disciple as claiming that the Israelites heard only the vocalized *aleph* of the word *anokhi* (I), roughly the sound "ah," directly from God. All the rest is interpretation. (*Anokhi* is the first word of the Decalogue: "I am the LORD your God, who brought you out of the Land of Egypt" Exodus 20:2.)[41] This is verbal content at its most minimal. Minimalism implies that the full normativity of revelation, as we see it spin out in Exodus 20–23, is a matter of participatory human response rather than a stenographic record of divine dictation. Revelation just *is* the human drawing out of possibilities implicit in an obscure, nonlinguistic, or threshold linguistic disclosure of divine presence.

That human beings are essential contributors to or participants in revelation does not imply that revelation is pervasively rational. Humans surely are not. It does imply, for Sommer, that revelation is pervasively normative and authoritative, however. He is unequivocal that any "authentic" Jewish understanding of revelation has to include the concept of law – the human participation in the revelatory event issues in legislation. (Hence, Sommer marginalizes an antinomian thinker like Buber. For Buber, revelation is God's presence; law is a failed attempt to hold on to that presence after it has departed.) Normativity in an ethical sense, without a legal instantiation seems insufficient for Sommer. Can the degree and kind of authority that law, especially *divine* law, requires be supported by Sommer's minimal and participatory theory? Here is where the ground underneath his theology becomes marshy, as Eagleton might put it.

The legal materials of the Bible, accumulated over the centuries, were telescoped "into one great revelation, beginning at Sinai and continuing through the career of our greatest teacher-leader, Moses."[42] The cumulative ascription of law to Moses constitutes a "Mosaic discourse," a tradition of legitimate and pious pseudepigraphy that functions to anchor communal religious/legal practice in a normative antiquity.[43] The sages of the Talmud and midrash speak of laws for which no biblical source exists as "given to Moses at Sinai." In one famous midrash, Moses comes to earth from heaven, sits in Rabbi Akiba's yeshiva, but is confused and discomfited by Rabbi Akiba's teaching. When Akiba says that the law that he is expounding and its reasoning were revealed to Moses on Sinai, Moses was relieved (B. Menaḥot 29b). The irony is that Moses was not previously aware that such a law *was* revealed to him.

Given a long, ongoing process of legal invention, ascribed to "Moses" but not actually written by Moses, why should the law have real authority?[44] If Sommer were only an academic biblical scholar and not a religiously observant theologian, this question would not arise. If he were a secular democratic political theorist, he might talk about the sovereignty of the people in a constitutional republic. One would think that such a secular stance would be inappropriate here, but the move he makes is similar. The historical tradition of the "constitution," created by human framers, translated into a Jewish "covenantal" idiom, is the main support for the authority of revelation on Sommer's account. And it has always been so, he argues. Sommer claims that rabbinic Judaism endorses "ex post facto holiness." God agrees to endorse, according to several rabbinic sources, laws enacted by Israel such as reading the Scroll of Esther on the holiday of Purim, as well as its other observances. Moses instituted several laws "on his own" and God agreed to uphold his innovations.[45] (But such interpretive moves are within an established legal system. Is it legitimate to extend this trope to ground the system *as a whole*?) Summarizing his view, Sommer asserts:

> Israel responds to God's command at Sinai by authoring specific laws, which, having endured for generations, can be understood to have been accepted and even legislated by God. We may further understand that God did not accept, or did not continue to accept, laws that did not endure .... *It is entirely possible in traditional Judaism to view a legal system as divinely decreed even though it is not divinely written.*[46]

The participatory theory of revelation anchors a "robust notion of obligation." "*Israel's observance of the law,*" Sommer concludes, "*helps God to grant the law the status of divine bidding, just as Israel's intensive, committed, ongoing study of scripture helps God to speak through it.*"[47]

By way of criticism, Sommer's view brings to mind the physicist Richard Feynman's quip about gravity. At the time of Kepler, he writes, some people thought that there were angels behind the planets pushing them in their orbits around the sun. But by the time of Newton, it was clear that the angels were pushing the planets inward, toward the sun.[48] The humor, of course, comes from the learned reassignment of the angels' roles given that the underlying Newtonian theory of gravitation eliminates the need for angels altogether. Has Sommer's minimizing of divine agency effectively eliminated the role of the divine? Has the divine authority of the law been practically replaced by a purely human, self-reflexive authority, muted perhaps by a pious rhetoric? If one were a Straussian, one could speak about a "noble lie," but that would be inappropriate here. Sommer is committed both to genuine, traditional Jewish observance and to a radical theology that tries to vindicate observance in modernity. He sees this as a meaningful construal (and defense) of revelation, not as an abandonment of it.

There is no question that tradition can function as a kind of authority.[49] Normative tradition can be a ground for normative explanation. The claim that "this is the way we have always done things" can be a legitimate normative reason for why one did this thing in this way. But it can't be the only or the ultimate reason that one produces. When traditions come under pressure – for conceptual and ethical reasons – they need a stronger defense than the stalwart reiteration of their traditionality. That defense may well be found through further reflection on the tradition's own resources. Nonetheless, the tradition needs something that makes it over the fact/value divide and argues in favor of the maintenance of the controversial *traditum* in terms of higher order values. Sommer's repeated invocation of revelation as a humanly participatory process, of a retroactive grant of holiness to human endeavors, of divine approval for human innovation (which seems to be no more than a redescription of the longevity of Jewish practices) lacks *normative* force. Although these moves *describe* why someone might take a tradition to be normative, they fail normatively to *justify* its ways. He appeals to divine will and agency or to intuitions of them, invoking Rosenzweig's felt distinction between commandment (*Gebot*) and law (*Gesetz*) and Heschel's mystical distinction between a heavenly Torah and an earthly one, but these provide at best a numinous atmosphere, not an argument for authority.

To be fair, even a maximalist still needs an argument for why a "stenographic" revelation *ought* to be obeyed. That would lead us into familiar terrain in the philosophy of religion and in ethics. One could also justify the full authority of a legal system on secular grounds, but minimalism is *not* secularism. It is a theological position that wants the warrant of divine authority with vanishingly little, if any, assertion of that authority by the divine. This is flatly problematic and quite possibly absurd. But is this absurdity a result of Sommer's own modernist (or postmodernist) excursions or has he hit upon a problematic dialectic that is genuinely buried in the tradition, surfacing fully only now? Generations of Jews thought that revelation provided solid, objectively normative guidance, in the form of indisputably divine law. Now it seems that this normativity, and the way of life that finds its source and meaning in it, is nothing more than a shared, shifting, intergenerational subjectivity.

Nonetheless, the search for objective normativity continues. An illuminating case is the debate between the Jewish natural law theorist, David Novak, and the historian of rabbinic Judaism, Christine Hayes. Natural law, an inheritance of Hellenism, asserts the existence of independent, objective grounds for the rightness of action, discoverable by right reason. Rabbinic thought on Hayes's telling rejects any such objective normativity. It relies on human trust in a radically personal God, who reveals his will in history. These two construals of ancient Judaism map roughly onto the objective/subjective distinction for normativity and its meaningfulness. They represent another iteration of the theorizing of revelation and the search for stable meaning.

RABBINIC DIVINE LAW VERSUS NATURAL LAW

Sommer's provocative treatment of revelation emphasizes the human role in its origination and promulgation. The stress is less on its reasonableness than on its authority. Given the role he ascribes to human participation in constituting that authority, however, revelation is presumably saturated with the rationality of its creators. "Moses" had his reasons for devising the laws that "he" did. The question of the rationality of law, of whether it emanates from the reason or the will of its presumed divine Creator, was an urgent one in post-biblical Judaism. Within the orbit of the Hellenistic and Roman worlds, the discussion about rationality, will, and law rested on a dichotomy of types of law, as briefly mentioned earlier in this chapter. Natural law – unchanging, universal, and true – reflected, for Greeks and Romans, the ideal type of law. Natural law was divine;

it expressed the Good or the Logos. It was unwritten, eternal, and unchanging. Against the ideality of natural law was conventional law. The latter was a product of the will of its human, political framers. It varied from city to city and approximated well or poorly the ideal principles of natural law. These two types of law tracked the fundamental Greek philosophical distinction between nature and custom, *physis* and *nomos*, the former having the higher dignity.[50] In the Greco-Roman world, the virtuous, ideal way of life was a life according to nature. Fulfilling our essential, permanent nature, especially as rational animals, made us most godlike.

Against this, rabbinic Judaism conceived of Jewish law as emanating from the *will* of a personal God.[51] God's element, so to speak, was history, not nature. God entered history at Sinai and gave Israel a written law. It was not universal, unchanging, or in correspondence with the deepest truths of nature; it was particular, adapted to the circumstances of a single nation, and not bound by correspondence with objective truths. It had all of the characteristics, except for its putative divine authorship, of Greco-Roman *conventional* law and none of the traits of what Greeks and Romans took to be divine law. Hence, the rabbinic sages had either to endure the mockery of educated pagans or defend the Torah and its claim to being the highest law, the most perfect divine revelation. To do so, they had to argue against the natural law paradigm, with its consistent view of rationality, as shared by gods and humans. The particular, apparently not quite rational features of Jewish law were not mere quirks of convention, but solemn duties imposed by the mysterious will of the Ruler of the universe.

This characterization of the rabbinic project of understanding the nature and content of divine revelation stems from the work of Christine Hayes. Hayes focuses on the rabbinic rejection of the pagan (and eventually Christian) natural law framework. Although that framework reenters rabbinic Judaism in medieval philosophy, early rabbinic thought, according to Hayes, self-consciously repudiates it. By contrast, David Novak has long argued that divinely revealed Jewish law presupposes natural law; there are rationally available, general, normative principles on which revelation builds.[52] The rabbis, for Novak, accept and endorse this view. Thus, Novak sees a profound affinity between classical natural law theory and the rabbinic understanding of divine revelation. He sees Judaism as having its own internal formulation of natural law – the seven commandments of the Children of Noah. Novak argues both for an historical interpretation of the rabbinic project as responsive to natural law considerations *and* for the normative use of natural law as an element of constructive Jewish theology. (Novak is primarily a theologian; Hayes is entirely an historian of religion. Her aim is to reconstruct ancient views. Although the disagreement between Hayes and Novak is primarily over historical interpretation, the scholarly matters at issue have consequences for normative, constructive theology.[53]) Hayes thinks that Novak is wrong about how the rabbis understood the grounds of Jewish law. If she is correct, Novak's larger project of a Judaism in conformity with what the natural law tradition calls *recta ratio*, right reason, could falter.[54] Let us briefly explore the debate between them for what it says about how to understand the nature of revelation, its authority and rationality, and whether, indeed, it is necessary for the normative guidance of human beings.

To get a sense of what the early rabbis rejected, consider Philo of Alexandria (died, c. 50 CE), who *did* assimilate Jewish law to the pattern of natural law. The Patriarchs, such as Abraham, observed the law before Sinai; this indicates that the Torah is tantamount to the law of nature. Indeed, for Philo, the pure natural law that Abraham intuited with his reason is superior to a law that is "heard": "For anyone who contemplates the order in nature and the constitution enjoyed by the world-city whose excellence no words can describe, needs no speaker to teach him to practice a law-abiding and peaceful life…"[55] Philo is then faced with the problem of maintaining the specific observances of Jewish law. If its core is natural law and if natural law is available through reason, why is a particular, written law still valid? Philo's solution is to analogize the rational core of the law to the soul within the body. The soul is more important than the body and is its animating principle, but it cannot do without the body. The dependence of the spiritual on the material mirrors the dependence of the rational essence of the commandments with their practical enactment. The wise man knows that the commandment of circumcision, for example, has a clear rational purpose: It is meant to chasten the passions. But the wise man should still endorse the actual *act* of circumcision on the body, not just the rational end it intends.

Philo's synthesis of Platonism and Judaism was not the way of the rabbis. Hayes' portrayal of divine law, as understood by the rabbis, shows how that law is willing to flout such criteria of classical natural law as truth, rationality, and unchangingness. That is, the rabbinic understanding of revealed, divine law is often untroubled by its correspondence – more precisely, its lack of correspondence – with "stable authentic truth."[56] Truth has formal, judicial, and ontological dimensions. "Formal truth" can be taken to mean that there is a single right answer (legal monism) to legal questions. Hayes shows that rabbinic law glories in pluralism, "the existence of multiple, equally authentic answers."[57] "These words" and "those words" – even when the words contradict one another – can be the "words of the living God" (B. Eruvin 13b). Less dramatically, law often overrides or flouts the conclusion to which formal logic would lead. Often norms of legal reasoning, such as a fortiori deduction, are overridden by the use of scriptural citations. The connection between formally correct legal conclusions and actual decisions needn't be strict.

"Judicial truth" picks out the tension between purely legal judgments and competing considerations. Even when the truth of a case is known, it can be overridden by concerns for other values, such as peace.[58] God must ignore the truths about his creatures in order to judge them compassionately. God and human beings cooperate in determining the law. Indeed, God not only consents to "human assistance in defeating the strict justice of his own decrees … he *needs* it." God depends "on human intervention to defeat him in the execution of his own decrees."[59] Human partners, astonishingly, free God from the implications of His own "law of justice and true judgment."[60]

"Ontological truth" gets at the question of whether the rabbis are concerned about law mapping "mind-independent" reality. Are they "realists" or "nominalists"? Does law draw its power from its own self-generated universe of discourse, or does it track facts about the world? Hayes claims that rabbinic texts "create a rhetoric of epistemological uncertainty about the law that is not resolved by appeals to an objective standard of some kind."[61] For example, the laws of the calendar presumably have to account for an objective fact situation regarding the phases of the moon and the seasons. "Nevertheless, these facts can be overruled in the determination of the law. In their references to the calendar, several rabbinic texts employ an explicitly nominalist rhetoric – asserting the court's right to subordinate astronomical fact to other considerations."[62]

In an imaginative aggadah, God defers to the lower court on the decision of when to declare the new month. "When all the ministering angels assemble before God and ask, 'Lord of the universe when is the new year?' he answers them: 'You're asking me? You and I should ask the lower court'."[63]

In other legal systems, legal fictions are tolerated. If overindulged, however, they undermine the credibility of law. In rabbinic law, Hayes maintains, legal fictions do not undermine confidence in the law because the law's authority is *not* predicated on the expectation that it aligns with truth. The divorce of divine law from truth at the hands of the rabbis is only "scandalous" on the presupposition of the natural law teaching that underlies much of the Western tradition of law.[64] It is not scandalous, according to Hayes, on the rabbis' own "nominalist" normativity.[65]

Hayes makes similar claims with regard to the criteria of rationality and unchangingness. Let us look briefly at two bits of evidence. With regard to the rationality of divine law, the Torah (Numbers, chapter 19:2) specifies a paradoxical statute: One who has been in contact with a human corpse requires ritual purification. An elaborate concoction, made from a completely red, unblemished calf, which has been killed, burned, and reduced to ash, is applied to the impure person. The person becomes purified, but all of those who prepared the substance become impure. How can something which purifies also contaminate at the same time? The Torah refers to the law as a *ḥoq*, a statute that is not at all transparent to reason. While medieval rationalists, such as Saadia Gaon and Maimonides greatly reduced, as we have seen, the "irrationality" of such statutes, at least some among the early rabbis celebrate it. They see the paradoxical implication of the law as evidence for its divine origin. A classical collection of midrash, *Pesiqta de-Rav Kahana*, for example, begins with the assertion:

> Who can bring forth a clean thing out of an unclean thing? Is it not the One?
> Like Abraham out of Terah, Hezekiah out of Ahaz, Mordecai out of Shimei, Israel out of the nations, the world-to-come out of this world?
> Who did it? Who commanded it? Who decreed it?
> Is it not the One? Is it not the Unique One of the World?[66]

Hayes notes, "Only the unique god of the world can decree the irrational."[67]

With regard to unchangingness, rabbinic law can be highly flexible. Unlike natural law, it needn't embody permanent moral norms. Most notoriously, the rabbis sometimes criticize divine law – even its divine Author – for perceived failures of justice and righteousness. In various texts, "God is compared to a king whose abusive or unethical behavior is challenged by a member of his inner circle."[68] In Numbers Rabbah (19:33), Moses challenges God's decree to visit "the guilt of the parents upon the children (Exodus 34:7)." Moses argues with God, bringing biblical evidence of righteous children being born to evil parents. It is not appropriate, he argues, for children to be punished for the sins of their parents. "The Holy One, blessed be he, said to him [Moses], 'You have taught me something. By your life, I will nullify my decree and establish your word.'" God thus learns from Moses, "annuls his decree, and establishes a new rule of individual punishment."[69] Neither God nor the revealed, divine law is understood to be perfect, unchanging, or static. In a way that would be utterly objectionable to natural law-oriented Greeks and Romans, "The divine law's perfection is not diminished but constituted by the fact that it is particular, flexible, responsive, and on occasion multiform rather than universal, static, and uniform."[70]

An important test case – and the bone of contention between Hayes and Novak – is Noahide law (or as rabbinic texts themselves say "the seven commandments of the sons of Noah"). Biblically, God commands Adam and Eve not to eat of the trees of the knowledge of good and evil, and of life. Normativity enters the human sphere with an explicit divine command. But the rabbis see a fuller set of commands latent in the text. They exegete Gen 2:15 to derive seven commandments.[71] The standard list includes six negative ones – idolatry, blasphemy, illicit sexual relations, bloodshed, robbery, eating flesh from a living animal – and one positive one, that is, setting up courts of justice. These laws may have been intended as a moral–legal minimum for humanity as such – Novak's view. Or they may have been intended to portray the stark differences between Israel and the nations – Hayes's view. On the latter, the rabbis use Noahide law to problematize the premise of a moral commonality between Jews and non-Jews. On Novak's view, the rabbis theorize Noahide law to *undergird* that premise.

What is the axiological status of the Noahide laws within rabbinic literature? There are discrepant views within the literature itself. On one view, the full revelation of law, for Israel, at Mt. Sinai is the final installment of a tradition of normative guidance going back to the garden. Sinai is continuous with Eden, so to speak. On another view, Sinai breaks with Noahide law and supplants it. The rabbis overturn Noahide law for Jews; after Sinai, it is no longer valid. (Some texts even show God *retracting Noahide law for non-Jews*, as they were unable to keep even that minimum.[72]) For Hayes, such views show that the rabbis could not have considered Noahide law to be tantamount to classical natural law. Rather than serving as a common moral floor for all humanity, it inscribes differences between Jews and non-Jews (so it is not universal). It can be suspended (so it is not eternal). And it is the product of divine command (so it is not embedded in nature in a way that unassisted reason can discern; it is not, that is, dependent upon some truths about nature or human nature).

On Hayes's reading, the main Talmudic discussion of Noahide law (B. Sanhedrin 57b) self-consciously argues against the possibility of a natural law reading of the prohibition of murder, surely the best candidate for a principle of natural law. It is only because of a scriptural verse (Genesis 9:6) that we know murder is prohibited. "Once the prohibition of murder has been "denaturalized," R. Papa restores its universality but *on the basis of a second verse, not on the basis of natural law reasoning*! In this remarkable passage, the universality of the prohibition against murder is shown to depend on revelation alone."[73]

If Hayes is correct, then the rabbis largely believed that humanity gets it morality from either a continuum or a series of disjunctive episodes of divine revelation. Morality and the laws that encode it are a disclosure, not of reason but of divine will. Divine will operates along the lines of what the Greco-Roman world would see as political governance, the imposition, by a ruler, of conventional law on the city. Any attempt, such as Novak's to ascribe features of natural law – true, rational, unchanging, eternal standards of normativity – on Torah law is unhistorical, on Hayes's analysis.[74]

Novak's response is essentially to contest a key premise of Hayes. Hayes insists that for the rabbis to hold natural law views, "natural law" has to mean what it meant in the ancient Greco-Roman world, which was roughly the moral–legal–metaphysical theory of Stoicism. Novak counterargues that ancient philosophical natural law is the wrong construct to apply. There is an *inherent* biblical and then Judaic constitution of natural law. Novak seeks an internal expression of natural law theorizing.[75] The Bible and the rabbis theorized a functional equivalent of classical natural law because human beings, reflecting with "right reason" on norms, *have to do so*; they are drawn by their reason to views of this kind. While far from isomorphic, biblical–rabbinic natural law is in some ways analogous to Greco-Roman natural law (and, therefore, in other ways disanalogous) because it does within the Jewish monotheistic context something like what classical natural law does in the pagan (and eventually Christian) context.[76]

For Novak, Greco-Roman philosophical natural law is inadmissible to the rabbis because it assumes a conception of nature, which they cannot share. (Thus far, he agrees with Hayes.) Nature is a category, which, on the (Stoic) philosophical account, comprises all beings, including gods and humans. Even if the polytheism could be amended into monotheism, God cannot be included in nature; no biblical or rabbinic monotheist sees God as "natural," as if God were the "apex of cosmic nature" or nature's "most important being."[77] Novak seconds Leo Strauss in saying that the Bible has no such conception of nature – nor could it and be a document of monotheism. Nonetheless, the Bible and rabbinic Judaism conceive of an order to the world, which the Greek concept of nature also picks out, under the concept of justice (*mishpat*). *Mishpat* functions like *natura* but indicates "the intelligible order that the Creator-God has placed *within* the created cosmos" rather than the "substance *within* which … all intelligent beings, whether divine or human, are contained."[78]

Mishpat, although divinely willed and created, is discovered by human beings, using right reason, in the course of their conduct. It is the discovery that "there exists a set of norms universally binding on all humans throughout all historical time and all political space, and that these norms can be formulated through discursive human reasoning."[79] It functions as a necessary (but not sufficient) condition for human beings to have just interhuman relations, indeed, for human beings and God also to have just relations (covenants). It expresses God's rational design of the world, a kind of ethical *a priori* that human beings cannot do without and remain human. They discover that their conduct is only morally intelligible (as right, just, etc.) because of it. *Mishpat* is not the sum total of justice; it is its presupposition. As in classical natural law, it is a limit, a minimum on which real communities, both Jewish and non-Jewish need to build. It is not a telos or goal, much less concrete practical content.[80] Novak claims that both classical natural law and biblical–Judaic *mishpat* are properly understood to have God as their ultimate warrant. (That seems correct in a sense, but what Plato, Aristotle, and the Stoics meant by "God" – which is often interchangeable for them with "gods" – is far from biblical monotheism.[81]) Hayes, I think, would see Novak's reading as moral theorizing at some remove from the rabbinic texts it takes as examples.

Although Novak certainly does not abandon or abuse the texts, he has shifted the ground from an historical–exegetical discussion over the presence, or not, of a certain set of normative ideas in two ancient cultures to a theoretical discussion of what normativity requires. His claims are frankly metaphysical and metaethical. From his point of view, the rabbis cannot help but constitute something analogous to classical natural law because that is what the logic of justice requires – in any society. Even though he tries to answer Hayes's criticisms point by point, there is a "ships passing in the night" quality to the response, most likely because of their fundamental, methodologically discrepant starting points.

To bring the discussion back to our point of departure, if Hayes is correct, revelation, as understood by the rabbis, was *absolutely necessary* to ground normativity as such insofar as they rejected the kind of natural law grounding operative in Stoic philosophy (with Platonic and Aristotelian anticipations).[82] If there is no reasoned access to normativity, then revelation is absolutely necessary. On Hayes's understanding of Judaism, revelation is essential; reason, at best, is scriptural, not philosophical. If Novak is correct, then reason can discover normativity, *mishpat*, in the natural, that is, *created* order, through its own attention to human conduct. Novak's is a theological natural law theory.[83] God has installed *mishpat* into the Creation; nature is not simply natural; it is already normative, expressing the will of its Creator. Nature is already revelatory. Special revelation – Sinai – is not necessary for normativity per se. That already exists, albeit in a form so minimal that it is not even sufficient for gentile societies. (Hence, the requirement under Noahide law to establish courts of justice, which Novak takes to imply institutions to build on minimal natural law principles to create a fully livable social world.) The Sinaitic revelation *was* necessary, however, in order to build a world for Jews (and others, such as Christians, who incorporate the "Old Testament" into their revelation) not only to live justly but to live meaningfully, to live in communion with God. Jews and gentiles have parallel enterprises of normative social construction based on nature and revelation, general and special, through the use of right reason.

Although Novak requires revelation no less than Hayes's rabbis, he gives much more scope to a natural law grounding and coloration of normativity. We discern it as an a priori *lex ratio*, rather than as a *lex voluntas*, that is, as a law of reason rather than a law based on will. We encounter it as a law expressive of divine reason rather than of sheer divine fiat. Novakian divine law has objectivity. What is good for human beings and essential to their well-being is inscribed in the world that God has created. There are objective goods and objective values that are revealed by rational reflection on nature and on human nature. (These need to be fully articulated by further revelation, in the case of Sinai, or by further insight and trial-and-error praxis in societies untouched by Sinai, but basic objectivity is assumed.) By extension, we might say that there can be objectively valid meanings, construed by *recta ratio*, derived from reflection on objective goods and values.

These matters remain, of course, unsettled. The debate between Hayes and Novak is about how to read the ancient Jewish sages with regard to the grounds of normativity. It has, therefore, a limited historical scope. But beyond this, the question of how we should understand revelation is also unsettled. How could it not be? The issues get to the heart of what one considers to be Judaism. While not every position is open to debate, there are few limits on what is debatable.[84] Assuming that we find revelation to be a cogent notion in the first place, we continue to ask: Is revelation continuous with expressions of moral reason or is it exceptional? Is revelation principally concerned with morality or is it about other matters, such as holiness, which is not reducible to ethics? Is revelation primarily a matter of divine command or of something akin to natural law; put differently, does God only command a good that is broadly intelligible to us, or must we struggle to develop new standards of intelligibility to accommodate God's norms? Those who emphasize a broad scope for ethics cannot help but touch on the themes of natural law as opposed to sheer divine voluntarism and its theory of divine commands.[85]

There is a certain truth to both sides. The God of Hayes's rabbis is a complicated literary character. He doesn't only command; he cajoles, entreats, and pleads. He is self-critical, open to the challenges of those he loves. He laughs. The Jews are in a dialogue with him. He asks for their trust; that is the basis of his authority. He asks for their love. Their willingness to give it to him – their caring about him – is the basis of his sovereignty, a term somewhat ill at ease with the discourse of love. The God of Novak's natural law is a philosopher's god, a cosmic architect who inscribes value into his handiwork. He reveals his will in nature – a cryptic kind of revelation – and in overt acts such as lawgiving on Mt. Sinai. Even though the Jews can also enter into dialogue with him, he lacks the intimacy of the character in rabbinic midrash and Aggadah. That level of description is permitted by the philosophical theologian only as a kind of poetry, vivid but somehow inessential. It is otherwise with the rabbis themselves. The Jewish tradition enshrines both approaches.

At issue is the question of what (or who) we should trust as our guide to discerning the values by which we should live and the meaning that we should make of them. Should we repose our trust in the sacred narratives of the past and find the stories of divine encounter and protection a sufficient foundation for our lives today? Or should we seek some basis in "true, eternal, and unchanging" normativity discerned by right reason and located at the basis of the sacred stories (as the philosophically inclined might think)? Is right reason necessary or superfluous, a mark of our dignity as rational creatures or a mark of our arrogance toward the Infinite? The god of Hayes's rabbis offers us a life, based on trust in a God whom we have chosen to trust. There are no guarantees other than our own faith that we, and our ancestors, have chosen well. The philosophical theologian's way, by contrast, seeks a rational basis, a rather more objective guarantee. These look quite different, but there may not be much difference between them. Both are fueled by hope, an emotion (or, arguably, a virtue) in uneasy alliance with reason.

The quest for rational reliability, represented by the natural law tradition, and the trust reposed in a lover by the one who loves are both fundamental to human life. Although the claims made on their behalf are not per se absurd, a trace of the absurd is found when the claims are pressed too far. Jews have, for the most part, synthesized reasoned faith with loving trust. Jews have disdained to "believe because it is absurd."[86] They have sought justification for their convictions and commitments by appealing to ancestral memory, history, texts, relationships, as well as reasoned argument. But none of these justifications can bear the full weight that the search for well-supported meaning puts on them. They tend to run in circles, assuming what they set out to secure.

Among medieval thinkers, Yehuda Halevi, to give one example, rejected a purely rationalistic approach. He did not want to base his defense of Judaism on universalistic arguments for divine existence, such as the cosmological proof. He wanted to start with memory and "history," with a particularistic story of love and trust. Halevi argues the superiority of Judaism, the "despised religion," over its Christian and Muslim competitors by pointing to the massively public nature of its divine revelation. The whole nation stood at the foot of Sinai, in contrast to the relatively private experiences of Christianity's and Islam's founders. But this approach is only credible if one is antecedently convinced that such a revelation occurred and has an objective meaning that all can, at least initially, accept. In Halevi's world, the debunkers of Judaism – Christian and Muslim – accepted the historicity and significance of Sinaitic revelation. But that is hardly the case for modern debunkers – or even for earnest modern seekers. It is the cogency, let alone the reality, of revelation per se which is in question. A Halevian argument today would be question-begging. It would be difficult, perhaps absurd, to try to vindicate it.

On what, if anything, can late modern defenses of Jewish conviction and commitments be based? One influential thinker, Yeshayahu Leibovitz, opts for decisionism: One must simply make a free, ungrounded choice. There are no experiences, memories, evidence, or arguments on behalf of one choice over another. Jewish commitment is a leap. One just decides to accept a norm – in Leibovitz's case, that one must worship God – and then everything follows.[87] Such decisionism, however, comes at a high cost. Abandoning reason *on principle* is performatively contradictory. It is a triumph of the absurd.[88]

OBJECTIVE VERSUS SUBJECTIVE VERSUS NO MEANING IN LIFE

In the preceding section, we analyzed the religious view that if we want to have a life worth living, we need a revelation that instructs us in how to live beyond what ordinary human beings could discern or imagine. Only a way of life that, by hypothesis, has been given in the form of divine guidance can be ultimately meaningful. Left to our own devices, our "telic visions" will merely mirror our conventional concerns. Revelation helps us look through the looking glass.

We also saw how difficult it is to make good on those claims, even within the horizon of theism. Revelation is paradoxical. It must be sufficiently continuous with our concepts of value to be intelligible to us, but it must also be discontinuous enough to put our values into question and invite us into another order of value and meaning. It is easy to err toward one pole or another, either transposing our rationality or transcending it. Furthermore, the revealed way should have an imperative, objective quality to it; it should be more than just another human preference. It should be anchored in the depths, sunk in something fixed and beyond our view. One can imagine such a ground, but actually giving a conceptually lucid account of it is difficult. Jewish thought – or in Hayes's case, historical scholarship on Jewish thought – finds that it cannot do so without pressing claims that risk absurdity. Revelation moves the discourse from an immanent to a transcendent frame, but it does not settle the problem of objective versus subjective grounds for (its version of) normativity.

Can philosophy do better? In this section, we consider three contemporary philosophers committed to a wholly immanent frame. Harry Frankfurt tries to work out the problem of a meaningful life by arguing for the subjective basis of such a life. Susan Wolf, in contrast, argues for the objective basis of a meaningful life. Finally, Rivka Weinberg looks at both kinds of attempts to secure grounds and concludes that neither can, in principle, succeed. Thus, she puts meaning in life beyond human grasp; human life is properly meaningless – a fact about which we should be "very, very sad."[89]

SUBJECTIVE MEANING

Harry Frankfurt sets out to address the ancient question of "how to live." His focus is not explicitly on meaning in life but on what our way of life, our goals in life, and our experience of life should be.[90] Nonetheless, this work is directly relevant to our inquiry for it bears on many of the relevant questions of meaning in life, a phrase that Frankfurt does occasionally use.

Frankfurt is clear, at the outset, that "morality" is too restricted a category to accommodate these concerns. Someone can be scrupulously moral and yet live a life that few of us would freely choose. (Highly moral people may be "emotionally shallow" or "lack vitality" or have "insipid ambitions," for example.) Frankfurt, like Fleischacker, wants to mark out a realm of concerns that go to meaning in life rather than the other-regarding conduct that he takes to dominate morality. Meaning will have to do with what is worth "caring about," with such matters as "aesthetic, cultural, and religious ideals" that are nonmoral.[91] He means by picking out such concerns to escape evaluating choices by a binary judgment of "selfish" or "moral," as if that exhausted the possibilities of practical reason.[92] As with Fleischacker's "telic visions," Frankfurt's nonmoral, authoritative ideals are deeper than the conventional norms of morality. They orient morality and help give it meaning.[93]

Frankfurt wants to move beyond the thin concept of what we want or "desire," to a thicker notion of what we care about – of what we regard as important to ourselves – and therefore love. Caring, taking as important, and loving are more complex than and different from wanting or desiring. They are not simply more intense forms of seeking the satisfaction of desire. They involve what Frankfurt elsewhere calls the "volitions of the second order."[94]

> Besides wanting to fulfill his desire, then, the person who cares about what he desires wants something else as well: he wants the desire to be sustained. Moreover, this desire for his desire to be sustained is not a merely ephemeral inclination. It is not transient or adventitious. It is a desire with which the person identifies himself, and which he accepts as expressing what he really wants.[95]

"Caring about" something, for Frankfurt, is foundational to a coherent life: It is "an activity that connects and binds us to ourselves .... Caring about something is essential to being the kind of creatures that human beings are."[96] We are not just swayed by our desires; we are able to reflect on them, to have attitudes toward them and toward ourselves. We are not "wantons," as he puts it elsewhere.[97] We take ourselves to be persons who experience an inner distancing from desire, who can experience a kind of freedom and agency with respect to our desires. Caring, taking as important, and loving are marks of distancing as well as identification. They are processes that form – a term that Frankfurt certainly does not use – our souls.

Our caring about things infuses the world with importance for us. "The totality of the various things that a person cares about – together with his ordering of how important to him they are – effectively specifies his answer to the question of how to live."[98] What then should we care about and what, if any, are the grounds for our caring? Is there a best way of life, a best set of things worth caring about? What deserves our love? Frankfurt believes that the kind of creatures we are, biologically speaking, sets limits on the answers to these questions. (Nearly everyone cares about staying alive, avoiding severe injury, disease, hunger, psychological distress, as well as positive things such as livelihood, reputation, and one's children.[99]) But this is merely a skeletal framework. Within those limits, there are no objectively fixed answers. The question of how people should live "is inescapably self-referential and leads us into an endless circle. No attempt to deal with the problem of what we have good reason to care about – to deal with it systematically and from the ground up – can possibly succeed."[100] Why?

Frankfurt claims that in order to answer the question "how should we live?," we need to be able to compare some forms of life to others. We need to distinguish what we should care about from what we needn't care about. We need to decide what has importance for us. But to do any of these things, we need criteria of evaluation. This is where the vicious circularity enters. Deciding on our criteria for what is important is *already* a decision about what is important. If we want to decide, say, whether a life in pursuit of wisdom has a higher value than a life in pursuit of money, our caring about the value of wisdom already acknowledges a choice-worthy kind of life. To propose a criterion is already to take seriously what it entails. "Formulating a criterion of importance presupposes possession of the very criterion that is to be formulated."[101] This circularity of reasoning preempts "well-ordered inquiry … because the prior question of how to identify and to evaluate reasons that are pertinent in deciding how one should live cannot be settled until it has first been settled how one should live."[102] The question of what one should care about has already been answered before the inquiry begins.[103]

Frankfurt draws from this that there can be no successful rational grounding for how we should live. It is a fantasy to think that we can demonstrate, from the ground up, the most reasonable account of how to live, that is, "incoherent and must be abandoned."[104] Frankfurt's privileging of the will over reason leads him to a kind of subjectivism about how we should live. The one thing needful in the face of our "restless uncertainty" is to "understand what it is that we ourselves really care about and to be decisively and robustly confident in caring about it."[105]

Nonetheless, we do seem to have reasons for what we care about; our confidence is not categorically irrational. The point, however, is that our reasons are post hoc, if articulable at all. We don't need to find reasons to care about our own health or survival. We don't deliberate our way toward good reasons for loving and protecting our children. We do not respond to commands of reason but, almost innately, to "commands of love." *A mode of caring about things rather than a rationally grounded set of principles constitutes our basic orientation in the world.*

Furthermore, one loves what one loves, for Frankfurt, not because one finds value in it and responds to it. Rather the act of loving creates the value. What we love acquires value *because* we love it.[106] It is not that we don't find value, say, in our children, whom we love. We do. It is just that their perceived value doesn't have priority or isn't the source of our motivation. It is "the other way around. The particular value that I attribute to my children is not inherent in them but depends upon my love for them."[107] The caring about/regarding as important/loving mode has priority over the rational, reason-giving one. Frankfurt wants to bracket the scope of reasoning in favor of a mode of engagement expressed by caring and love. These are more than transient expressions of feeling. They are the "contingent necessities of love," which "express something that belongs to our most intimate and most fundamental nature." They are highly personal, "constituted by and embedded in structures of the will through which the specific identity of the individual is most particularly defined."[108]

Finally, for Frankfurt, what we most care about and love constitutes our "final ends," the intrinsic values that organize all of our instrumental activities. Intrinsic values or final ends are necessary if our lives are to be "meaningful," rather than "empty and vain."[109] It is love that is the "originating source of terminal value."[110] Were it not for love, nothing would be of value for us. The instrumental goods that serve the ultimate ones, would become ends in themselves. But they would be pointless, a labor of Sisyphus. Our lives would be "empty and vain," if we had nothing "terminal" to care about. That seems right. What is more questionable is the pervasive subjectivism of Frankfurt's account. The things we most care about become valuable because we, post hoc, ascribe value to them. Value grows out of our subjective reflection on things we love, with loving having priority over valuing. Ultimately, the meaning in our lives comes from acts of will, from (literally) self-sustaining care for and commitment to beloved persons, things, and projects. Are these arbitrary? Not entirely, insofar as Frankfurt appeals to our species nature and its limit setting role. But the contingencies of individual histories, experiences, and psychologies create infinite variations on the theme of caring. What people find important and care about is an empirical matter. The philosopher, on Frankfurt's account, is unsuited to prescribe objects of care.

Frankfurt's subjectivism cannot help us sort out what is worth caring about from what is not. Even if objective, intrinsic goods were to exist, that would not entail that we should care about them. Intrinsic goods do not obligate us to find them important.[111] What we care about is basic – fair enough. But it is hard to see how we could be content with the fundamental subjectivity of what we care about, find important, and love. Do we not constantly revise, through reflection, what we care about? Could we not come to doubt that our terminal ends are worth caring about? Isn't a belief in the objective goodness of our deepest commitments part of our confidence in having them? These questions are of central concern for Wolf.

OBJECTIVE MEANING

Susan Wolf argues that "meaning arises from loving objects worthy of love and engaging with them in a positive way."[112] Had she spoken only of "loving objects" in the sense, say, of pursuing one's passions whatever they may be, objectivity would not be salient. Specifying that objects must be "worthy of love," however, puts constraints on one's engagement.

A popular version of the meaningful life is a life that one finds personally fulfilling. One follows one's dreams and develops one's talents. One lives without boredom, listlessness, or slavish subjugation to a routine. One's inmost passions guide one's investment of energy and care. There is, of course, some truth in this. A subjective dimension of agreeable attitudes and feelings of the experience of engagement with things that one cares about is straightforwardly part of meaning in life. (Wolf calls this "the fulfillment view.")

It is, however, possible to care about things that are *not* worth caring about because of, say, their triviality or ethical perversity. It is possible to spend one's life pursuing foolish or misguided passions. The judgment of outsiders matters here. We would tend to find lives preoccupied with worthy values and projects more meaningful than lives squandered on low pleasures or aimlessly adrift. The point of view that generates such judgments, whether in others or in our own self-reflection, should not be dismissed.

Wolf asks us to consider the paradigm case of meaninglessness: Sisyphus rolling the stone up the hill for all eternity. She references Richard Taylor's gloss on the myth: If Sisyphus were given a drug that made him enjoy stone-rolling, made him think that it was a fulfilling activity, would that suffice to merit the ascription of a meaningful life? Taylor thinks that it would. Wolf rejects Taylor's subjectivism. Sisyphus's experience of fulfillment through perpetual stone-rolling lacks worthiness in our eyes; from an external point of view, Sisyphus is deluded. Sheer subjectivity must not be given the last word. Thus, according to Wolf, "meaning arises when subjective attraction meets objective attractiveness."[113]

To get a further intuition of the need for objectivity, Wolf references another popular view: One's life gains meaningfulness by devotion to things, projects, causes, etc. "larger than oneself." This also suggests an objective dimension. We put ourselves in service to something not ourselves; we sense that a self-serving life is deficient in meaning. Otherness is indicative of objectivity, of something beyond our own subjective fulfillment. (But this view has its own dangers. One can go terribly wrong in devoting oneself to something larger than oneself. A quick reference to the totalitarian political movements of the twentieth century should suffice.) Combining the fulfillment view and the "larger than oneself" view, we get a first, rough version of a balance between subjective and objective elements. Wolf calls this bipartite approach the "fitting fulfillment view" – a framework for meaningfulness that combines subjective satisfaction with objective worthiness.

Another way she develops these tentative intuitions of objectivity is to suggest that to have a meaningful life, at least in part, is to be able to see our lives as valuable "from a point of view other than one's own."[114] Invoking Nagel's "view from nowhere," she wants to use this conceit in a positive way. To overcome the suspicion or fear that our lives are objectively meaningless or insignificant, we want to believe that they matter from a perspective *other than* our own. That they matter to others, even though they may not matter from the truly impersonal point of view of the universe, is significant. That we have contributed to the good of others confers objectivity of a kind on our endeavors and hence on our lives. Even if we contribute something unrecognized, the idea that, in principle, something of value has been brought into the world by us can satisfy a criterion of objectivity.

> Our interest in being able to see our lives as worthwhile from some point of view external to ourselves, and our interest in being able to see ourselves as part of an at least notional community that can understand us and that to some degree

> shares out point of view, then, seem to me to be pervasive, even if not universal. By engaging in projects of independent value, by protecting, preserving, creating, and realizing value the source of which lies outside ourselves, we can satisfy these interests.[115]

Wolf is alert to an objection. That one loves objects worthy of love and engages with them in a positive way, with worthiness defined by what some community or notional collective considers valuable, a critic could say, just kicks the can down the road. Why should a collective's view of value be any better grounded than that of an individual?[116] Wolf is frank about accepting an "endoxic method." The *endoxa*, according to Aristotle, were "the things that were accepted by everyone, or by most people, or by the wise (Topics I.I 100b 21–23)."[117] Unlike Plato's Socrates, who sought to show that the opinions of people were hopelessly confused, Aristotle begins his ethical analysis with their basic soundness. Wolf, in treating the fulfillment view and the larger-than-oneself view as valuable, albeit partial, perspectives, exemplifies the endoxic approach.

Nonetheless, she worries that "if an individual's valuing something isn't sufficient to give the thing real value ... it is hard to see why a group's endorsement should carry any more weight."[118] She acknowledges that her proffered forms of objectivity – the judgment of others and one's admission of the possibility that one's own judgment about values could be wrong – may be too weak. They are a promissory note on objectivity. But she doesn't think that a more robust version is available.

> In claiming that meaningfulness has an objective component .... I mean only to insist that something other than a radically subjective account of value must be assumed. Nonetheless, I must confess that I have no positive account of nonsubjective value with which I am satisfied. Radically objective accounts of value are implausible and obscure, but the most obvious conceptions of value that fall between those and the radically subjective are problematic as well.[119]

She is thus left in the unstable position of rejecting a radically subjective account of meaning in life without being able to provide much content for a "reasonably complete and defensible nonsubjective account." This is an "unsolved problem in philosophy."[120] Frankfurt, I believe, would disagree. He would think that Wolf's attempt to constitute a viable objectivism is wrongheaded.

Wolf makes use of the incompleteness of objectivity. She finds value in the very fact of puzzlement about objective value; puzzlement itself makes an important contribution to meaningfulness. If meaning in life needs objective value, our ongoing, if inconclusive, wrestling with the problem of objectivity may itself sharpen our appreciation of meaning. Worries about objectivity drive us to focus on the uniqueness of meaning as a category irreducible to subjective satisfaction or compliance with objective moral norms. By refusing to accept pure subjectivism, we implicitly reject, for example, hedonistic versions of meaning in life. By refusing to accept objectivity in a strong sense, we reject equating meaning with morality, that is, with an external and overriding criterion on what we must do or be to have a good life. Wolf wants her unstable position to be critical and heuristic. Thus, although it may not provide much content, it can still do much work. This is why the problem of the meaning of life and its entanglement with objective value "matters."[121]

Aristotle, as well as the natural law thinkers who adapted his thought, did not think that the problem of objective value was unsolved. Aristotle had a normative biology or anthropology. He had, that is, an account of what was distinctive to human beings, of the content of their good, and of what ends they should serve. Aristotle's thought was, of course, vulnerable to the prejudices of his day, as any reader of the *Nicomachean Ethics* or of the *Politics* soon notices. (The *Ethics*, e.g., claims that little people may be "neat and well proportioned, but cannot be beautiful (1123b 7)." In the *Politics*, Aristotle endorses slavery; there are slaves by nature (Book I:5 1254a 18). In the case of opinions about ethics, Aristotle held that there were substantive, not just formal standards by which to judge them, such as their contribution to human flourishing. They weren't free-floating, as they seem to be for Wolf. While Wolf uses an endoxic method, she severs the endoxa from any account of the human good. She disdains to argue for such an account or to engage with thinkers, such as those in the natural law tradition on one side or in the natural science tradition on the other, who do. One wonders how so tentative, cautious, and minimal account – its precision, elegance, and philosophical rigor notwithstanding – could withstand an absurdist, let alone a nihilistic critique.

NO MEANING

Unlike Wolf, Weinberg focuses on the meaning of – not in – life. She specifies the relevant meaning of "meaning" as "point." She is emphatic that life is pointless. ("Some people worry that life is pointless. That's because it is."[122]) This is not a flippant or glib remark on her part. She believes that the logical grammar or conceptual structure of meaning forces us to admit that life as a whole cannot have a point. Individual projects and activities within life can have a point, but the whole cannot. (That is, she wants to – and does – avoid the fallacy of composition wherein what is true of the constituents of a group is ascribed to the group as a whole.) What is her argument for this stark conclusion?

Weinberg distinguishes between the point of an activity and the activity itself. We engage in an activity to accomplish some valued end. We hammer nails into boards to build a shelter. We build a shelter so that we can dwell in it and be protected from the elements. It is because we find ourselves to be valuable that value flows downward on the instrumental activities that serve us. Whether the activity is straightforwardly goal-directed, such as building a hut, or apparently atelic, such as having coffee with friends, there are in all cases intrinsic goods that are served by "pointful" activities. The innumerable activities in which we engage are "somewhat safe from the perils of pointlessness," but "the only little problem is that the effort or enterprise of leading our entire lives is pointless."[123] The episodic purposefulness we have within life categorically fails to apply to life as a whole. We do not and cannot have answers to "What is our justified valued end? Why live?"[124]

The problem here is a logical one. Valued ends are external to the activities and projects that serve them. But there are no ends external to existence; all ends are within the scope of the lives that pursue them. Thus, all of our activities and projects have a point only within our lives, which leaves life itself literally, categorically pointless. We have no perspective external to our lives from which to evaluate the meaning of those lives. Lives, logically, lack ultimate meaning. "Human life includes its entirety, leaving nowhere for us to reach for a valued end to serve as a point for leading and living it."[125] The chain of justification for why we should do anything ends within life; there is no justification beyond life for life per se. The values that guide us to do what we do can be justified. That I care about my children or my health or my country is justifiable (all things considered). What cannot be justified, insofar as the point that makes for justification is in principle lacking, is why I should lead a life at all. Weinberg refers to the first range of justifications as "everyday meaning" and the second as "ultimate meaning."[126] Weinberg is committed to keeping the everyday cogent despite the absence of the ultimate. "Our lives may be full, even meaning*ful*, overflowing with purposeful projects and enterprises but conducting life itself isn't one of them. It can't be."[127]

It doesn't matter, on Weinberg's view, whether values, and hence meanings, are grounded subjectively or objectively. Whatever the ground of values is, it does not extend beyond the horizon of the living human beings whose activities reveal the axiological relation between means and ends, projects and their points. Weinberg insists that life itself cannot be a valued end; it is only an enterprise to serve a valued end, of which there is none. "Life itself is a biological state, not a reason at all and [it] isn't a reason for leading a life any more than a jump is a reason for jumping ...."[128] It seems odd to say that life per se is not valuable or meaningful, but Weinberg's constitution of meaning as "having a point" constrains her here. Life is dependent upon a point beyond life, and no such point exists or can be known by us. Life is only "biological," a kind of container for episodic projects and everyday meanings. If this is the tragic truth of the matter, why is suicide, as in Camus, not the only serious philosophical question? Weinberg asks:

> Why do we keep on keeping on? Yes, we have Everyday Meaning, and that is no small thing. It enables us to lead a meaningful life. But it does not negate noticing that there is this other kind of meaning—Ultimate Meaning, which we have reason to want, and it is a sad aspect of the human condition that we cannot have it. There is no contradiction between appreciating Everyday Meaning and wondering, still, why are we bothering to lead a life at all? (p. 9)

On Wolf's view, a life infused with everyday meaning can certainly be a good life. But there is something insufficient about it. For we do tend to treat our lives as a whole; we run or lead them *as if* there were a point to the whole enterprise. The will-o'-the-wisp of ultimate meaning becomes part of the sense and satisfaction of everyday meaningfulness. Everyday meaningfulness suffers a loss of meaning when ultimate meaning is revealed as a sham. This need not lead to suicide, however. "It just means that we recognize a particularly sad aspect of the human condition …." (9) The ultimate meaninglessness of our lives makes them tragic, everyday meaning notwithstanding. All of our striving, creating, and shaping as valuing, purposive agents take place within our lives, but our lives are just "containers" for these projects and activities; they have no point as such. There is a disproportion between our engagement with value in life and the absence of value of our lives as such. That our lives as such are pointless "should make us sad because it [the sadness] is a fitting response to the facts" (p. 10).

Weinberg's is an absurdist view. The disproportion between the intensity of our engagement with value in life, our sense that there must be value in a comprehensive, final sense, and our sad recognition that there is neither value nor meaning to our lives as a whole exemplify absurdity. She doesn't want us to scant or diminish the force of this absurdity, but neither should we let it paralyze us. To an extent, it can't help but tinge our motivation for the valued activities and projects that lead to meaning *in* life. But it doesn't seem able to defeat them altogether on Weinberg's account. It gives us tragic stature and bearing, one supposes. But that doesn't make our lives any less pointless. The rock-solid conviction of pointlessness points toward, perhaps embraces, nihilism – a modern philosophical cashing out of the implications of absurdity.

Although it is admirable that Weinberg confronts us with the question of the meaning of life rather than preemptively make the concessions that reduce the question to meaning in life, it is troubling that she finds no ultimate value in human life per se. If there isn't basic goodness in life, in being as such, it is not only ultimate meaning that fails. It is not clear why any given activity or project should count as good if the very life that they serve is not good. Why wouldn't all activities and projects be a labor of Sisyphus? Weinberg tries to insulate – to some degree – everyday meaning from the absence of ultimate meaning. But why shouldn't everyday meaning simply collapse if life as such, the literal existence condition for activity, were worthless?

Both Judaism and philosophy run into persistent problems in grounding value and securing meaning; both encounter the absurdity built-in to the process. Judaism's transcendent turn toward revelation runs into complexities and doubts about the grounds of *its* normativity. Judaism reaches toward a version of objectivity – the expression of divine will – but the God of Israel is not a general who must simply be obeyed. Revelation is subject to reciprocity. The Jews constitute the divine way as much as, if not more than, the Divinity does. Revelation does not command from an objective height; revelation relies on, indeed, invites the covenantal participation of the Jews to determine its own meaning. Nor can the immanent framework of contemporary philosophy secure meaning without worries about the adequacy of its grounds. Frankfurt's subjectivism of love assumes an extensive ethical context which his theory cannot justify. Wolf's objectivism assumes that widely shared opinions are morally reliable, a view that seems endlessly falsified by history. Weinberg wants an environing context for our shared everyday meanings but, unable to find one, pronounces life ultimately meaningless. She gives us a promissory note on nihilism, which James Tartaglia, in Chapter 4, will be happy to cash. Given the headwinds both revelation and secular meaningfulness face, can we be redeemed from ultimate meaninglessness? Is local, subjective or transsubjective meaning the best we can do? To the question of redemption, we next turn.

NOTES

1 For a careful study of subtle allusions to the Torah in Kohelet, see Thomas Krüger, "Die Rezeption der Tora im Buch Kohelet," in his *Kritische Weisheit* (Zürich: Pano Verlag, 1997), pp. 173–193. Krüger argues that Kohelet makes frequent reference to verses, ideas, tropes, and laws of the Torah but does so in a critical spirit, often trying to substitute creation and human experience for revelation as the ground of wisdom about how to live in the world.

2 Benjamin Storey and Jenna Silber Storey, *Why We Are Restless: On the Modern Quest for Contentment* (Princeton: Princeton University Press, 2021), p. 3. The Storeys use the term to describe Montaigne's moderate and worldly ideal of human happiness.

3 Lenn Goodman, *On Justice: An Essay in Jewish Philosophy*, 2nd edition (Oxford: Littman Library of Jewish Civilization, 2008), p. 122. On whether nature is "enough" or whether the phenomenon of value, properly conceived, requires transcendence, see John F. Haught, *Is Nature Enough?* (New York: Cambridge University Press, 2006), p. 153. Haught's basic move is to argue that the naturalization of value is self-undermining. If the analysis of the human responsibility to seek the truth comes down to an evolutionary story involving genetic replication, then the motivation for seeking the truth is eviscerated. Naturalism with respect to morality founders on absurdity. This kind of argument is

comparable to Plantinga's "evolutionary argument against naturalism." See Alvin Plantinga, *Where the Conflict Really Lies: Science, Religion & Naturalism* (New York: Oxford University Press, 2011), pp. 307–350.

4 The figure is from astrophysicist, Adam Frank. See www.nytimes.com/2021/05/30/opinion/ufo-sightings-report.html?action=click&module=Opinion&pgtype=Homepage (accessed May 31, 2021).

5 See Steve Stewart-Williams, *God, Darwin, and the Meaning of Life* (Cambridge: Cambridge University Press, 2010), p. 187.

6 Cf. Pesikta Rabbati 15 cited in Christine Hayes, *What's Divine about Divine Law? Early Perspectives* (Princeton: Princeton University Press, 2015), p. 202.

7 For a Talmudic example of social judgment on well spent and poorly spent lives, see B. Berakhot 28b.

8 For the Platonic anticipations of natural law, see Tom Angier, *Natural Law Theory* (Cambridge: Cambridge University Press, 2021), pp. 1–2.

9 For a possible background to the decline of objective ideas of the good life in a democratic age, see Tocqueville on the democratic diversity of the human search for happiness in Benjamin and Jenna Silber Storey, *Why We Are Restless*, pp. 154–55. A philosopher whose sense of meaning in life is based on the essence of humans as rational beings is Peter Geach, although perhaps he is speaking more as a traditional Catholic than as a philosopher in Geach, *Truth and Hope* (Notre Dame: Notre Dame University Press, 2001), see, for example, pp. 17–33.

10 See especially John Finnis, *Natural Law and Natural Rights* (New York: Oxford University Press, 2011) on basic goods.

11 B. Berakhot 8a.

12 See Pesikta Rabbati 20: Had Israel not accepted the Torah, God tells the angels, neither He nor they would have a home (*dirah*) in the world. Cited in Isaac Heinemann, *The Reasons for the Commandments in Jewish Thought*, trans. Leonard Levin (Boston: Academic Studies Press, 2009), p. 19.

13 It is up to the Jews, for example, to restore (or perhaps only to proclaim?) God's greatness and sovereignty in the world. See B. Yoma 69b, for example.

14 Saadia Gaon, *The Book of Beliefs and Opinions*, trans. Samuel Rosenblatt (New Haven: Yale University Press, 1948), p. 158 (Treatise III, Ch. 7).

15 A recent, philosophically astute treatment may be found in Jonathan Jacobs, *Law, Reason, and Morality in Medieval Jewish Philosophy* (Oxford: Oxford University Press, 2010), pp. 29–30; 112–117.

16 Saadia Gaon, *The Book of Beliefs and Opinions*, p. 31 (Introductory Treatise, Ch. 6).

17 Ibid., p. 31.

18 Ibid.

19 Ibid., pp. 141–143 (Chapter 3, Section 2).

20 Heinemann, *The Reasons for the Commandments in Jewish Thought*, p. 54.

21 See especially B. Yoma 67b, Pesikta d'Rav Kahana 4. Cited in Heineman, ibid., p. 20. See also B. Berakhot 28b where R. Eliezer counsels his students to prevent their children from logical inquiry (*higayon*) and rather place them "between the knees of Torah scholars" when they are young. The commentators try to parse a type of logical inquiry that inclines toward heresy, rather than discouraging rational exploration per se.

22 Alexander Altmann, "The Encounter of Faith and Reason in the Western Tradition and Its Significance Today," *Journal of Religion*, Vol. 101, No. 3, p. 340.

23 See Michael L. Morgan, *Interim Judaism: Jewish Thought in a Century of Crisis* (Bloomington: Indiana University Press, 2001) and John Cottingham, *On the Meaning of Life* (New York: Routledge, 2003), p. 72.

24 Samuel Fleischacker, *The Good and the Good Book: Revelation as a Guide to Life* (New York: Oxford University Press, 2015), pp. 49–61.

25 Fleischacker, *The Good and the Good Book*, p. 35. Although Fleischacker doesn't mention him, Rawls comes to mind. For Rawls, societies should deliver justice (in the sense of fairness). Given that basic good, individuals are free to pursue "comprehensive schemes of the good," that is, the meaning-seeking projects for their own lives. These latter, however, are categorically different from the public justice that is secured by "public reason." In this way, politics and religious (or secular) telic visions, to use Fleischacker's term, do not compete or conflict. (Rawls hopes that they overlap and therefore provide additional, nonpolitical support for public justice.) See John Rawls, *Political Liberalism* (New York: Columbia University Press, 2005), p. 13. See also https://plato.stanford.edu/entries/rawls/#PolConJus (accessed June 15, 2021).

26 Fleischacker, *The Good and the Good Book*, p. 74.
27 Ibid., p. 64.
28 Fleischacker distinguishes sharply between revelation and its reception: "Revelation and its reception thus belong together by *contrast*; the relationship is lost if we ignore their differences ... [I]f revelation dissolves into its reception; if the Torah or Gospels or Quran themselves become merely one among many human attempts to grasp what God wants of us, rather than God's own communication to us, then we might as well return to our reason and experience alone as a source of insight into our highest good ...." Ibid., p. 98.
29 Ibid., p. 79. One might object that the burden of proof is on the theist. The claim that there is an all-powerful, hidden, permanently mysterious yet real Person above yet among all things is an extraordinary claim in contrast to the claim that, essentially, what you see is what you get as regards the world. The burden of proof is on those who make extraordinary claims. Arguably, however, the discovery of the entirely counterintuitive quantum realm so complicates what counts as reality that "what you see is what you get" empiricism also faces a heavy burden of proof.
30 Ibid., p. 104.
31 Ibid., p. 116.
32 Ibid., p. 117.
33 Remarking not on what was heard and by whom, but on where Moses was during the Sinai theophany, Sommer writes:

> The story of revelation in Exodus 19–24 defies a coherent sequential reading. Even more than most passages in the Pentateuch, Exodus 19 is full of ambiguities, gaps, strange repetitions, and apparent contradictions, as many scholars have shown. These oddities multiply when one reads the subsequent two narratives that treat the theophany at Sinai: Exodus 20:18–22 and Exodus 24. These texts present a bewildering aggregate of verses describing Moses's ascents and descents on the mountain. Moses seems not to be located at the right place when the Decalogue is given: God tells him to descend the mountain and then re-ascend with Aaron (Exodus 19:24), whereupon he descends (19:25); but before he reascends, the revelation of the law takes place (20:1) .... These oddities can be resolved, after a fashion, through harmonistic exegesis, but their presence already intimates that the extraordinary event chapter 19 describes was witnessed through a fog, or that the narrative of that event could not be articulated in human words; further, one senses that the text combines

> multiple recollections of an essentially unreportable event. (Benjamin D. Sommer, *Revelation and Authority: Sinai in Jewish Scripture and Tradition* [New Haven: Yale University Press, 2015], pp. 31–33)

Highly detailed analyses of the patterns of ambiguity in who heard what during the lawgiving may be found in pp. 35–41.

34 Choosing to work within the context of academic, "critical" biblical scholarship no doubt increases the amount of absurdity with which a modern Jewish thinker much cope. Fleischacker may be wise to ignore it, but it damages the *rational* acceptability of his view.

35 Sommer, *Revelation and Authority: Sinai in Jewish Scripture and Tradition*, p. 41. Italicization added.

36 Ibid., p. 48.

37 "Translation," a key concept for Sommer, seems problematic. Translation means conveying semantic content from a fully articulated source language to a target language. If the source is nonlinguistic, what is there to be translated?

38 Sommer, *Revelation and Authority*, pp. 86–87.

39 Cited in Ibid., p. 104.

40 Cited in Ibid., p. 29.

41 Ibid., pp. 89–95.

42 Greenstein, cited by Ibid., p. 143.

43 The term is Hindy Najman's, cited by Ibid., pp. 141–143.

44 Ibid., p. 144.

45 Ibid., p. 145. Especially striking is a quotation Sommer cites in support of his position from a contemporary Jewish philosopher, Jerome Gellman: "The saintly make God's word. Then they hear it ... God speaks to us after we create God's speech."

46 Ibid. Italics in original.

47 Ibid. Italics in original.

48 Richard Feynman, *The Character of Physical Law* (Cambridge: MIT Press, 1965), pp. 18–19.

49 For a rich discussion of the normativity of tradition and its associated problems, see Samuel Scheffler, *Equality and Tradition* (New York: Oxford University Press, 2010), pp. 287–311.

50 Tom Angier, *Natural Law Theory* (Cambridge: Cambridge University Press, 2021), p. 7.

51 Hayes, *What's Divine about Divine Law*, p. 2.

52 Novak's writings on this theme are extensive. The basic statement may be found in David Novak, *Natural Law in Judaism* (Cambridge: Cambridge University Press, 1998). A more recent statement is found in David Novak et al., eds., *Natural Law: A Jewish, Christian and Islamic Trialogue* (Oxford: Oxford University Press, 2014). I have also made use of an as yet unpublished response to Hayes, which Professor Novak shared with me.

53 Indeed, the motivation for work on this topic seems to be to warrant larger claims about the nature of Judaism and thus about the relation of Jews to non-Jews in the modern world. Seeing Judaism as grounded in natural law makes Judaism essentially moral and lessens the distance between Jews and their non-Jewish fellow citizens. See Daniel Statman, "Natural Law and Judaism" (unpublished manuscript provided by the author), p. 1.

54 The classic statement of natural law is found in Cicero, reporting on the Stoic, Laelius:

> There is one, single justice. It binds together human society and has been established by one, single law. That law is right reason in commanding and forbidding. A man who does not acknowledge this law is unjust, whether it has been written down anywhere or not .... That is why justice is completely nonexistent if it is not derived from nature .... We can distinguish a good law from a bad one solely by the criterion of nature. And not only justice and injustice are differentiated by nature, but all things without exception that are honourable and dishonourable. For nature has created perceptions which we have in common and has sketched them in our minds in such a way that we classify honourable things as virtues and dishonourable things as vices. (Cicero, *The Republic and the Laws*, cited in Jonathan Jacobs, *Law, Reason, and Morality in Medieval Jewish Philosophy* [Oxford: Oxford University Press, 2010], p. 157) Cf. also Angier, *Natural Law Theory*, p. 7.

55 *On Abraham* 13:60–61, cited in Hayes, *What's Divine about Divine Law?*, p. 123.

56 Hayes, *What's Divine about Divine Law?*, p. 172.

57 Ibid., p. 173.

58 Ibid., p. 186.

59 Hayes cites Exodus Rabbah 43:4 on Exodus 32:9–10. When God wants to destroy Israel for the Golden Calf, Moses implores God not to do so. God orders Moses to stand aside, but he does not. Moses, the midrash interprets, does not "implore" (*vayyeḥal*) God, he annuls (*yaḥel*) God's

vow – Moses saves God from having to destroy the Israelites by legally letting Him out of his implicit vow. See Hayes, *What's Divine about Divine Law?*, p. 193.

60 Hayes, *What's Divine about Divine Law?*, p. 194.

61 Ibid., p. 199.

62 Hayes cites Mishnah Rosh Hashanah 2:9–12. Hayes, *What's Divine about Divine Law?*, p. 200.

63 Hayes, *What's Divine about Divine Law?*, p. 202.

64 Ibid., p. 244.

65 For a good view of the human consequences of nominalism, broadly speaking, see David E. Cooper, *The Measure of Things* (Oxford: Clarendon Press, 2002), pp. 24–40.

66 Hayes, *What's Divine about Divine Law?*, p. 276. The opening verse is a rabbinic interpretation of a verse from Job 14:4: "Who can bring forth a clean thing out of an unclean thing? Not one." The rabbis read "not one" as "is it not the One?" This move in itself neatly encapsulates the jettisoning of conventional logic.

67 Hayes, *What's Divine about Divine Law?*, p. 277.

68 Ibid., p. 320.

69 Ibid., p. 321.

70 Ibid., p. 326.

71 Ibid., p. 332. The main rabbinic discussion of the Noahide laws is in B. Sanhedrin 56a–60a. Earlier discussions take place at Tosephta Avodah Zarah 8:4 and Genesis Rabbah 16:16. The various lists do not agree in all details.

72 Hayes, *What's Divine about Divine Law?*, p. 366. For a text, see Sifre Deut 343.

73 Hayes, *What's Divine about Divine Law?*, p. 365. Emphasis added.

74 Hayes, *What's Divine about Divine Law?*, pp. 355, 359, 367, citing Novak by name.

75 For the theoretical, speculative (rather than practical, political) character of rabbinic natural law according to Novak, see his *Natural Law in Judaism* (New York: Cambridge University Press, 1998), p. 151.

76 David Novak, "Response to Christine Hayes' *What is Divine about Divine Law?*" Unpublished manuscript; personal communication.

77 Novak, "Response," p. 2.

78 Ibid., p. 3.

79 David Novak, "Is Natural Law a Border Concept between Judaism and Christianity?" *Journal of Religious Ethics* 32: 242.

80 Novak, "Response," p. 10.

81 See Angier, *Natural Law Theory*, pp. 9–10.

82 See, for example, *Gorgias* 483e; *Rhetoric* 1.13, 1373b4–17.

83 For a critique of theological natural law from a perspective that, while not hostile to theism, nonetheless wants to avoid theological premises, see Angier, *Natural Law Theory*, p. 15. N.b. his criticisms of Novak.

84 An example of this in the Middle Ages is Maimonides's attempt to formulate rational dogmas for Judaism, itself highly controversial. He found thirteen beliefs to be necessary and sufficient, indeed, morally obligatory for a Jew in good standing. These were immediately challenged by later thinkers, including Hasdai Crescas, Joseph Albo, and Isaac Abravanel, who produced different lists and different rationales for what Judaism required rationally of its adherents. Each of these entails different views of the relations among the divine, the human, law, ethics, and reason. Some thinkers rejected the whole enterprise. See the classic study by Menachem Kellner, *Dogma in Medieval Jewish Thought* (Oxford: Littman Library, 1986).

85 For a historical and contemporary overview and evaluation, see Tamar Rudavsky, "Natural Law in Judaism," in Tom Angier, ed. *Natural Law Ethics* (Cambridge: Cambridge University Press, 2019), pp. 113–134. For the ambiguities that afflict the discussion, see Statman, "Natural Law and Judaism" (unpublished manuscript).

86 The statement "*credo quia absurdum*" is ascribed, wrongly, to the Church Father, Tertullian. See Peter Harrison ""I Believe Because it is Absurd": The Enlightenment Invention of Tertullian's Credo." *Church History* 86.2 (2017): 339–364.

87 Leibovitz's understanding of Judaism has learned from Hans Kelsen's legal positivism. Given a sharp dichotomy between facts and values, there is nothing in nature and history to support normativity. It rests entirely on the free and essentially arbitrary choice of individuals to accept a basic norm. As Yonatan Brafman writes about Leibovitz, "The normativity of this value, like all values, however, is only supported by an individual's free decision in favor of it. The positivism of halakha corresponds to the existentialism of value. The individual is confronted by a self-enclosed system of commandments, which he can only leap

into through an act of will." Yonatan Brafman, *Critical Philosophy of Halakha* (no publisher; no date). On Leibovitz and the absurd, see Avi Sagi, *Jewish Religion after Theology* (Boston: Academic Studies Press, 2009), especially pp. 67–106 on Leibovitz and Camus.

88 Leibovitz would not recognize his position as absurd. For a postmodern thinker (and critic of Leibovitz) Rav Shagar, who calls his own position absurd and embraces it, see Shimon Gershon Rosenberg, *Faith Shattered and Restored*, trans. Elie Leshem (Jerusalem: Maggid Books, 2017), pp. 23, 59.

89 Rivka Weinberg, "Ultimate Meaning: We Don't Have It, We Can't Get It, and We Should Be Very, Very Sad," *Journal of Controversial Ideas*, I:1 (April, 2021); see https://journalofcontroversialideas.org/volumes_issues/1/1 (accessed August 20, 2021).

90 Harry Frankfurt, *The Reasons of Love* (Princeton: Princeton University Press, 2004), p. 5.

91 Frankfurt, *The Reasons of Love*, pp. 8, 11.

92 Cf. Bernard Williams's rebuke of the morality system. Cf. also Wolf's "moral saints."

93 "... even after we have accurately identified the commands of the moral law, there still remains – for most of us – the more fundamental practical question of just how important it is to obey them." For that we need a larger frame, such as meaning in life provides. Frankfurt, *The Reasons of Love*, p. 9.

94 See Harry Frankfurt, "Freedom of the Will and the Concept of a Person," *The Importance of What We Care About* (New York: Cambridge University Press, 1998), p. 20.

95 Frankfurt, *The Reasons of Love*, p. 16.

96 Ibid., p. 17.

97 Frankfurt, "Freedom of the Will," p. 16.

98 Frankfurt, *The Reasons of Love*, p. 23.

99 Ibid., p. 27.

100 Ibid., p. 24. That the forum for caring and assessing what we happen to care about is internal is the basis for the judgment that Frankfurt is a subjectivist. "Subjective" here should not be taken to mean merely arbitrary or preferential, although Frankfurt exposes himself to that criticism. There is something deeply and constitutively personal about what one cares about, so it cannot be sustained by sheer whim. The

radical role that caring plays in forming one's self-conscious being weighs against arbitrariness. For Frankfurt's use of "subjective," see Frankfurt, *The Reasons of Love*, p. 56.

101 Frankfurt, *The Reasons of Love*, p. 26.

102 Ibid.

103 This is reminiscent of the problem of the relationship of revelation and reason, which surfaced in several treatments considered above. Revelation must be coherent enough with our already established moral orientation to be intelligible but different enough to be valuable and authoritative. We can't quite escape our own constitution of revelation, given the necessity of our acknowledgment of its morality.

104 Frankfurt, *The Reasons of Love*, p. 28.

105 Ibid.

106 Ibid., p. 39.

107 Ibid., p. 40.

108 Ibid., p. 48.

109 Ibid., p. 52.

110 Ibid., p. 55.

111 Ibid., pp. 56–57.

112 Susan Wolf, *Meaning in Life and Why It Matters* (Princeton: Princeton University Press, 2010), p. 8.

113 Ibid., p. 9.

114 Ibid., p. 27.

115 Ibid., p. 31.

116 Wolf herself admits that this is a problem.

117 Wolf, *Meaning in Life*, p. 10.

118 Ibid., p. 46.

119 Ibid., pp. 45–46. Presumably the objectivity provided by a revelation of God's would be "implausible and obscure."

120 Wolf, *Meaning in Life*, p. 47.

121 See, in general, the discussion in Wolf, *Meaning in Life*, pp. 48–53.

122 Weinberg, "Ultimate Meaning," p. 1.

123 Ibid., p. 3.

124 Ibid.

125 Ibid., p. 4. Even one's afterlife, should there be such a thing, belongs to one; it is part of one's life. It cannot, therefore, provide an external, ultimate point/meaning for life.

126 Weinberg, "Ultimate Meaning," p. 5. Weinberg distinguishes between "cosmic meaning" – our role in the universe and hence our significance or, as is pervasively assumed these days, our insignificance – and ultimate meaning. The latter, her preferred term, is about the impossibility of finding a valued end for life rather than a cosmic role for it.

127 Weinberg, "Ultimate Meaning," p. 7.

128 Ibid.

4 Redemption

When we think about the future, we seek, in part, the significance of human action. When we imagine a better future, we wonder to what extent human action can help bring it about. If we dread a dark future, we worry about our contribution to it. The future we hope for or fear is entangled with our action. It forces us to reflect on the meaning of our agency and so, in a fundamental way, on the meaning of our lives.

Even if we think that the future is undetermined, that it awaits our direction and design, it nonetheless has a strong grip on the present. The future holds the present hostage. One needn't be a determinist or a fatalist to see this. Samuel Scheffler has argued that our sense of the meaning of our lives depends on there *being* a future. If one were to learn that thirty days after one's death, the earth would be hit by an asteroid and all human life would perish, how would that affect one? One's own death (by asteroid) is not at issue. One is dying, say, of a disease. So, the coming catastrophe won't be a matter of personal experience. A possible answer is to say: "It won't affect me at all; I'll already be dead." If one had that attitude, doomsday would be a matter of indifference. But how many of us would think that way? To the extent that our lives have been meaningful, that they have mattered, we want everything that made them matter to continue. This includes both the people whom we cared about and the conditions under which our lives had significance.

We readily accept the idea that we and everyone we care about will someday be gone. But the realization that human life *as such* at a near and definite time would be gone, given Scheffler's scenario, would be devastating. Would the value and meaning of our lives survive that realization? Say that one had been involved in a stereotypically meaningful activity such as research on cancer therapies. One has been dedicated to curing cancer. This project has organized one's adult life in a comprehensive way. The meaningfulness of that life has depended not only on advancing toward a cure for cancer but on their being people who can be cured of it. If there were no human future, given doomsday by asteroid, one's life would suddenly become – arguably – much less meaningful. It could now seem, retrospectively, absurd. Nothing that heretofore had meaning, such as the creation of art, of fundamental scientific discovery, and of achieving greater justice, better government, and human rights, could retain meaningfulness under such catastrophic circumstances. The instrumental value of all of one's activities, undertakings, and projects has been nullified. (Do they retain any intrinsic value? Perhaps there is an argument to be made there.) The upshot is that mere futurity is a condition on meaning; the future has veto power over the prospect of meaning in the present.[1]

Hans Jonas has a related insight. He described the condition of ethics in the twentieth century as fundamentally different from that of previous centuries.[2] He claimed that in earlier times, one could assume that the earth as such would endure. The arena of our moral agency – of the benefactions (or injuries) that we do for (or inflict on) one another – would remain as a stable, taken-for-granted backdrop for ethics. In the twentieth century, however, the possibility arose of making the earth uninhabitable. The threat of nuclear war and environmental degradation – climate change had not yet come into focus when Jonas was writing – changed our moral condition. We could no longer blithely assume that no matter how we acted, the world would endure. For Jonas, the preservation of the earth *as a home* had itself to become a criterion for ethical theory and action. The planet as such went from ground to figure. The future thus intrudes dramatically on the meaning of action in the present.

Scheffler's worry is more radical than that of Jonas. Jonas assumes that ethics, which now must consider the fate of the earth as a criterion for moral decision, remains eminently meaningful.

He wants to expand the scope of human moral activity to include a new, crucial dimension of concern. For him, the basic belief that human action matters remains intact. Jonas is a traditional moralist. Scheffler, by contrast, raises the prospect of a certain kind of future – a future without us – where little that we now think matters would continue to matter. The loss of a significant human future has a corrosive effect on the present. While Jonas' worry is actionable, that of Scheffler is merely a thought experiment. Yet, Scheffler makes a plausible point. Without the continuity of human life, our judgments about the meaning of life, about our agency as a meaningful dimension of life, become hard, if not impossible, to justify.

The ad absurdum extreme is raised by the physicist Brian Greene who posits a doomsday scenario to the universe as such. He observes that:

> The future we tend to envision, even if only implicitly, is one that's populated by the kinds of things we care about. Evolution will surely drive life and mind to take on a wealth of forms supported by a range of platforms – biological, computational, hybrid, and who knows what else. But regardless of the unpredictable details of physical composition or environmental backdrop, most of us imagine that in the vastly distant future, life of some stripe, and intelligent life more particularly, will exist and it will think.[3]

This, however, is a future that, after our brief moment in cosmic time, Greene disallows.

> Planets and stars and solar systems and galaxies and even black holes are transitory. The end of each is driven by its own distinctive combination of physical processes, spanning quantum mechanics through general relativity, ultimately yielding a mist of particles drifting through a cold and quiet cosmos ... [I]n a universe that will ultimately be devoid of life and consciousness, even a symbolic legacy – a whisper intended for our distant descendants – will disappear into the void.[4]

Here we are no longer talking about the end of humanity, or of conscious life, or of the sun and its planets, but of *everything*. No cosmic structure will remain. On the scale of billions of years, everything is indeed *hevel havalim*, a "mist of particles." Not content to write in a strictly scientific mode, Green confronts the challenge of this possible physical scenario to meaning. Does cosmic extinction undermine meaning? Not quite. Greene finds "nobility in being" and basically counsels that we make the most of our moment, building self-constructed meaning on our wonder at the universe and gratitude for our ability to understand it.[5] What is remarkable is not Greene's proposal for meaning – a kind of contemplative carpe diem – but his willingness to think that something four billion years off should matter to us *now*. He takes seriously that a definitive end to everything could undermine meaning here and now.

I think that he is right to do so. The implications of the end are not to be shrugged off just because they are incomprehensibly remote. Their measure must be taken. Even though the end has no emotional impact, unlike Scheffler's asteroid scenario, it has conceptual and axiological consequences. It makes it seem that we find our lives, agency, ethics, and projects meaningful only because we suspend our thinking about the furthest future. We shrink our temporal horizon to imaginable, humanly scaled time. But without those blinders, meaningfulness totters. The assumption of an extreme view from nowhere puts all of our values, projects, and meanings under judgment. Given the long-term futility of any human aspiration or agency, the scenario forces us either to ignore the far future as irrelevant or to imagine it, against the presumed evidence of physics, as ultimately conducive to our well-being. Both of these seem like acts of wishful thinking. The cosmic doomsday scenario, the nihilist might argue, mocks both our hope and our sense of absurdity. It is a kind of objective proof for the truth of nihilism. Far enough out, nothing will matter. Ultimate non-mattering bleeds back into our present and weakens our confidence that anything really matters now. It exposes a chasm between the ultimate and the proximate.

Our values and projects matter only within a framework that ignores the ultimate physical fact about reality: It is destined to become unreal.

A REDEMPTIVE FUTURE?

It is not only physics that contemplates time at cosmic scales. Monotheism does, too. It trades in this kind of language. God looks from creation to consummation, absolute beginning to ultimate end. "Before the mountains came into being, before You brought forth the earth and the world, from eternity to eternity You are God ... in your sight a thousand years are like yesterday that has passed (Psalms 90:2, 4). God's perspective, as it were, comprises eternity. Although that perspective is not our perspective, we stipulate it and reflectively scale our mortal concerns to it. Jews are no strangers, as it were, to speaking about the beginning and end of everything.

Although Greene provides a plausible physical scenario for cosmic extinction, perhaps the thought is nothing new. Religious traditions of east and west have always told us that everything is transient. For Jews, "The grass withers, the flower fades, but the word of the Lord endures forever" (Isaiah 40:8). Only God, who is beyond this transient universe, endures. Nonetheless, the modern physics-based supposition of cosmic finitude might be different. If there is no contrast term – divine eternity as against cosmic temporality – our being left with nothing but transience might well be novel, at least for a culture shaped by the Bible. (Arguably, Buddhists learned to live with total transience millennia ago. It's flux, impermanence, dissolution all the way down and all the way out.[6]) If what we glimpse with our view from nowhere is ultimate nothingness, how can that not corrode the meanings by which we live here and now?

Add to this the problem that, with scientific monism, we lose the idea of an immortal soul as an identity- and worth-conserving essence. Although dualism has its defenders, talk of the soul in the old dualistic sense functions today more as a poetic or moral affirmation than as an ontological claim, at least among philosophers.[7] If we, qua souls, were to have eternal life outside of the perishable universe, the nonfuture proposed by Scheffler or Greene would lose its bite. But without something like an immortal soul, we belong only to a natural world seemingly headed toward dissolution. Poetic uses of "soul" cannot rescue us from that. Lacking a belief in the immortal soul, Ecclesiastes sensed the absurdity of radical finitude.

This far horizon of our scientific and moral imagination affects the ancient trope of redemption, an important biblical way of envisioning the future. The Bible's dominant conception of redemption is this-worldly. This-worldly redemption is only viable given a *world*. If in some billions of years, there is no longer a world, no longer anything, redemption too will be of a moment, our brief moment in cosmic time. Perhaps redemption within that moment would suffice. But that is not how the Jewish tradition, at least, has imagined it. Redemption seems conceptually to require eternity in order to underwrite its value and power. It, very roughly, signifies a resolution of the tragic dimensions of the human condition. It is an ultimate relaxation and resolution of the tensions, contradictions, paradoxes, harms, and absurdity of human life. It, of course, requires that there be humans to be redeemed.

The Bible sometimes envisions redemption as restorative, a return to Eden, so to speak, and sometimes as a rupture, a breakthrough to something radically different. The second possibility can entail an apocalyptic dimension, a catastrophic upheaval before the redemptive resolution arrives. Jewish eschatology, containing both impulses, has strong internal tensions.[8] Although yearning for a resolution of the human condition might be a human universal, what drives the Jewish belief in redemption are specific memories and the hopes that they engender. Just as God redeemed His people Israel from bondage in Egypt (Exodus 6:6), God will redeem His chosen people at the end of days. God is faithful to His covenant, His promises, and His people. The figure of the messiah – a royal descendant of the House of David – works as God's agent in the redemptive process.[9] On some versions of messianism, such as Maimonides's, the messiah is a fully human political figure, a worldly king. On other versions, the messiah takes on a more supernatural role.

For "realistic messianists," redemption will consist of the Jewish people returning from exile, rebuilding their temple, exercising righteous self-government in their own land, and establishing a society in which none are maltreated and all have dignity. The other nations will come and worship on God's holy mountain in Jerusalem. All will acknowledge God's universal sovereignty and live out the ethical and political consequences of that acknowledgment. The earth will be full of the knowledge of God as the waters cover the sea (Isaiah 11:9).

How will such an ultimate resolution of the human condition, in general, and the travails of the Jewish people, in particular, come about? Classical Judaism has a number of scenarios. (As is typical of Jewish belief, their disharmony with one another is less a scandal than a spur to further reflection.) On all accounts God plays a decisive role. But human beings are hardly bystanders. There is at least a contested role for human action. For some ancient Jewish sages, human agency helps advance the realization of the salvific future (e.g., B. Yoma 86b; Exodus Rabba 25:16). Some texts assert that if all Jews were to keep the Sabbath, God would bring the redemption. On the view of R. Eliezer, repentance is the condition for redemption; the Jews will not be redeemed unless they return to God (B. Sanhedrin 97b). His contemporary, R. Yehoshua, disputed this. The coming of the redemptive kingdom rests on God's initiative alone (B. Sanhedrin 97b–98a). Human action, far from contributing to redemption in a positive way, only drives the world into deeper degradation. Human depravity is such that our actions only make things worse (e.g., Midrash on Psalms, Psalms 45:3).[10] Here, human agency has an ironic effect. Unremitting human moral corruption brings redemption in a negative way: God will intervene when things can't get any worse.

For Rabbi Yehoshua, God, knowing the way the world will course into the future, has set a time for the end. It is *not* something that can be hastened by human initiative. How or if human action is meaningful with regard to redemption is unsettled. If one were to push hard on this aporia, one might find a trace of the absurd. Given doubt about whether anything that human beings can do contributes positively toward fundamental amelioration of the human condition, hope for the future will always be vulnerable to skepticism. We cannot live without hope. But we cannot corral the doubts that accompany it either. Doubts about what human beings might accomplish can be resolved by faith in what God will accomplish. But that higher order resolution is also subject to doubt.

The redemptive future is sometimes pictured as a utopian return to an Edenic existence or, more chastely, as a realistic return to political sovereignty. In the latter strain, the world will go on in its accustomed ways. Everything will be the same, the Talmud tells us, except that Israel will not be oppressed by the gentile nations. Foremost among the expressions of realistic messianism is the statement in B. Berakhot 34b (in parallel with B. Sanhedrin 99a) where the sage Samuel asserts that "There is no difference between this world and the days of the Messiah except [that in the latter there will be no] bondage to foreign powers, as it says: For the poor shall *never* cease out of the land (Deuteronomy 15:11)."[11] This statement takes the Torah's word that the poor shall "never" cease from the land to extend even into the days of the messiah. It thus concludes that the difference between the messianic time and the present will be minimal, although highly significant. Israel's liberation from servitude to alien political power is a crucial shift, albeit within the bounds of a stringent realism. The ongoing reality of poverty implies a deflationary idea of redemption. This deflationary view can narrow our hopes and straiten our more utopian expectations. On the other hand, the deflationary view creates a space for a realistic messianism to emerge – a messianism, that is, that one can enact. Tying the messianic advent to human action gives our agency meaning. But it is also full of danger.

If the difference between the messianic age and the present age is only a matter of degree *and* if (contra Rabbi Yehoshua) human action can precipitate the messianic age, then it is always possible for human beings to imagine that they can do something to "force the end." The rabbis, especially after the disastrous Bar Kokhba uprising against Rome in 132–135 CE, accordingly played down the importance of messianism altogether. A famous (and highly realistic) statement is "If there was a plant in your hand, and you are told: 'Behold, the Messiah is here', go and plant the plant, and then go forth to welcome him" (Avot de-R. Nathan xxxi, 33b–34a).[12] This statement assumes that essential features of the world will remain so unchanged by the advent of the messiah that one might not notice his arrival while one is at work in one's field. Nor *should* one interrupt one's work to investigate whether he has arrived. This realistic eschatology was taken up by Maimonides and his rationalistic successors.

The stringently realistic, deflationary view, although attractive to rationalists such as Maimonides and some modern Jewish thinkers, is an outlier. Realism notwithstanding, both the Bible and Talmud interpolate a miraculous dimension to redemption. The redemptive consummation of history will be marked by the resurrection of the dead (*teḥiyat ha-metim*), at least of those who were righteous in life.[13] Righteous persons will be corporeally resurrected *en masse* at the appointed time. Redemption will take the form of blessed this-worldly life for those then living and for the resurrected ones who join them. The righteous of the past who participate in the future messianic kingdom will be compensated for their previous suffering. (Thus, the injustice of only future people enjoying the kingdom is preempted.) These various strands of redemption narrative are greatly elaborated in rabbinic literature and rationalized into (more or less) coherent accounts in medieval Jewish philosophy.[14] In all of these stories, an imagined future reconciles the contradictions, suffering, outrages, and injustices of the past (and present). The obscurity and absurdity of our present will be clarified and dissipated in a luminous future. The full meaning and significance of being human will be revealed.

The this-worldliness of a future-oriented redemption within a historical horizon, whether realistic or miraculous, has been accompanied by another story – a redemption beyond time in an afterlife. Although the Bible has an idea of resurrection, the idea of a fully conserved personal identity transposed to heaven (or hell) lies beyond the Hebrew Bible. The Bible imagines a kind of continuity in Sheol, a watery realm under the earth. But Sheol is not a place of judgment, of reward or punishment, as is heaven or hell. It is a place beyond worldly life – a place of distance from God. It is a nod to the significance of personhood, an unwillingness to consign it to complete extinction, albeit without wanting to embellish or elaborate an afterlife. Nonetheless, Sheol should not be considered a version of redemption.

A full-blown afterlife is redemptive, at least for the righteous. It is a recompense for the faithfulness of individuals in this life. The Bible knows little of a heaven where the righteous go after death. The resurrection of the dead is its favored postmortem trope. Rabbinic literature, however, articulates many depictions of heaven. Although some are full of sensuous pleasure, they needn't be. This is in keeping with the moral seriousness of rabbinic piety:

> Rav was wont to say: The World-to-Come is not like this world. In the World-to-Come there is no eating, no drinking, no procreation, no business negotiations, no jealousy, no hatred, and no competition. Rather, the righteous sit with their crowns upon their heads, enjoying the splendor of the Divine Presence, as it is stated: "And they beheld God, and they ate and drank" (Exodus 24:11).[15]

Nonetheless, the midrash can wax about the beauty of heaven. It is full of paradisiacal groves, with scented trees and flowers. Strikingly, the great martyrs and teachers continue to teach Torah there. Indeed, God is teaching Torah in the heavenly study hall.[16] The inexhaustibility of Torah, one imagines, mitigates the threat of an infinity of boredom in the afterlife. The philosopher Bernard Williams proposed the prospect of boredom as a strike against the desirability of immortality.[17] The rabbis would vigorously dissent.

The rabbinic idea that deep, abiding absorption in the Torah itself constitutes consummate blessedness is an instance of another dimension of redemption, which Cass Fisher has called "actualized redemption."[18] On this view, luminous clarity, resolution, and unshakeable meaning are *not* eschatological or postmortem; they can be found at the heart of the present moment. This view needn't reject a future redemption for all of the righteous, but that is not its center of gravity.[19] Its focus is less on the injustice of life than the unholiness of it. What becomes central is a proleptic realization of redemption now – a displacement of messianic longing by an idealized/actualized holy life in the present. The present mode of being of the Tzadik or saint (in Hasidism) or of the true "halakhic man" or second "Adam," in Rabbi Soloveitchik's thought, is what redemption will look like in the future. But the future is not in the foreground. To the extent that this holy way of being is presently instantiated, redemption has partly arrived, a foretaste of a fullness to come.[20] Thus, Soloveitchik writes:

> Being redeemed is … an ontological awareness. It is not just an extraneous, accidental attribute – among other attributes – of being, but a definitive mode of being itself. A redeemed existence is intrinsically different from an unredeemed. Redemptiveness does not have to be acted out vis-à-vis the outside world …. Cathartic Redemptiveness is experienced in the privacy of one's in-depth personality …. When objectified in personal and emotional categories, cathartic Redemptiveness expresses itself in the feeling of axiological security. The individual intuits his existence as worthwhile, legitimate, and adequate, anchored in something stable and unchangeable.[21]

Redemption becomes the conviction or experience of eminent or ultimate meaning here and now.

This strand may be rooted in an early impulse of rabbinic Judaism. If Jacob Neusner is correct, ancient Judaism shifted from a messianic, eschatological anticipation/activism toward a sacramental concept of a redeemed, that is, a holy life. The catastrophic failure of the Bar Kohhba revolt in 132–135 CE was the background for the shift. The founding document of rabbinic Judaism, the Mishnah (edited in its final version around 200 CE), proposed an alternative to the vicissitudes of history and politics, of war and destruction: an ahistorical, static world of holiness. The Mishnah depressed messianism and elevated "timeless sanctification."[22] In the Mishnah's vision, human action narrowed to faithful obedience to the law. (An echo of this vision may be found not only in Soloveitchik, as above, but in Franz Rosenzweig's depiction of the Jews as an already redeemed community, living in cyclical, ritual time, beyond history and politics. Although the world is not yet redeemed – all are not yet one in the oneness of God – the Jewish people, in its communal, ritual life, anticipates the ultimate redemption.[23]) It was also the case, however, that such a vision was unsustainable. The old history and politics-oriented trope of messianism was reintroduced by the Mishnah's commentary literature, the Jerusalem and the Babylonian Talmuds. Messianism as a historical hope, dependent on divine and, to some extent, human action reentered Jewish thought. Judaism was not ultimately willing to opt entirely for timeless sanctification over meaningful human action.

In what follows, we will consider some modern Jewish philosophical treatments of this-worldly redemption. Realistic messianism, with its tempered, demythologized view of a messianic age and its relative confidence in the efficacy of human moral action has seemed a better candidate for modern Jews than apocalyptic, utopian, or frankly supernatural versions of redemption. Moral action per se has fundamental value in Jewish thought. But how far does the writ of its meaning run? The modern Jewish thinkers – we shall consider Hermann Cohen, Steven Schwarzschild, and Kenneth Seeskin – construe the meaning of action qua contribution to redemption in a highly rationalistic way. Nonetheless, the elimination of mythic, fantastic elements does not prevent absurdities from arising. Human action has built in futility and hence a trace of the absurd.

But perhaps, from the stern perspective of nihilism, all of these pious hopes for human action or for finding deep, unimpeachable meaning in human experience are mere wishful thinking. In the philosophical section of the chapter, we will consider James Tartaglia's critique of ascribing any transcendent meaning to human agency, indeed, to human existence. He takes nihilism as the simple truth of our being in the world: Ultimately, nothing means anything. This needn't, for Tartaglia, embitter us. Indeed, realizing nihilism as a basic truth about the world frees us to live without the burdens of higher expectations. Ironically, nihilism becomes a kind of resolution of the human dilemma – a secular surrogate for redemption. If that is correct, however, it seems even more absurd than the piety it scorns.

REDEMPTION: MAIMONIDES

Modern Jewish reflections on redemption, especially in a philosophical key, draw from Maimonides. Maimonides presents a highly rationalistic picture of the messianic age. In his code, the Mishneh Torah, Maimonides writes:

> The Messiah will arise and restore the kingdom of David to its former might. He will rebuild the sanctuary and gather the dispersed of Israel. All the laws will be reinstituted in his days as of old .... Do not think that the Messiah needs to perform signs and miracles, bring about a new state of things in the world, revive the dead, and the like. It is not so .... Rather it is the case in these matters that the statutes of our Torah are valid forever and eternally. Nothing can be added to them or taken away from them. And if there arise a king from the House of David who meditates on the Torah and practices its commandments like his ancestor David in accordance with the Written and Oral Law, prevails upon all Israel to walk in the ways of the Torah and to repair its breaches, and fights the battles of the Lord, then one may properly assume that he is the Messiah. If he is then successful in rebuilding the sanctuary on its site and in gathering

> the dispersed of Israel, then he has in fact proven himself to be the Messiah. He will then arrange the whole world to serve only God, as it is said: "For then shall I create a pure language for the peoples that they may all call upon the name of God and serve him with one accord" (Zephaniah 3:9). Let no one think that in the days of the Messiah anything of the natural course of the world will cease or that any innovation will be introduced into creation. Rather, the world will continue in its accustomed course. (Laws of Kings: chapters 11–12 (selections))[24]

Maimonides goes on to explain that the utopian view of Isaiah 11:6 ("The wolf shall dwell with the lamb, the leopard lie down with the kid") and all similar passages must be understood as parables. Israel is the vulnerable animal that will dwell securely among the heathen nations, now emptied of their violence by their conversion to the worship of the one, true God. He confirms his realist view by citing the famous dictum of Samuel noted above.

Maimonides' realist view was taken up and given currency by a rationalist follower, Rabbi David Kimchi (d. 1235).[25] It also provoked dissent. A contemporary commentator on the Mishneh Torah, Rabbi Abraham ben David of Posquieres (d. 1198), rejected the assertion that nature will remain the same. Does the Torah not promise that dangerous beasts will be banished from the land? The Torah's promise contradicts Maimonides's postulate of an unchanging nature.[26] For his part, Maimonides cautioned his readers not to dwell on the symbols and images of the messianic age. "Therefore, a person should never occupy himself a great deal with the legendary accounts nor spend much time with the Midrashim dealing with these and similar matters. He should not regard them as of prime importance since devoting himself to them leads neither to the fear nor to the love of God" (Laws of Kings,12:2).[27]

Maimonides does not want us to indulge in eschatological fantasies. He takes the rabbinic descriptions of a paradisiacal age and, while not refuting or completely demythologizing them, minimizes their importance. Furthermore, the messianic age must *not* be understood as a reward for righteousness. There is no question of a crude quid pro quo. Redemption is a condition for the complete devotion to wisdom, that is, to the Torah. The messianic age will remove the externalities that inhibit us from total dedication to the way of wisdom and truth. In the messianic age, we will at last have the liberty to join a fellowship of the righteous where all our days can be spent in study. Both the messiah and the rest of us (even the resurrected ones) will eventually die and go on to the last stage, the world to come. That is the world of eternal knowledge of God achieved in the presence of God. The "'crowns on their [the righteous'] heads' signify the immortality of the soul being in firm possession of the Idea which is God the Creator. The 'crown" is precisely the Idea which great philosophers have explicated at length."[28] The righteous will exist *eternally* qua souls, "forever involved with the existence of God the Creator, who is the cause and source of its existence and goal."[29]

It is important to underscore that Maimonides does not view this state of complete beatitude as a reward for a life well lived. Redemption is not compensation. The Torah, as divine wisdom, is a good in itself. The learning and living of it is of intrinsic, not instrumental, value. One doesn't learn and practice Torah for the sake of some allegedly higher good, some further reward. Torah is its own reward. Knowledge of God – the core of the Torah – is the ultimate end. A life – indeed, an afterlife – lived in pursuit of this knowledge is the only truly meaningful life. All of our worldly activity should be focused on this end (with a crucial caveat):

> Nevertheless, even though this is the end we seek, he who wishes to serve God out of love *should not serve Him to attain the world to come.* He should rather believe that wisdom exists, that this wisdom is the Torah; that the Torah was given [to] the prophets by God the Creator; that in the Torah He taught us the virtues, which are the commandments, and vices, that are sins. As a decent man, one must cultivate the virtues and avoid the sins.

> In so doing, he will perfect the specifically human which resides in him and will be genuinely different from the animals. When one becomes fully human, he acquires the nature of the perfect human being .... His soul thus attains the eternal life it has come to know, which is the world to come ....[30]

As a virtue ethicist, Maimonides would have us perform what is right for its own sake. The highest virtue is the intellectual love of God. We enact this now when we are living in the highest way. Thus, Maimonides teaches a version of "actualized redemption." We can experience consummation now, although the enduring enactment of this virtue in the world to come still awaits. Insofar as our living in the highest way is an actualized redemption, the focus of redemption shifts from a this-worldly social–political messianic kingdom to a transcendent state of intellectual–spiritual *communio dei*. Now, in the midst of this world, it is imperfect. Then, in the eternity of the world to come, communion will be consummate and constant. (Is this resistant to Williams's worry about the boredom of immortality? Our nature would be so radically changed that we would no longer be the kind of being who could feel boredom. But would we then no longer be ourselves?)

Modern Jewish philosophical reclamations of messianism and redemption tend to appropriate the realistic this-worldly dimension of Maimonides's vision and to bracket the metaphysical dimension of beatific communion. The loss of the latter puts all of the weight on the ethical and political dimensions of the former. That is too much weight, I will argue, for the hopeful vision of a redeemed world to bear. It invites, more than does Maimonides's integrated ethical–metaphysical vision, absurdist consequences. These emerge in the leading modern Jewish rationalist, Hermann Cohen (1842–1918).

REDEMPTION: HERMANN COHEN

Hermann Cohen saw in the messianic idea the highest realization of the implicit promise of monotheism.[31] Cohen fuses elements of

Maimonides with an idealist interpretation of Kant. (Cohen's "neo-Kantianism" makes for the rejection of the metaphysical side of Maimonides' vision of the afterlife.) He adopts Kant's progressive reading of the trajectory of human history and crowns it with the Jewish concept of a this-worldly messianic age. The one humanity, created by the one God, will recover its oneness in the fullness of the future through its hopeful and persistent practice of ethics in the present. Ethics is the heart, although not exactly the entirety, of religion for Cohen. Ethics is actionable and social. When directed to society as a whole, ethics implies the pursuit of a morally grounded socialist politics.[32] Human action can be realized by politics. A morally infused politics is, for Cohen, the work of realistic messianism. This is the content and ultimate end of Judaism.

For Cohen, Israel's central philosophical insight is that God is unique. "Hear, O Israel, the Lord our God, the Lord is One!" (Deuteronomy 6:4) does not assert that there is one God as opposed to many gods, in a numerical sense.[33] Rather, it asserts the uniqueness of God: God is wholly unlike everything in his creation. For Maimonides, who shares this central insight, the uniqueness of God has primarily metaphysical and epistemological consequences. For the neo-Kantian Cohen, the uniqueness of God is correlated with the uniqueness of the Jewish people who are in turn constituted by their unique ethical task. That task is to work for the redemption of humanity by acting in a way that preserves and honors the ethical ideal of human unity.

The factual pluralization of humanity into nations requires an ideal counterweight. The idea of a unified humanity is made present in the concept of the one people, Israel. Israel is not just another people; it did not come into being in a *natural* way and, furthermore, its very existence is constituted by an *ethical* calling. Until the actual achievement in history, via ethical–political action, of the messianic age, the Jews are required to retain their exemplary oneness as a sign, symbol, and, tragically, a provocation to the nations. The Jews – one people in all the earth – are made to suffer, with sufferings of divine love, for the messianic cause, which flows from the deepest logic of monotheism.

The biblical prophets discovered the idea or ideal of a unified humanity made in the image of God. This insight gives rise to the emotion, indeed, the Hebraic virtue, of compassion. Compassion recognizes the poor, the widow, the orphan, the marginal one, and the ethnic or national other as our fellow human being. That recognition, however, is not enough. To make compassion historically effective as a force for political and social justice, one needs science. One needs Jerusalem and Athens or, in Cohen's idiom, the prophets and Plato. Cohen trusts that the modern sciences of sociology, politics, and economics, fueled by prophetic compassion, can buttress a scientifically based socialism that can work toward the holy task. Cohen's is a religious socialism, articulated politically along social democratic lines. It is in this sense that Cohen embraces a political messianism as the principal object of meaningful, redemptive human action. A hopeful, rational faith in God culminates in the messianic idea of a united humanity, living together in peace and justice. The path to this eschaton, the messianic praxis, is social ethics realized through democratic socialism.

Cohen's philosophy, the leading modern expression of Jewish rationalism, struggles mightily to wed Kant's theory of knowledge and ethics to traditional Jewish faith, as exemplified by earlier, demythologizing rationalists such as Maimonides. Yet Cohen, who stands much further than Maimonides from traditional religion, wagers more on the significance of human agency than his Talmudic and medieval predecessors. For Cohen, democratic socialism is both praxis and telos. The commandments of the Torah, reconceptualized along mostly ethical lines, must suffice to bring about the messianic age. Strictly speaking, however, Cohen's view is that *the messianic age is always approaching but will never fully arrive.*[34] This is because the tasks of ethics are infinite.

Cohen visualizes this infinitude as an asymptote, a curve infinitely approaching but never intersecting an axis.[35] We can progress, if we will, toward perfection, but we will never achieve it. Nonetheless, progress is real; social amelioration can occur; ever higher levels of political and economic justice can be achieved. Like Kant, Cohen believes that history ought to be interpreted as a narrative of progress. This has less to do with description than with normative orientation: We *ought to* believe that our moral and political acts improve the world in order to sustain confidence in our own action and hope for redemption. Without that confident teleology, no commitment to ethics could be sustained. These themes are taken up by Cohen's late twentieth-century protégé, Steven Schwarzschild.

REDEMPTION: STEVEN SCHWARZSCHILD

Steven Schwarzschild, an explicit devotee of Cohen, gives Cohen's view that the messiah cannot, in principle, arrive a precise formulation:

> The eternal futurity of the Messiah, translated into operational language, asserts that no smallest time-unit nor any smallest space-unit in the universe is as yet, or will ever have been, redeemed. Indeed, what is asserted is that the universe is always infinitely different from what God wants it to be and what we must, therefore, make it, insofar as this lies within and perhaps beyond our power.[36]

Schwarzschild acknowledges that the view that the messiah cannot come but "will always be coming" is a "radical assertion." He makes it for two reasons. First, the infinite postponement of the messiah militates against mythologizing him, a temptation "to which, above all, Christianity has fallen prey."[37] Second, "it makes humanity's ethical (and, indeed, scientific) tasks not an interim obligation but a perpetual (if you please, metaphysical) destiny."[38] The eternal delay of the messianic advent gives rise to an "eternal moral striving." "The striving toward total human morality on earth ("the Messianic kingdom") continues beyond any and all individual human lives: This is what we call "history." It consists of the infinite and, therefore, never-completed spiritualization of the human universe. "The regulatively postulated completion of that infinite historical process of spiritualization is what is called 'the coming of the Messiah'."[39]

Schwarzschild is building here on Cohen's view that the concept of eternity should properly be understood not as an infinite stretch of time but as an absolute, continuous moral obligation. In his Kantian, ethicizing manner, Cohen claimed that eternity (*Ewigkeit*) means that there can be no rest (*keinen Stillstand*) for the pure, that is, ethical will and for one's self-consciousness as a moral being.[40] Eternity becomes a "regulative concept." That is, it orients thought and will and governs action rather than identifies some alleged metaphysical truth about time.

On Schwarzschild's account, following Cohen, Jewish messianism as a Kantian regulative idea is the telos that orients moral striving. The messiah cannot (literally) come because the messiah is an ideal, a fictive depiction of a norm. Furthermore, the concept of the messiah is not only a normative goal but a normative ground. Schwarzschild argues that "messianism in fact operates ... as a direct *producer of moral values* and as an intermediate criterion of proper action in any and every situation."[41] Just as in Kant the (quasi-messianic) Kingdom of Ends is to be the regulative ideal for practical reason, so in Schwarzschild, the (unreachable) end of the messianic age should launch and orient moral action. The unbridgeable logical gap between "is" and "ought" necessitates an insuperable historical gap between our age and the messianic age. But if the messianic age is incapable, in principle, of arriving what sense is there in referring to it as an "age" at all?

Unlike Cohen, Schwarzschild does not allow theological views to map completely onto ethical ones. Schwarzschild invokes God's grace, which will close the gap that no human action can bridge. Yet, he also seems to retract it as soon as he invokes it:

> God's saving hand may force the end at any time that he determines .... The final upshot, then, of the dialectic of grace and ethics in Jewish eschatology is this: salvation may come about by works or by grace, but, in the first place, grace is indispensable to works themselves, and, in the second place, salvation by grace

> alone would be such a horrifying experience – morally atrocious and experientially painful – that humanity will not choose it as the way to the goal: "May he [the Messiah] come, but let me not see it." Thus, ethics remains the only actionable course."[42]

Schwarzschild thus admits that God, through grace, could bring the messianic age and could close the otherwise enduring gap but that such a miraculous eruption would be "horrifying." Precisely why it would be horrifying he does not say; he relies only on the rabbinic belief in the "birth pangs of the messiah," citing a twice repeated saying in B. Sanhedrin 98b of sages who hope for the messiah but do not want to be alive in the days immediately before his coming. The Talmudic saying assumes the apocalyptic tradition, which postulates great travail prior to the messianic advent.

More is going on in Schwarzschild's usage of this doctrine, however, than the assumption of its literal truth, in which one doubts he actually believed. Schwarzschild is insisting here on human moral integrity. Human beings should choose the way of ethics over passive reliance on grace insofar as it would be "horrifying" to be given a world one is unworthy of receiving. How could less than moral persons live in a fully realized moral world? Unless that world, however asymptotically, is achieved through human moral performance, humans could not inhabit it without destroying it, hence the imperative of realism over apocalypticism. Accordingly, ethics remains the only plausible option for messianism. Judaism, Schwarzschild concludes, is "actionable messianism."[43]

In commenting on his Cohenian understanding of messianism shortly before his death, Schwarzschild wrote "infinite ideals rather than empirical expectation are, or ought to be, the incentive to human life and history."[44] Messianism as infinite task precludes the false hope that typifies utopianism. It fully embraces the goal of achieving the *summum bonum* for human beings on earth and in history. Yet it also affirms that the *summum bonum* cannot be achieved; it can only be ever more finely approximated. Redemption on this account is nonutopian, but it also reveals a trace of the absurd. This is because while messianism as an infinite task cannot be *falsified*, it can also not be *realized*. The obligation to work for it has the immaculate aloofness of the categorical imperative. And yet we must try in all of our deeds to aim at its realization. This inner tension may symbolize nothing more than the mishna's classic statement that "it is not your duty to finish the work, but neither are you free to desist from it" (Pirkei Avot 2:16) or it may be more deeply problematic. It may open an abyss of paradox and hint at the absurd.

Schwarzschild, although stressing the necessity of human action, continues to try to balance it with divine grace. He writes that to see Jewish history as solely the province of human action is "to leave God and his covenantal promise out of account."[45] Schwarzschild seeks to balance, in his language, ethics and metaphysics. Ethics alone runs into absurdity. Metaphysics alone runs into futility. The linkage of the two undergirds resilient Jewish faith. His thinking is more faithful to traditional Judaism, on my reading, than that of Cohen or Seeskin. But, in both, the tension between human action and Divine grace in bringing about the messianic age remains unresolved.

REDEMPTION: KENNETH SEESKIN

The gap between messianic realism and ethical perfectionism generates absurdity. Accepting a realistic account of messianism, we think that our actions in the world can contribute to a redemptive "resolution of the tragic dimension of the human condition." Yet, on Cohen's and Schwarzschild's highly Platonizing accounts of the ethical ideal, ideals by definition cannot be realized. Our local instantiations of the Good necessarily fail to capture the full, ideal amplitude of value. The axiology in play holds that value is but another name for "what Plato called the idea of ideas, the good, God."[46] Our likeness to God permits, indeed requires, that we act ethically. But our unlikeness ensures that our ethics falls short. The result is an "infinite deferral" of the messiah, which is to say, of the messianic age.[47]

This is partially alleviated in Schwarzschild by his traditional faith in divine grace. It remains fully problematic in Cohen.

Seeskin senses the absurdity at the heart of an infinitely deferred messianic advent and makes it thematic.[48] His solution is to relax the tension between messianic realism and ethical perfectionism through diminishing expectations. His depiction of the messianic age goes beyond Samuel and Maimonides. The age *will* arrive, with sufficient human striving, but it will provide no more than a decent institutional and political framework in which moral lives will still need to be led. Building on Maimonides, Seeskin envisions no miraculous transformation of human nature.[49] The age will banish neither vice nor sin. What it will do is give human beings continual opportunities to practice virtues, improve their moral judgment, increase their knowledge of God (qua moral exemplar), and work toward ethical advancement. The hard work of morality will not cease in the messianic age. By contrast, it will become the focus of life:

> Let us therefore admit that there will always be things a morally responsible person needs to do and decisions a morally responsible society needs to make. Let us also admit that the Messiah will not change this. The legislature will still meet, courts will still decide cases, and voices of dissent still need to be heard. All the Messiah will do is get society to make its decisions in conformity with moral demands rather than a chorus of individual interests.[50]

Seeskin thus holds onto the infinite moral task but puts it at the level of the individual. The messianic age will be substantially like our own but better in crucial ways. It will be a durably good society, a kind of Kantian cosmopolis of perpetual peace. Messianism becomes an achievable social, economic, and political framework in which individuals can conduct their infinitely demanding ethical lives. A certain amount of moral transformation, of "moral awakening," will take place, as better education – a kind of liberal, democratic "knowledge of God" – spreads in the good society.[51] Nonetheless, intellectual and value pluralism – goods not envisaged by Maimonides – will flourish. What will not flourish are invidious, mythical, and cruel misunderstandings of religion: "In simple terms, redemption implies the end of fanaticism. What it does not imply is the end of dissent. Instead of fanatics, we will have the opposite: skeptics, atheists, agnostics and a range of other options to consider."[52]

A free, dignified, sovereign society will allow people their own experiments in living and continuous refinement of mind. In short, the messianic age will be like a lifetime of work and study at a fine university, with free tuition. Such is Seeskin's modern American take on the divine yeshivah of rabbinic imagination. It is, in its "realistic" way, quite utopian.

Although Seeskin breaks from Cohen and Schwarzschild in arguing that the messianic age *is* achievable if only we had enough political and moral will, his view is not free from absurdity. Infinite deferral is no longer conceptually necessary, but it is not quite clear why God is necessary on his highly naturalistic view. Following Maimonides, the age will be one where the "earth is full of the knowledge of the Lord," which means that many people will be aware of – and inspired by – God's exemplary moral goodness. They will strive to be holy, that is, to be morally exemplary. But, given that the age comes as a result of human striving, what exactly does God have to do with it? For neither Cohen nor Seeskin does God actually intervene or act in history. There are no miraculous dimensions to messianism. Allowing for Schwarzschild's qualified dissent, such is redemption on the modern Jewish account.

Cohen, Schwarzschild, and Seeskin work within a Kantian context. For Kant, God is an idea that must be thought in order for ethics to have validity in an otherwise natural, causally governed world. All we can really know of God is that the moral world and the physical world can't hang together without a concept of divinity. God is, minimally, a postulate that makes for the ultimate coherence of the moral law and the laws of nature.[53] Belief in God (*Glaube*) is less a cognitive commitment to the existence of a supersensible being than it is an attitude of hope.[54] To believe in God is to believe in the possibility of our betterment with God's assistance, although how that assistance might be possible is uncertain. Hence, the necessity of hope.

Cohen has somewhat different worries than Kant, but he too avoids ontological language when it comes to God. For Cohen, God is not a supernatural entity with independent agency, miraculously intervening in nature and in history. The concept of God is "correlated" with the concept of humanity, which means that the two ideas are inseparably linked – and linked in a such a way that ethics is essential to the definition of both.[55] Cohen speaks constantly about God and what God does – forgiving humans on the Day of Atonement, for example. But this apparently pious, naïve discourse doesn't have any ontological purchase.[56] When decoded, it is about ethical commitments and transformations, and moral projects and processes. Although Cohen gave religion ever more thickness of description and ceased explicitly to reduce it to ethics, the ethical meaning of religion remains primary if not exhaustive. There are no supersensible entities to be described in Cohen's discourse, because no supersensible entities exist. God is an ethical Idea.[57]

The absence of God in any sense other than as a correlate of the ideal concept of a moral humanity persists in Seeskin. Seeskin's Maimonidean God is, in principle, "distant." Thus:

> Revelation is not a case of God's choosing to speak with Moses but of Moses' coming to understand the will of God. Repentance is not a case of God's granting mercy to y but of y's deciding to redirect the course of her life. Love is not a case of God's dispensing special favors on z but of z's coming to feel awe and humility in the presence of God.[58]

There is no primary religious experience or encounter with God. We reach God conceptually, through peeling away positive ascriptions and negating any predicate that we can imagine applies to God.

Seeskin's apophatic or negative theological method has a broadly ethical upshot. Demythologizing God and the messianic age wards off complacency, passivity, chauvinism, and gnosticism. But it also cuts any cords between God and history. God doesn't seem to do anything in the world, post-Creation, other than invite our moral adoration and emulation. The moral ideals of the Torah and the prospect of a humanly achieved messianic age are unfalsifiable on empirical grounds. That, of course, is in the nature of moral ideals. If they were subject to a veto by majority vote, that is, by how the majority of any given society actually behaves, they would lose their authority. A society deeply marked by personal, social, and political injustice, Seeskin wants to say, does not invalidate justice. It puts itself, rather, under severe critique, from a God's eye ethical point of view.

The Holocaust, for example, does not invalidate Cohenian (and biblical) ideals of humanity. We would not be in a position to denounce the infinite evil of Nazism if the idea of a shared humanity founded on respect for human dignity died at Auschwitz. This ideal cannot be falsified by history; it is exempt from empirical impeachment. Seeskin resists the Hegelian move of seeing the instantiation of ideas in history and, with the passing of an age, the demise of an ideal. He seeks, like Cohen, a transcendental ground for ethics. The upshot for messianism is that, from the empirical fact that no human society has so far achieved redemption, we should not infer that redemption is, in principle, unachievable. One ought to "weaken one's commitment to the principle of induction: [that] what has happened in the past limits what is reasonable to expect from the future."[59] Induction can be relied on for natural occurrences. But a future shaped by human decisions implies, he believes, greater openness and possibility. Although still non-miraculous, profound and unprecedented change may be possible, that is, what we ought to hope for and, indeed, work for.

Why hope over despair? Why action over passivity? I don't think that Seeskin (or Cohen or Schwarzschild) arrives at rational grounds for this fundamental choice. (Nor do I think that he or they can.) Seeskin writes:

> Religion stands in defiance of history. If the record of history is all we have, and a repeat of history all we can hope for, then religion must bow to the demands of *realpolitik*. I take the lesson of the Hebrew prophets to be that society can and must aspire to something more – not just in the next life but in this one, for without such an aspiration, we run the risk that realism will become another name for defeatism, and defeatism and excuse for despair.[60]

The option for hope – the rejection of defeatism and despair – is too basic to be given a rational ground. Perhaps one can say that any argument for hope presupposes it. (By mounting an argument, I would hope to convince myself or you that hope is better than despair.) Hope has a reason that reason doesn't know, as it were. The production of reasons for hope has a circular quality; the decision has already been made.

The thoroughgoing modern transposition of messianism into a non-miraculous key saves it from the excesses of superstitious religiosity but not from a trace of the absurd. Its God is absent and quiescent. Its insistence on a hopeful moral faith is based on the moral necessity of a hopeful moral faith. Its argument, as noted, is circular. If the circularity is vicious, the argument undermines itself. If the circularity is virtuous, we can do no better. The nihilist is convinced the circularity is vicious. Jews and others who are, as the prophet Zechariah put it, "prisoners of hope (Zechariah 9:12)" are convinced that this is the virtuous core of a trusting faith.

Jewish realistic messianism gives human agency, indeed, human life as a whole – a meaning, point, and purpose. It integrates the value of moral action into a meaningful story about the human future in which we try to overcome the tragedy, suffering, and evil of the human condition. It is courageous to affirm the value and meaning of hope, especially in the absence of traditional faith in a God who enters history. The future is entirely in our hands; "that is all there is."[61] It focuses meaning on purpose. Defying history and repairing the world are what we ought to be about in life. The expectation that we can, against the grain of all history and without a miracle, succeed is what Jewish faith looks like on the modern redemptive story. We should believe both that there are no guarantees of our success and that the ideals that fund our praxis are somehow written into, if not the starry heavens above, then the moral law within.

But the starry heavens above are not irrelevant. The singular focus on human action in resolving the contradictions of the human condition does not take into account the *hevel havalim* of cosmic extinction. That is beyond its purview. But if we are right, as I suggested at the beginning of this chapter, not to avert our eyes from that presumed "end of days," the modern Jewish redemptive view looks insufficient. It doesn't have the resources to cope with the challenge of ultimate extinction and thereby may well concede the argument to nihilism. To counter that challenge, it would need to reappropriate something like Maimonides's version of an afterlife, a genuinely transcendent scenario at odds with its basic, this-worldly tendency. To the extent that modernist versions of redemption reject transcendence, their hopes seem somewhat absurd.

NO REDEMPTION: JAMES TARTAGLIA

In Chapter 1, we observed that A. J. Ayer approved of Macbeth's characterization of life as "a tale told by an idiot, full of sound and fury, signifying nothing," while disagreeing with the "aura of disillusionment" that emanates from the speech. Tartaglia is very much in agreement.

He describes himself as "happy" to be called a nihilist.[62] To be a happy nihilist is to recognize the truth of the matter – that life is ultimately meaningless – and to do so without undue or overwrought emotion. It is simply to get things right, as one might correctly understand the street grid of one's town and make one's way around it. It is pleasing to get things right. Of course, this particular fact of the matter – that one's life along with everyone else's lives is meaningless – is a more important fact than those of urban geography. So, getting it right brings an extra measure of satisfaction.

Counterintuitively, for Tartaglia, nihilism is not a belief or a system of beliefs (an "ism") as much as it is the *factual content* of a belief. It is a "fact" that life is meaningless. One can state these facts: Life is a biological phenomenon. Life evolved on earth. Life has no overall purpose.[63] Qua fact, nihilism should occasion neither disappointment nor stern resolve – no more of an emotional response to it is warranted than toward those other facts about life.[64] Given its fact status, all of the various emotional responses, whether those of bravery or of despondency, are equally arbitrary and unnecessary. We needn't be, unlike Weinberg, "very, very sad." The discovery that life is meaningless would warrant disillusionment if one had thought that life was full of meaning. But one would have been wrong. The factual status of nihilism undercuts any ground for value-fueled disappointment with it. Tartaglia commends an attitude of equanimity:

> For nihilism is not bad. It cannot be. If reality is meaningful, then the meaning of human life might be good, bad, or neither. Thus if reality exists for a reason, this might reveal that human life serves a good purpose. Or it might reveal that some or most of reality serves a good purpose that human life runs counter to. Or it might be that the reason has nothing to do with human notions of good or bad. But if there is *no* reason that reality and hence humans exist then there is no good meaning against which the meaninglessness of human life might be counted bad in comparison. So if nihilism is true, it cannot be good or bad. Rather, nihilism's implication that life is meaningless is best viewed as simply a fact about life ....[65]

If one had started, *per impossibile*, with a calm acceptance of nihilism, then disappointment, anger, bitterness, cynicism, Ecclesiastes-like absurdity, and so on could not have gotten a grip. Of course, for most of us, coming out of the swamp of illusions watered by our historic, religious cultures, we can't help but have started in the wrong place as to seeing life as it is. Most of us thought that life per se is meaningful. Nihilism can't but discomfit us. Nonetheless, we can take this fact onboard and work it into our worldviews. We can learn to live with it, reconstructing our philosophies of life (and of much else) in light of the fact. Essentially, Tartaglia wants to train us to think and live well in light of this discovery.

Why does Tartaglia take nihilism to be a description of fact simpliciter rather than a philosophical belief about a purported fact? He takes the question of the meaning of life – not, in his view, the lesser, evasive, uninteresting questions of meanings *in* life – to be equivalent to: "Why do human beings exist?"[66] This question has a causal sense (How did human beings get here?) *and* a teleological one (What are human beings for?). Both senses are necessary to get to meaning. Thus, any empirical answer – the kind of in principle factual story that science provides – is insufficient to answer the question insofar as it can only address the causal dimension. A scientific answer about mammalian evolution would just initiate a regress. The existence of hominids and hominins calls for further questions about why they exist(ed), which calls in turn for further regressive questions about why antecedent forms of life existed, and so on. Any naturalistic or physicalist answer, however final as to why reality per se exists, leaves unanswered what really motivates the question, which is, "What are human beings (or existence as such) for? Is there a reason (= a value, a purpose) for which human beings exist?" Yet, given what we know of the physical universe as the objective context in which the question is raised, there is no reason to expect a different kind of answer than the brute, causal one.

Tartaglia is committed to what he calls "objective thought" about the objective context for life. He takes this to be the "final context." It may be the case, following Heidegger, that abstract, scientific (objective) thought may have grown out of our humanly immediate interaction with the world, but once emerged, it has a near monopoly, contra Heidegger, on understanding the world correctly. "[E]ven if Heidegger is right that objective thought grew out of our everyday understanding of the world, it does not follow that the understanding that it provides is less fundamental. This is because objective thought's abstraction from human concerns provides a *more comprehensive and explanatorily powerful way* of understanding the world ...."[67]

For Tartaglia, the silence of objective thought on meaning does not so much leave the question open as settle it in the negative. This is because there is no real (explanatorily powerful) alternative to the objective context, the context, that is, where causal explanations rule.

Curiously, that is not because Tartaglia is just a garden variety physicalist. He repudiates physicalism. Much of his book is a working out of the implications of a kind of *transcendence*, without which he thinks that consciousness, for example, is inexplicable if not metaphysically impossible. He endorses a version of transcendence when it comes to explaining consciousness (as well as time and universals).[68] But he doesn't think that transcendence applies to the context in which we ask – and look for an answer to – the meaning question. Why is this?

A "transcendent context" for the question of why human beings exist would posit something beyond the objective world as the domain in which meaning could be discovered. Tartaglia admits that this is logically possible. He treats this as an idle possibility, however. He doesn't believe that it is a live option.

> Thus, if the physical universe were transcended by a final context of meaning, then an account of the purposes of things would not culminate in the brute fact of the meaninglessness of existence, but rather in the fact of purposeful existence .... However, although we cannot rule out the possibility, we have no good reason to believe it either. For even if the physical universe does exist within a transcendent context, there is no reason this should be a context of meaning or one in which human life has an overall purpose. All this is possible, *but possibility is cheap*.[69]

"Possibility," he writes elsewhere, "is superstition's life-blood."[70]

Tartaglia is convinced that it is futile to posit or search for a transcendent context. It is too discontinuous with everything we know through objective thought about physical reality to be worth stipulating. Furthermore, the urge to do so seems to be rooted not in the objective world as such but in the teleology-seeking propensity of our minds. That we are used to "applying teleological concepts" is no indication that a teleologically ultimate transcendent context applies or exists.[71]

In sum, Tartaglia is convinced both of the objective reality of the physical *and* that reality exceeds the physical; consciousness is the paradigmatic example of this. Sentient experience is *not* part of the objective order of things. Nonetheless, whatever use some minimal, indescribable transcendent order has for making sense of consciousness (and of our experience of time and our use of universals), it does not extend to meaning. Given the promiscuity of possibility, we can't rule out, but neither can we rule in, a final context that might make sense of our lives. We can imagine a transcendent, teleological context that could prove nihilism false – religions do this all the time – but we don't and can't have one. Thus, with no real possibility of a more than a notional alternative, nihilism – the fact of the meaninglessness of life – stands. There's nothing to do, unless we want to flee from the metaphysical truth, other than to accept this fact and live in light of it.

How do we accept this "fact" and still find meaning in our lives? Rather like Weinberg, Tartaglia sees a metaphysical gap between ultimate meaninglessness and proximate "social meaning" or "social worth." We live in "frameworks" of culturally and socially contrived values and meanings. It has always been so. It is what blinds us to the truth of nihilism, although flashes of awareness break through the framework from time to time. Tartaglia does not exactly want to disabuse us of the socially manufactured meaning that we have but only to show us its arbitrary, nonultimate character. When viewed as if from nowhere, from the perspective of nihilism, the meanings by which we live lack grounding. Furthermore, from the metaphysical height of nihilism, he wants to show us that none of the various ways modern philosophy has tried to ground social meaning really work. Modern philosophy wants to substitute "meaning in" for "meaning of," thinking that by changing the question it will avoid having to admit the nihilistic answer. Were modern philosophy to realize that nihilism is nothing to be avoided, it wouldn't have to artificially inflate the value of social meaning. It could let social meaning be the unjustified, arbitrary, culturally conditioned framework that it is. We can commit to the latter and take it seriously while recognizing that it is fundamentally a charade.

Tartaglia consistently reaches a view that empties humanly recognizable value from objective thought and from the objective world. (Recall: "Objective thought's abstraction from human concerns provides a more comprehensive and explanatorily powerful way of understanding the world ....") Value resides in the human world – by fiat or agreement – but has no deeper anchorage when seen from the detached perspective from which we pursue questions of fact or from which we ask the meaning question. Thus:

> None of this [the meaninglessness of reality] implies that things cannot be good or bad *within* life; murder is bad, as I see it, because there is a well-informed social consensus to evaluate it as bad. The consensus is not wrong because there is no good reason for humans to exist, because now that we do, we have found plenty of good reasons to carry on.[72]

The "consensus" that murder is wrong needs no ground other than our social agreement. Having decided "to carry on," despite the lack of a reason to exist in the first place, the species, one imagines, has a right to set up some groundless ground rules. (Recall Ayer's need for "a rule.") The rules, however, are not licensed by our reason-free "thrownness" into being, nor are they grounded in the biological imperatives that characterize our existence as parts of nature. We have outstripped those imperatives. All that is of human value is invented and arbitrary.

It is imperative, for Tartaglia, that we all recognize this. Openings for such understanding constantly present themselves. We notice, for example, that the very young play games, the very old devise things to pass the time, and others, during their "productive" years, are involved in a framework of activities that satisfy, if they are lucky, their ambitions and desires. From the midst of life, we can look at what the young and the old do as trivial, manufactured pastimes. We take our own activities to have importance and meaning. But with further reflection, we can realize that our activities are equally time-filling and arbitrary. Our action is meaningful only relative to the "framework," which is a product of fiat and consensus. From an abstract perspective, where the meaninglessness of life becomes fully apparent, all of these activities are equally inessential. "In truth, the same situation holds throughout life: *there is nothing we ever have to do.*"[73] In all cases of human activity, "the purpose is made up within a life that has no purpose of its own."[74] Our "highest" purpose seems to be to make sense of why we cannot make sense of life. When we accept the brute fact of meaninglessness – nihilism – we come to the blank signpost at the end of the road of sensemaking.

There is no redemptive agenda here. No "authentic" life beckons. Tartaglia commends the view from nowhere not to liberate us but merely to help us "view our lives more objectively by viewing our goals as another aspect of life to be described." There are no ethical ends to realize here; the objectivizing view is "completely indifferent to questions concerning autonomy and self-determination."[75] We "need" to step back from our socially constructed framework of practical activity only to grasp something theoretical: "that there is no overall point to life." This perspective is so denuded of human value that from its vantage point, Tartaglia remarks, we appear to ourselves as no more than noisy objects. "The quickest and easiest way to do this [i.e. achieve a detached view] is to retreat to a physical perspective and think of human life as consisting in bodies moving around and making noises."[76] By doing so, we become so disengaged that we cannot view our actions *as* actions but only as meaningless happenings, which, outside the social framework, they are.

What is so valuable about discovering the fact of nihilism, of living in awareness of its truth? Why ought we to assume a stance that delivers (a presumed) truth? Of what value is truth? Is it more than just another socially meaningful epistemic/ethical norm? Does truth have a transcendent value such that it is compelling outside of the framework? It is hard to see how it could have such value on Tartaglia's account, but, on the other hand, truth does seem to be a kind of deliverance from beyond, from outside of the framework of social meaning. If there is a transcendent context in which to put the objective world and arrive at an answer to the question of the meaning of human existence, truth would seem to be its sign or trace. It is unclear what sense Tartaglia's intimation of normativity – we ought (or "need") to step outside the framework to realize the truth of nihilism – can have unless the imperative of pursuing truth is a nonarbitrary goal.

What is difficult to accept here is not the deflationary but familiar claim that ultimate meaning is, in principle, unavailable; it is the etiolated picture of normativity and human agency. Tartaglia imagines a world so brute that reality asks nothing of us. "There is nothing we ever have to do." When we encounter a person who cries to us for help; when we encounter the plea in the eyes of another not to hurt them; when we encounter an abandoned corpse that ought to be buried; when we have a child that needs to be cared for and loved – are these phenomena adequately explained by our voluntary adherence to arbitrary, culturally contingent social norms? Do we know, with Tartaglia-level conviction that there is no natural normativity that underwrites the authority of the claims that beings make on us? Do we know that value is not built into being? Why is Tartaglia so certain that we can achieve a purified, value-free perspective that reveals to us a world devoid of value and meaning? Recall the view of Stroud in Chapter 1, that purging value and value properties from the world is only possible if we can secure a "metaphysically purified" perspective in which brute facts appear without any evaluative accompaniment.[77] But to secure such a perspective, we would need a metaphysical argument. That argument could not avoid relying on values such as validity, truth, coherence, and reasonableness. The needed value-free perspective would be self-impeaching. "Objectivity" in Tartaglia's "objective thought" is itself a value. An objective claim comes with the demand that we believe it. It is hard to see how the implicit normativity of fact is merely an artifact of social and cultural practice. Our human orientation toward truth and toward a normatively demanding rationality seems to run deeper than the values supported by "social meaning."

Tartaglia's divestment of value from our being human is an act of violence toward ourselves. If we can't recognize our actions as actions because we ought to see ourselves as noisy objects, subject to the laws of physics, we subvert our aspiration to reach explanatory adequacy. If Tartaglia rejects the objective view as insufficient when it comes to explaining our intuitions about sentience, why should he accept its sufficiency when it comes to explaining our intuitions about the value and meaning of our lives?

Tartaglia's picture of isolated, anomic selves, who detach from the social framework in order to view its norms as alien and arbitrary, who find reality a blank biological slate devoid of teleology and value, and who are driven by desires and so devise projects to fulfill them is a modern picture. Its moral anthropology is that of Cartesian selves, existing as bare egos, as centers of consciousness prior to sociality, community, history, and tradition. (Recall Jacobi's critique of Fichte qua nihilist.) It assumes that all commitments are acts of will made in furtherance of the desires of an atomized self. It denies our fundamental, constitutive sociality. It denies that if we transgress the proper claims that beings make on us – the baby in its sheer being claiming that we care for it – we transgress nothing more than the norms of some contingent frameworks that we ourselves have chosen. On Tartaglia's view, we do not transgress against a deeper norm of being, for there are no such norms. The persons who inhabit the

Tartaglian picture may pride themselves on being metaphysically clear-sighted, objective knowers, but they are hypocritical actors, to the extent that they are actors at all. They have to commit themselves to their chosen projects in order to live, but they can't believe, if they are honest, that their projects have any real worth. Their projects are at most ways of maximizing the chances of fulfilling desires that are themselves arbitrary and meaningless. *It is impossible for ultimate meaninglessness not to seep down and infect social meaningfulness, at least for thinking beings.*

Tartaglia doesn't accept this criticism. He claims that "there is nothing to" the view that

> [J]ust because our goals are not imposed from on high, and we realize this, it does not follow that we cannot commit to them; because the framework is the principal source of our commitment and gets on perfectly well without metaphysical reinforcement. We see this clearly in sport, where commitment is often total, with or without the waning motivation of religious glorification through athletic achievement.[78]

No doubt some athletes believe that the immanent goods of health, success in competition, excitement, flow states, fame, wealth, etc. are sufficient criteria for a life worth living. One would not want to deprive them of such social meanings. But although sports is a pastime or, for a few, a career, is it a life? Are games sufficient to fill a life or, to put it in another way, is life only a game? The metaphor is incompatible with moral seriousness. Nor can serious moral claims, dilemmas, demands, heroism, and tragedy be illumined on this model.

Tartaglia's answer is to deny that ethical normativity *has* any distinctive force or stature. It is just a kind of strong desire that has been systematically misrepresented by the social framework. He deflates the "feeling that one has to do things" (already a trivialized and self-impeaching formulation of ethical obligation) into a "particularly strong form of desire."[79]

> What has happened is that our desire to do things has disguised itself as *having* to do things, as if there were a meaning of life impelling us. Feeling that you have to do something is a particularly strong form of desire .... The social framework we live within, which has been building up over the course of history makes it seem that our lives have an overall point, thereby disguising desires as absolute imperatives.[80]

This is all an illusion, however. Tartaglia levels distinctions among types of "desire," such as the desire to play golf versus the desire to earn a living to support yourself and your loved ones versus the desire not to harm people gratuitously. Although one can rank these in importance from the viewpoint of the social framework, they are all *mere desires* from the detached perspective. Equivalent in their objective meaninglessness, none can properly be construed as "absolute imperatives." There are no such things.

The entire ethical field of life with others, of responsibilities, as Jewish sources say, *beyn adam l'ḥavero*, between persons, essentially disappears. These responsibilities, redescribed as the desires of isolated selves, cannot disclose a deeper meaning. "[E]ven if my life has a strong social narrative that dovetails with various other lives from start to finish ... there remains a clear sense in which there would still be no overall point to my life. It may have a point within other lives, but only *within other lives that have no point.*"[81]

Although Tartaglia is not a cruel nihilist from a nineteenth-century Russian novel who actively works to shatter the social framework and can envision nothing beyond ecstatic destruction, his theoretical view comes to the same thing. The insistence that the lives of others "have no point" undermines commitment to the protection, love, respect for, and responsibility to others as a central theme of one's own life and a pillar of its meaningfulness. It undermines the justice of their claims if we always have to qualify them by thinking "yes, they are just from a social point of view but they are ultimately meaningless." That is one thought too many. We cannot find meaning in ethical relations with others when we "need" to remind ourselves that their lives are as worthless and meaningless as our own. Told that the ultimate truth about us is that we are physical objects, moving around and making noise, we can't help but see our agency as no more meaningful than the acquisitive behavior of any other noisy, mobile animal.

Nihilism leaves us perfectly free to pursue all kinds of goals, ethical ones included, if that is what we think best, or "if that is what you desire; or what society expects of you; or simply for no reason. Nihilism tells us that life has no overall goal, but we can still act as if it did; though any such commitment is our own, not an imposition from reality."[82] Nothing steps out of the world to confront us, to make ethical claims on us. It is all a matter of agent-centered goals and desires. To the extent that Tartaglia has a theory of value, it grows from this assumption.

Although value is "not essential" to what life is, "we value many things, including ourselves. We might not have done so, so this value is not essential to what we are, or to the other things we value. But our capacity to think about and value anything has made us contingently valuable."[83] Thus, whatever arises in the world that can be called a value is an artifact of human desire. That human beings exist, meaninglessly, in the world has occasioned that value exists, meaninglessly, in the world in consequence of human desiring/valuing. Valuing is a fact – but not, as it were, a value. Tartaglia doesn't have a language to ground value qua value. He aims at a philosophical explanation of the normative – that is, of what normativity qua phenomenon is – without entering into normative explanation. That is, he prescinds from standing within the space of value and offering reasons, justifications, defenses, indeed, explanations for which values ought to prevail, what they mean, and so on.

Tartaglia's project is to bracket humanly significant value from objective reality and then to insist that valueless/meaningless objective reality ought to have the last word. This is absurd. I fail to see where the "ought" comes from. So does Tartaglia.

Confronted with philosophical nihilism, we need to choose between a stance that finds value, and hence the possibility of meaning, in being as such and an axiological vacuum, which empties everything of genuine significance. If the choice between these two contrary positions is groundless, it is fully absurd insofar as it would make our choice entirely arbitrary. Although I think that a trace of the absurd confronts us, we have good reasons to choose against nihilism. Our philosophical and religious predecessors have given us indications of the way to go.

Kant sensed a version of this problem. He sought to secure grounds for human freedom, and hence human moral agency, in a universe he believed to be mechanical, causal, and deterministic. Kant denied traditional metaphysics, with its talk of God, the soul, and immortality, the status of knowledge. Although he denied (theoretical) reason a constitutive role, reason, nonetheless, could not simply walk away. Reason remained responsible to life. It needed to make affirmations that preserved our freedom and morality and that sustained the values that religious faith in God once endorsed. Kant argued that reason in its moral capacity had a "need" to affirm God in order to orient our thinking toward moral ends. Critical, theoretical reason, having devastated some of our metaphysical beliefs, could not leave us in a nihilistic vacuum. Moral (practical) reason had its own legitimate needs, without which human life would be less than human.

> But now there enters *the right* of reason's *need*, as a subjective ground for presupposing and assuming something which reason may not presume to know through objective grounds; and consequently, for *orienting* itself in thinking, solely through reason's own need, in that immeasurable space of the supersensible, which for us is filled with dark night.[84]

Under the circumstances occasioned by his own critical philosophy, Kant held that the practical need of reason *outweighed* its theoretical needs. Theoretical reason can get the metaphysical situation right and judge "the first causes of everything contingent." But doing so is optional, a luxury of critical thinkers. Practical reason is more demanding. It is useful not merely "if we want to judge, but because we *have to judge*. For the pure practical use of reason consists in the precepts of moral laws."[85] We have to judge because we have to live. We have to live ethically. We are not, Kant said, "volunteers to morality." To be born is to have been signed up. Being human as such makes claims on us; there are things that we have to do in virtue of our very being as human beings.

For Kant, while theoretical reason is not able to prove (or disprove) the existence of God, practical reason cannot work without believing in God. Practical faith gives "objective reality to the concept of the highest good, i.e., to prevent it, along with morality, from being taken merely as a mere ideal ...."[86] Kant would have no truck with Tartaglia's theoretical endorsement of nihilism-cum-practical assertion of social value and meaning. For Kant, the practical is not a fiction; morality is as real as it gets for human beings.

Although there is much to question in the Kantian account, what is worth preserving is a profound commitment to the ethical domain, to what Martin Buber calls "the interhuman," as constitutive of human nature and stature. Kant recognized the potentially destructive consequences of his critique of theoretical reason. He gave us a rich portrayal of the "metaphysics of morals" not merely as compensation for the weakening of speculative metaphysics but as a domain that is more important, more humanly significant, than that mapped by theoretical reason. Without being able to believe in the centrality of the ethical as the meaning of the human, life would be meaningless. If the consistent assumption of the objective stance leads us to nihilism, to deny what reason needs to affirm about human dignity under the moral law, so much the worse for the objective stance.[87] As Hilary Putnam once put it, "Deconstruction without reconstruction is irresponsibility."[88] Nihilism abandons the work of reconstructing an integrated metaphysical–ethical whole and so falls into irresponsibility.

If we can reclaim the significance of the ethical as the domain in which a worthy and meaningful life can be achieved, we needn't be intimidated by the abstract view as invoked by nihilists, physicalists, and other conversation-stopping reductionists. We can focus on the quality of human action, both in terms of ethical praxis and moral virtue, as the condition for the meaningfulness of life. The Jewish sources, with their fraught tension between incremental amelioration and complete redemption, endorse this approach. They validate human action as something that fundamentally matters. But they, at least traditionally, resist portraying it as the only thing that matters. To the extent that an ultimate resolution of the tensions and tragedies of the human condition is possible, our action cannot be the only thing that matters. But neither could we move in the direction of redemption without it.

NOTES

1 Samuel Scheffler, *Death and the Afterlife* (New York: Oxford University Press, 2016), p. 18

2 Hans Jonas, *The Imperative of Responsibility* (Chicago: University of Chicago Press, 1985).

3 Brian Greene, *Until the End of Time* (New York: Vintage Books, 2020), p. 11.

4 Ibid., p. 13.

5 Ibid., pp. 322–323. For a critique of physics-inspired doomsday projections, see Stephen Toulmin, *The Return of Cosmology* (Berkeley: University of California Press, 1985), pp. 36–39.

6 And yet, Buddhist "emptiness" sustains an ethics of compassion! Transient reality may be, but emptiness does not lead to nihilism in the modern sense.

7 William G. Lycan, "Giving Dualism Its Due," *Australasian Journal of Philosophy*, 87:4 (2009), pp. 551–563. See www.acsu.buffalo.edu/~dh25/seminarofthesoul/Lycan%20-%20Giving%20Dualism%20its%20Due.pdf (accessed January 23, 2022).

8 The great essay on the struggle between the restorative and the apocalyptic in Jewish "messianism" is Gershom Scholem, *The Messianic Idea in Judaism* (New York: Schocken Books, 1971), pp. 1–36.

9 For an excellent set of studies on diverse conceptions and traditions of Jewish messianism, as well as their philosophical implications, see Michael Morgan and Steven Weitzman, *Rethinking the Messianic Idea in Judaism* (Bloomington: Indiana University Press, 2015).

10 Scholem, *The Messianic Idea in Judaism*, p. 13.

11 Cited in Ephraim Urbach, *The Sages*, trans., Israel Abrahams (Cambridge: Harvard University Press, 1994), p. 308 (emphasis added).

12 Ibid., p. 667.

13 For a history of resurrection, see Jon D. Levenson, *Resurrection and the Restoration of Israel* (New Haven: Yale University Press, 2008).

14 Saadia Gaon (d. 942) harmonizes these various tendencies – afterlife vs. resurrection; individual vs. collective redemption; human vs. divine initiative, inter alia – in chapters 6–8 of the *Book of Doctrines and Beliefs*.

15 B. Berakhot 17a. For the righteous, being in God's presence is sufficient nourishment. It is like eating and drinking in this world. Cf. Rashi ad loc.

16 See, for example, Louis Ginzberg, *Legends of the Jews*, I:1. See www.sefaria.org/Legends_of_the_Jews.1.1?lang=bi (accessed January 20, 2022).

17 "The Makropulos Case: Reflections on the Tedium of Immortality" in Bernard William, *Problems of the Self* (Cambridge: Cambridge University Press, 1973), pp. 82–100.

18 The term is Cass Fisher's. For a study of "actualized redemption," that is, redemption in the present, see Fisher, "Actualized Redemption in the Thought of Franz Rosenzweig and Rabbi Joseph B. Soloveitchik," *Naharaim* 2020, 14(2), pp. 173–207. See www.degruyter.com/document/doi/10.1515/naha-2019-0016/html (accessed January 13, 2022).

19 For Scholem, this presentist view characterizes Hasidic teaching. See his "The Neutralization of the Messianic Element in Early Hasidism," in *The Messianic Idea in Judaism*, pp. 176–202.

20 In a related way, Michael Oakeshott writes of actions that are worth doing in themselves, without regard to consequences or the achievement of ends. In action done out of a deep sentiment of enacting one's worth, "Doing is delivered, at least in part, from the deadliness of doing, a deliverance gracefully enjoyed in the quiet of a religious faith." Michael Oakeshott, *On Human Conduct* (Oxford: Clarendon Press, 1975), p. 74.

21 Joseph B. Soloveitchik, *The Lonely Man of Faith* (New York: Doubleday, 2006), pp. 33–34. Cf. Joseph B. Soloveitchik, *Halakhic Man*

(Philadelphia: Jewish Publication Society, 1983), p. 70. For a comparable view, see Martin Buber, *I and Thou*, trans. Walter Kaufmann (New York: Simon & Schuster, 1970), p. 130. Buber describes one's realization that God needs one as much as one needs God as "the meaning of your life" (*der Sinn deines Lebens*). God needs to be the meaning of your life. See also Buber, *Between Man and Man*, p. 98.

22 Jacob Neusner, *Foundations of Judaism* (Philadelphia: Fortress Press, 1989), p. 34.

23 The Jewish people "is at its goal and knew that it was at its goal," according to Rosenzweig in the *Star of Redemption*, cited in Fisher, "Actualized Redemption," p. 185. See also Annette Aronowicz, *Jews and Christians on Time and Eternity* (Stanford: Stanford University Press, 1998), pp. 97–102.

24 Cited in Scholem, *The Messianic Idea in Judaism*, pp. 28–29. Cf. Maimonides's earlier formulation of the days of the messiah in *Perek Ḥelek*, his introductory essay to his commentary on Mishnah Sanhedrin, chapter 10, in Isadore Twersky, *A Maimonides Reader* (Springfield, NJ: Behrman House, 1972), pp. 402–417.

25 Cf. Radak ad loc, where Radak follows Maimonides's demythologizing interpretation but affirms that, although the beasts will not change their nature and cease to kill and eat prey, righteous Israelites living in the land of Israel will nonetheless not be attacked by them in the days of messiah. The popular, if not uncontroversial, commentary of Radak helped "mainstream" Maimonides' rationalistic interpretation. The above treatment of Maimonides and Radak, as well as that of the modern Jewish thinkers Hermann Cohen and Steven Schwarzschild that follows is adapted from my chapter "Messianic Hope," in Robert W. Jensen and Eugene B. Korn, *Covenant and Hope* (Grand Rapids: Eerdmans, 2012) and is reprinted by permission of the publisher.

26 On Ravad's (R. Abraham ben David) view, the beasts will actually change their nature in the land of Israel but will not change in other nations. With regard to the world at large, therefore, the text should be understood, as Maimonides does, allegorically. With regard to Israel, it should be understood in the straightforward, nonallegorical (*peshat*) sense.

27 Cited in Scholem, *The Messianic Idea in Judaism*, p. 29.

28 Twersky, *A Maimonides Reader*, p. 412.

29 Ibid.

30 Ibid., p. 416 (emphasis added).

31 This treatment of Hermann Cohen is drawn from Alan Mittleman, *Hope in a Democratic Age* (Oxford: Oxford University Press, 2009), pp. 206–213 and is used by permission of Oxford University Press.

32 For a thorough study, see Steven S. Schwarzschild, "The Democratic Socialism of Hermann Cohen," *Hebrew Union College Annual* 27 (1956), pp. 417–438. In Schwarzschild's words: "The messianic belief is primarily the belief in the ethical norm of a united humanity created by the moral endeavors and history-shaping actions of men .... Messianism is thus only the religious term for socialism" (pp. 427–428). For the original source, see Hermann Cohen, *Ethik des Reinen Willens* (Berlin: Bruno Cassirer, 1904), p. 528: "ihrer Politik nicht anders ist, als was wir heutzutage Sozialismus nennen." (Their [i.e., the Hebrew prophets] politics is nothing other than what we today call socialism.).

33 Hermann Cohen, *Religion of Reason Out of the Sources of Judaism*, Simon Kaplan, trans. (Atlanta: Scholars Press, 1995) p. 35.

34 Ibid., pp. 207, 305.

35 Cohen's idea of an infinitely deferred messianic age, which can only be approached asymptotically, is built on Kantian foundations. See *Critique of Pure Reason* A663/B691. For discussions, see Kenneth Seeskin, *Jewish Messianic Thoughts in an Age of Despair* (New York: Cambridge University Press, 2012), p. 82, and Martin Kavka, *Jewish Messianism and the History of Philosophy* (New York: Cambridge University Press, 2004), pp. 94–128.

36 Steven Schwarzschild, *The Pursuit of the Ideal*, Menachem Kellner, ed. (Albany: State University of New York Press, 1990), p. 211.

37 Ibid., p. 212.

38 Ibid.

39 Ibid., p. 215.

40 See Cohen, *Ethik des reinen Willens*, p. 387. Cf. *Religion of Reason*, p. 255 on the eternity of humanity, which is based on the eternity of the value of human unity. To my ear, Cohen equivocates between the presumably discarded temporal sense of eternity (=forever) and the infinite value sense.

41 Schwarzschild, *Pursuit of the Ideal*, p. 218 (emphasis added).

42 Ibid., p. 225.

43 Ibid., p. 219.

44 Ibid., p. 254. Seeskin gives us a sharper variant of Schwarzschild's Platonizing idealism: "Ethics means to have an alternative to reality." See Kenneth Seeskin, *Jewish Messianic Thoughts in an Age of Despair* (New York: Cambridge University Press, 2012), p. 168.

45 Schwarzschild, *Pursuit of the Ideal*, p. 86.

46 Ibid., p. 251.

47 Seeskin, *Jewish Messianic Thoughts in an Age of Despair*, pp.79ff. See also, Kenneth Seeskin, *Thinking about the Prophets* (Lincoln: University of Nebraska Press, 2020), pp. 57–58.

48 Seeskin, *Jewish Messianic Thoughts*, p. 99.

49 Ibid., p. 34.

50 Ibid., pp. 100–101.

51 Ibid., p. 192.

52 Ibid., p. 187.

53 Immanuel Kant, *Critique of Practical Reason*, Lewis White Beck, trans. (Upper Saddle River: Prentice Hall, 1993), pp., 130–138.

54 Andrew Chignell, "Rational Hope, Moral Order, and the Revolution of the Will," in Eric Watkins, ed., *The Divine Order, the Human Order, and the Order of Nature: Historical Perspectives* (New York: Oxford University Press, 2013), pp. 197–218.

55 Cohen, *Religion of Reason*, pp. 86–88. I take "correlation" in a logical sense of concepts being mutually dependent. The concept of God cannot be thought without the concept of the human, where both concepts are given an ethical significance. See Alexander Altmann, "Hermann Cohen's Begriff der Korrelation," in Hans Tramer, ed., *In Zwei Welten* (Tel Aviv: Verlag Bitaon, 1962), p. 379.

56 For Cohen, God has being – is a unique Being – but God does not "exist." "Existence," in his language has to do with sensible (i.e., empirical) reality. Being is conceptual. "Uniqueness, therefore, also entails the *distinction between being and existence.* The share of reason in monotheism is strongly confirmed in this distinction. For existence is attested by the senses, through perception. On the other hand, it is reason that, against all sense-appearance, bestows actuality upon existence, discovers and elevates the nonsensible to being, marks it out as true being." Cohen, *Religion of Reason*, p. 44. Cf. Frederick C. Beiser, *Hermann Cohen: An Intellectual Biography* (New York: Oxford University Press, 2018), p. 2.

57 Beiser writes:

> Thus the concept of God has an essentially normative meaning for Cohen; the fact that God does not exist is irrelevant for the simple reason that normative truth or validity is independent of existence. For Cohen, we must recognize the concept of God in the same way, and for the same reason, that we recognize our moral obligations; God is indeed the source of all our moral obligations; but that does not mean, of course, that he exists. (Beiser, *Hermann Cohen*, p. 359)

58 Kenneth Seeskin, *Searching for a Distant God* (New York: Oxford University Press, 2000), p. 21. How does Seeskin's negative theology avoid Hume's critique of apophasis in *Dialogues Concerning Natural Religion* (Part 4; para 1), where Hume argues that believing in an unknown and unknowable God is tantamount to believing in no God at all? For a discussion of how a sincere theist can overcome Hume's critique, see John Cottingham, *Why Believe?* (London: Continuum, 2009), p. 55.

59 Seeskin, *Jewish Messianic Thoughts*, p. 168.

60 Ibid., p. 194.

61 Ibid., p. 170.

62 James Tartaglia, *Philosophy in a Meaningless Life: A System of Nihilism, Consciousness, and Reality* (London: Bloomsbury Academic, 2016), p. 6.

63 Ibid., 56.

64 Ibid., p. 5.

65 Ibid.

66 Ibid., p. 1.

67 Ibid., p. 130 (emphasis added).

68 Roughly: Just as waking consciousness provides a "transcendent context" in which to understand dream-experience, waking consciousness itself needs a transcendent context in which the phenomenon of experience can be situated and explained. Experience, on Tartaglia's view, cannot be put into the context of the objective world without eliminativism (e.g., Dennett) or functionalism (e.g., Putnam) or some other revisionism that distorts the phenomenon beyond recognition. He considers all physicalist reductions of consciousness to fail. He also considers idealist ontologies of consciousness to be misleading. The transcendent context that he hypothesizes allows experience to have an irreducible integrity. However, our only scientific

ways of talking about it – through returning it to the objective world – necessarily and systematically misrepresent what is really going on. We are forced to use objective language to characterize experience but this is metaphysically misleading. Experience does not belong to the objective world, but to a transcendent context. This strategy, however, is more a formal move than a substantive-ontological one. It is somewhat similar to a nonontological, purely logical reading of the Kantian "thing in itself."

69 Ibid., p. 52 (italic in original).

70 Ibid., p. 169.

71 Ibid.

72 Ibid., p. 6.

73 Ibid., p. 21 (emphasis added).

74 Ibid., p. 23.

75 Ibid., p. 25.

76 Ibid.

77 Stroud, *Engagement and Metaphysical Dissatisfaction*, p. 96.

78 Tartaglia, *Philosophy in a Meaningless Life*, p. 175.

79 Ibid., p. 22.

80 Ibid.

81 Ibid., p. 55 (emphasis added).

82 Ibid., p. 172.

83 Ibid., p. 6. It is not clear what it means to say that "human beings are contingently valuable." It would make more sense to say that human beings produce and traffic in contingent values.

84 Immanuel Kant, "What does it mean to orient oneself in thinking?" in trans., Allen W. Wood, *Religion and Rational Theology* (Cambridge: Cambridge University Press, 2001), p. 10.

85 Ibid., p. 12.

86 Ibid.

87 For a splendid historical study of Kant and his successors on nihilism, ethics, and metaphysics, see Nisenbaum, *For the Love of Metaphysics*, p. 44.

88 Oral communication, c. 1997.

Conclusion

The rabbis criticized Kohelet because he seemed to scant the life of Torah. Perhaps they were also dubious about his fundamental stance. Kohelet's highly individualistic, skeptical temperament, which makes the book appealing to the modern, meaning-seeking reader, has troubled some traditional interpreters.[1] Kohelet, like Job, gave voice to a lonely, perplexed "I." Even in the social dimension of his life, his acquisitive ego dominated. He sought more wealth, more property, more power. When, with advancing age, the presumptive value of those goods weakened for him, he raised questions about what they were really worth – what anything was really worth. He assumed an abstract, disengaged, austere view – a view from the perspective of an impersonal cosmos. To this he added a dismal fixation on the certain demise of all flesh. The austere view and the somber certainty further undercut the value of the goods he had spent his life pursuing. Meaningfulness cratered. Finding something that remains, something that gives life the possibility of joy, is the project of the book. But once again, the results have to satisfy a fundamentally isolated, perplexed, and skeptical observer. He is, in a way, trapped. If Kohelet had allowed himself to be integrated into a richer world of sociality and normativity, would his questions – and answers – have arisen in the form he bequeathed to us?

I don't want to reduce his struggle for meaning to a psychological matter, nor do I want to offer anodyne advice about the importance of friends, family, and community (as important as these are!). His struggle is a genuine one. I do, however, want to weaken the dichotomy that appears in Kohelet and runs through many of the philosophical treatments that we have considered. I want to demote it from a dichotomy to a distinction. The dichotomy goes like this: Either one goes along contentedly with everyday meaning/social meaning or one rises to a height of metaphysical insight and attains a justification-shattering view from nowhere. The former stance is then assumed to be deluded and lazy; the latter, although deeply problematic, is thought to be honest and brave. The person who is content with the world of social meaning is living an absurd life, by default. Her world is structured by illusions. The person who rises to a metaphysical perspective has come to recognize the prior absurdity but although, in a sense, liberated from it, she must return to it with full awareness of doing so. This generates a new wave of absurdity. Nihilism is one answer to relieving the tension – life just is meaningless. Living courageously with absurdity and its irresolvable contradictions is another.

Throughout this book, I have accepted this picture and have tried to argue that Jewish thought has evolved ways of coping with it. The acceptance comes both from believing that Nagel has articulated a real phenomenon, thereby formulating a genuine dilemma, and from my personal experience of living with this fraught alternation of perspectives. Nonetheless, I think that ceding *too much* authority to this picture is a mistake. As mentioned in Chapter 1, the abstract view is a *method*, a way of bracketing our egocentricity, our anthropocentricity. It does not clinch noetic access to the world-in-itself or any such thing. It is a way of complicating our taken-for-granted beliefs and extricating ourselves from self-interested reasoning. Its results, as to truth, are another matter.[2] This is to say that the abstract view *is also underwritten by a structure of value*; it is not a holiday from value. Its emphasis on achieving truth about the world and our place in it is a normative commitment. Value undergirds human thought and action in an ineluctable way.

With regard then to Kohelet's attainment of a "view from nowhere," the rabbis who pushed back were not reactionary conservatives; they were quite properly defending the legitimacy of a world of value and meaning. That world needs a voice to respond to the dissolutive metaphysical perspective – whether that of ancient skepticism or of modern scientism.

Thinkers such as Weinberg or Tartaglia believe that, given the achievement of an austere perspective on fact and value, we come to realize the limited scope of the latter. For them, value begins in what Yeats memorably called, "the foul rag and bone shop of the heart." At the height of awareness, we see only a cosmos of pallid facts. We supply the color and attraction of value out of our own self-assertive vitality. The metaphysical awareness offered by the austere view is taken to be an awareness of the absence of value – the default condition of the universe until human self-interest enters the cosmic picture. The absence of value entails the stillbirth of meaning. With nothing to make meaning of, meaninglessness results.

Opposed to this is a biblical story where the cosmos, as a created order, is itself good. This is to say that the goodness that we find in life – if our lives have been such as to afford the discovery – is basic and objective. The concept of creation fuses fact and value. The warrant for this is that value is ineluctably part of our epistemological and practical activity. The very process of scientific discovery, which purports, in the hands of the positivists, to deliver value-free snapshots of reality, is laden with value. The truth that it seeks is a value. The claims that it makes ought to be believed (but only insofar as they are true). The procedures by which science works are normative. The level at which explanatory projects in the sciences and elsewhere rely on values is basic and inextricable from their operation. We start, therefore, as mentioned in Chapter 2, not with a blank, value-free, indifferent, brute factual, material world but in a world alive with value.[3]

Of course, one could object that it is impermissible to infer from our value-laden way of knowing the world a conclusion about how the world is as such. That truth has a debt to value should not be taken to imply, the critic might maintain, that the world about which truths are discovered itself has value. But how can the critic differentiate such a thing-in-itself world from the value-inflected world about which we can sensibly speak? The world in itself, if prised from our ways of knowing it, would be so aloof from human description that we could not say if it was value-free or value-full; we could not say anything about it. Thus, rather than confidently assert that the world, when viewed abstractly, as if from nowhere, is valueless – that life lacks value or that nihilism is a "fact" – one should desist from making such pronouncements.

No less than nihilists, religious people who reject the absurdist sensibility that I have tried to articulate do not want to desist from making such pronouncements either. Accepting revelation as a story about the furniture of the universe, as it were, not simply as a story about the mysterious ground of value, they do not want to admit their ignorance about ultimate things. Humility can be as scarce in religion as in philosophy. The philosopher Bryan Magee, who sees ignorance as one of the most fundamental features of the human condition, criticizes religious believers for an "unjustified evasion, a failure to face up to the reality of ignorance as our natural and inevitable starting-point."[4] Religious people, he relates, initially accept his claim about ignorance due to its likeness to "mystery," but then move unjustifiably to equate ignorance with "the noumenal 'God'."[5] This is cheating, for Magee. They can't have it both ways. Ignorance is ignorance, full stop.

Magee makes a good point. We contradict ourselves when we accept our basic ignorance but then characterize it in a way that implies knowledge. We can avoid Magee's criticism, however, by continuing to deny knowledge while affirming hope. We can't know that the mystery is the ground of value, but we can hope that this is so. We can hope that the goodness of being manifests something of the ultimate. We can have faith that our work in the world, especially in its ethical dimension, advances that insistent but fragile goodness. We can believe that something calls to us from the depths and asks for our response. We have a right to construe revelation as such a call, as well as to see in mysterious encounters and experiences possible traces of the ultimate. None of these constitute knowledge claims. They constitute an orientation toward the world. Nothing requires us to take these fundamental features of our human reality and cordon them off from reality as such. We can be chaste about ignorance but open to the possibility of a relation between the values constitutive of human life (such as truth, beauty, and goodness) and the ultimate. This may well be a religious stance, but even staunch secularists find it hard to overcome.[6]

It is, therefore, not completely surprising that Tartaglia's argument has a "religious" structure. On his account, consciousness, time, and the most general concepts (universals) are rooted in a transcendent context about which we can say nothing. This is akin to apophasis or "negative theology." Everything that is most important comes from a mysterious level of being about which we must remain ignorant. Humanity is thus dependent on a transcendent domain beyond description or characterization. But rather than stopping there and letting mystery remain mysterious, Tartaglia needs to characterize the mystery as meaningless, to void it of potential significance, of its potential as a signifier. Mystery gets flattened into the "fact" of nihilism. It is right for religion to oppose this flattening. This is part of what religion does. For a Jew, to be a "prisoner of hope" is to stand in hope before mystery. It is to take a hopeful stance toward the unknown ultimate.

The abstract view has authority, but it does not have a monopoly on it. It is a dialectical aspect of our epistemic and existential engagement with the world. The Ivan Ilych-like experience of meanings being shaken, of our valued projects, our "loves," to use Harry Frankfurt's language, becoming problematic is not due to an encounter with ultimacy per se. It is due to *our* alternation of perspectives. It is part of the normal give-and-take of a questioning soul. The view from nowhere is a stance within one's cognitive repertoire that serves to check uncritical beliefs. It is part of our experience of being creatures of reason and will; it is a method, not an epiphany from some beyond. The alternation of our perspectives – from here to nowhere and back again – does not overcome our ignorance of the ultimate, nor does it wash out the goodness of being; it enriches it through revealing our own internal cognitive and volitional complexity. The alternating perspectives heighten the need for us to better integrate our minds and hearts. The organic unity, which Nozick identifies with value, thus becomes apparent in our own inner worlds. It calls for a kind of spiritual discipline by which we strive for an internal unity of being.

Finding meaning is a way of striving for this internal unity. When we secure meaning in the face of absurdity, we quiet the commanding voice of the abstract view and recommit to the values that have guided us. Our grasp of them becomes more confident, and their scope more capacious. We secure a higher, more durable sense of being at home in the world. Standing before mystery, we know that whether life is ultimately meaningful, and in what way it does not originate in rational argument, nor can it be settled by one. The best meanings we construe (or find) express insights so deep as to elude explicit articulation. Meaning commends and underwrites a way of life; it must be embodied and enacted. In judging whether a life was meaningful, we are also judging the quality of a life. It is at that level that meaning succeeds.

I find these meanings narratively encoded in the story of creation. I read it as an affirmation of the goodness of being. This goodness is radical but not yet durable; its growth and stability depend upon us. From my earliest young adult rediscovery of Genesis (in a religion course in my freshman year of college), I thought that the creation stories held profound insight. I saw in them an unexpectedly sophisticated meditation on chaos and order, on nature and humanity, on creativity, freedom, limits – on the tragic and the good. The bible stories from childhood that I dismissed as fairy tales in early adolescence became alive with meaningfulness for me in late adolescence, fifty years ago. This has never ceased. Does the rather distilled philosophical construal that I take from the text express its genuine meaning or only my arcane reading of it? I doubt that this is a worthwhile question. The text invites our participation in construing its meaning. The quality of our interpretation is tied, not only to technical background knowledge but also to the virtues we bring as interpreters. Do we honor the text by treating it charitably? Do we open ourselves to its voices as responsible readers or do we try and ram our own preconceived views down its throat? Do we allow it to live within us and let ourselves live with it? Judaism supports a vast polyphony of interpretation if only one begins with the right spirit.

The story of creation and those of revelation and redemption are rubrics for personal meaning-seeking. But they also organize large-scale diachronic and communal frameworks of meaning. Participation in this enterprise also requires an ethical spirit. One must take not only a canonical text seriously, even lovingly, but one must take the Jewish traditions of interpretation that have developed over the millennia seriously, at least if one wants to be part of the conversation. As personal as meaning is, the communal dimension of the pursuit is vital. No matter how keen or insightful any one of us might be, there is something to be said for standing on the shoulders of giants. Entering into a world of collective Jewish meaning, articulated over centuries by innumerable fine minds, enlarges and enriches.

In line with this view, one of the common tropes of meaning – about which this book has said little – is that meaning is to be found by getting beyond oneself and identifying with a larger entity. This can run from something as morally basic as serving others in decent, caring ways to something as insidious as subordinating oneself to a cult, a gang, or a Führer. People who take that route to meaning have tried to flee, perhaps, a life they took to be meaningless. Their new engagements, though wrong or evil in mounting degrees of intensity, might well be meaningful, at least in a subjective sense and with the proviso that the subjects who find such activities meaningful expose themselves to moral judgment. Precisely because of the abuse of this version of meaningfulness, so evident in the political and moral history of the last century, I have found it unpromising to try to develop it. Here, however, we see a more promising instance. Associating oneself with a meaning-seeking community that is respectful of individual contribution and dissent and that can give an ethically adequate account of itself is properly meaningful.

This does not entail that everything done in the name of such a community will pass moral muster or that one should completely assimilate to the community and practice a kind of self-abnegating masochism. Here the view from nowhere can help. We can abstract from our immediate engagements and view them in a comprehensive way. We can thereby remember dimensions of value, meaning, and commitment that might have been demoted or obscured in our communal immersion. There is no end of asking more from ourselves and from our communities. If Kohelet had had a richer understanding of the value of the human world, perhaps he wouldn't have come to his utterly deflationary view.

Absurdity is a fact of life; nihilism is not. Meaning can be quite dull and conventional, or it can result from hard wrestling with genuine dilemmas. The traditions of philosophy and Judaism can help us confront our existential challenges. The two can be allies, not zero-sum competitors. We have good reason to trust what is best in them rather than to go it alone. For as Kohelet said, "Two are better than one" (Ecclesiastes 4:9).

NOTES

1 Soloveitchik, *Out of the Whirlwind* (Brooklyn: Ktav, 2003), p. 155. For a more popular approach to the self-limitation of Kohelet, see Emanuel Rackman, "An Optimist Sees Pessimism in Ecclesiastes," www.rabbirackman.com/an-optimist-sees-pessimism-in-ecclesiastes/ (accessed August 3, 2022).

2 Chapter 1, p. 48, subsection "Defining Terms: Absurdity."

3 Chapter 2, p. 1; see the very first line.

4 Bryan Magee, *Ultimate Questions* (Princeton: Princeton University Press, 2016), p. 31.

5 Ibid.

6 See, for example, the last book of Ronald Dworkin, *Religion without God* (Cambridge: Harvard University Press, 2013).

Bibliography

Altmann, Alexander, "The Encounter of Faith and Reason in the Western Tradition and Its Significance Today," *Journal of Religion*, 101 (2021).

Altmann, Alexander, "Hermann Cohen's Begriff der Korrelation," in Hans Tramer (ed.), *In Zwei Welten* (Tel Aviv: Verlag Bitaon, 1962).

Angier, Tom (ed.), *The Cambridge Companion to Natural Law Ethics* (Cambridge: Cambridge University Press, 2019).

Angier, Tom, *Natural Law Theory* (Cambridge: Cambridge University Press, 2021).

Arendt, Hannah, *The Life of the Mind: Thinking* (New York: Harcourt, 1978).

Aronowicz, Annette, "Heschel's Yiddish *Kotsk*: Some Reflections on Inwardness," in Stanislaw Krajewski and Adam Lipszyc (eds.), *Abraham Joshua Heschel: Philosophy, Theology, and Interreligious Dialogue* (Wiesbaden: Harrassowitz Verlag, 2009).

Aronowicz, Annette, *Jews and Christians on Time and Eternity* (Stanford: Stanford University Press, 1998).

Ayer, Alfred J., *The Meaning of Life* (New York: Charles Scribner's Sons, 1990).

Beiser, Frederick C., *Hermann Cohen: An Intellectual Biography* (New York: Oxford University Press, 2018).

Bergman, Shmuel Hugo, *Dialogical Philosophy from Kierkegaard to Buber* (Albany: SUNY Press, 1991).

Berlin, Isaiah, "The Apotheosis of the Romantic Will," in Henry Hardy and Roger Hausherr (eds.), *The Proper Study of Mankind* (New York: Farrar, Strauss, and Giroux, 2000).

Braude, William, Kapstein, Israel, and Poupko, Yehiel, trans. *Pesikta de-Rab Kahana* (Philadelphia: Jewish Publication Society, 2002).

Brooke, John Hedley, *Science and Religion* (Cambridge: Cambridge University Press, 2014).

Buber, Martin, *Between Man and Man*, trans. Ronald Gregor-Smith (New York: Macmillan, 1965).

Buber, Martin, *I and Thou*, trans. Walter Kaufmann (New York: Simon & Schuster, 1970).

Camus, Albert, *The Myth of Sisyphus*, trans. Justin O'Brien (New York: Vintage Books, 2018).

Chalmers, David, "Facing Up to the Problem of Consciousness," *Journal of Consciousness Studies*, 2(3) (1995).

Cherry, Shai, *Coherent Judaism* (Brighton: Academic Studies Press, 2020).

Chignell, Andrew, "Rational Hope, Moral Order, and the Revolution of the Will," in Eric Watkins (ed.), *The Divine Order, the Human Order, and the Order of Nature: Historical Perspectives* (New York: Oxford University Press, 2013).

Cohen, Hermann, *Ethik des Reinen Willens* (Berlin: Bruno Cassirer, 1904).

Cohen, Hermann, *Religion of Reason Out of the Sources of Judaism*, trans. Simon Kaplan (Atlanta: Scholars Press, 1995).

Cooper, David E., *The Measure of Things* (Oxford: Clarendon Press, 2002).

Cottingham, John, *On the Meaning of Life* (London: Routledge, 2005).

Cottingham, John, *Why Believe?* (London: Continuum, 2009).

Crosby, Donald A., *The Specter of the Absurd* (Albany: SUNY Press, 1988).

Deutsch, David, *The Beginning of Infinity* (New York: Penguin Books, 2011).

Dupre, John, *Darwin's Legacy: What Evolution Means Today* (Oxford: Oxford University Press, 2006).

Dworkin, Ronald, *Justice for Hedgehogs* (Cambridge: Harvard University Press, 2011).

Dworkin, Ronald, "Objectivity and Truth: You'd Better Believe It," *Philosophy and Public Affairs*, 25 (1996).

Dworkin, Ronald, *Religion without God* (Cambridge: Harvard University Press, 2013).

Eagleton, Terry, *The Meaning of Life: A Very Short Introduction* (Oxford: Oxford University Press, 2007).

Feynman, Richard, *The Character of Physical Law* (Cambridge: MIT Press, 1965).

Finnis, John, *Natural Law and Natural Rights* (New York: Oxford University Press, 2011).

Fisher, Cass, "Actualized Redemption in the Thought of Franz Rosenzweig and Rabbi Joseph B. Soloveitchik," *Naharaim*, 14 (2020).

Flanagan, Owen, *The Really Hard Problem: Meaning in a Material World* (Cambridge: MIT Press, 2007).

Flanagan, Owen and Caruso, Gregg, *Neuroexistentialism: Meaning, Morals, and Purpose in the Age of Neuroscience* (New York: Oxford University Press, 2018).

Fleischacker, Samuel, *The Good and the Good Book: Revelation as a Guide to Life* (New York: Oxford University Press, 2017).

Fox, Michael V., *The JPS Bible Commentary: Ecclesiastes* (Philadelphia: Jewish Publication Society, 2004).

Fox, Michael V., *A Time to Tear Down and a Time to Build Up* (Grand Rapids: William B. Eerdmans Publishing, 1999).

Frankfurt, Harry, *The Importance of What We Care About* (New York: Cambridge University Press, 1998).

Frankfurt, Harry, *The Reasons of Love* (Princeton: Princeton University Press, 2004).

Gaon, Saadia, *The Book of Beliefs and Opinions*, trans. Samuel Rosenblatt (New Haven: Yale University Press, 1948).

Geach, Peter, *Truth and Hope* (Notre Dame: Notre Dame University Press, 2001).

Gertz, Nolen, *Nihilism* (Cambridge: MIT Press, 2019).

Gillespie, Michael Allen, *Nihilism Before Nietzsche* (Chicago: University of Chicago Press, 1995).

Goldman, Alan H., *Life's Values* (New York: Oxford University Press, 2018).

Goodman, Lenn E., "Kohelet and the Search for Meaning," in David Birnbaum and Martin S. Cohen (eds.), *Search for Meaning* (New York: New Paradigm Matrix, 2018).

Goodman, Lenn E., *On Justice* (Oxford: Littman Library, 2008).

Goodman, Lenn E., "Value and the Dynamics of Being," *Review of Metaphysics*, 61 (2007).

Greene, Brian, *Until the End of Time* (New York: Vintage Books, 2020).

Grice, H. P., "Meaning," *The Philosophical Review*, 66 (1957).

Habermas, Jürgen, *An Awareness of What Is Missing* (Cambridge: Polity, 2010).

Halbertal, Moshe, "If the Text Had Not Been Written, It Could Not Be Said," in Deborah A. Green and Laura S. Lieber (eds.), *The Shapes of Culture and the Religious Imagination* (Oxford: Oxford University Press, 2009).

Hallamish, Moshe, *An Introduction to the Kabbalah*, trans. Ruth Bar-Ilan and Ora Wiskind-Elper (Albany: SUNY Press, 1999).

Haught, John F., *Is Nature Enough?* (New York: Cambridge University Press, 2006).

Hayes, Christine, *What's Divine about Divine Law?* (Princeton: Princeton University Press, 2017).

Heinemann, Isaac, *The Reasons for the Commandments in Jewish Thought*, trans. Leonard Levin (Boston: Academic Studies Press, 2009).

Heschel, Abraham Joshua, *Kotsk (Yiddish)*, Volume II (Tel Aviv: Ha-Menorah Verlag, 1973).

Hickey, Lance P., *Hilary Putnam* (London: Continuum, 2009).

Humphrey, Nicholas, *Soul Dust: The Magic of Consciousness* (Princeton: Princeton University Press, 2011).

Jacobs, Jonathan, *Law, Reason, and Morality in Medieval Jewish Philosophy* (Oxford: Oxford University Press, 2010).

Johnston, Mark, *Saving God: Religion after Idolatry* (Princeton: Princeton University Press, 2009).

Jonas, Hans, *The Imperative of Responsibility* (Chicago: University of Chicago Press, 1985).

Kant, Immanuel, *Critique of Pure Reason*, trans. Norman Kemp Smith (New York: St. Martin's Press, 1965).

Kant, Immanuel, *Groundwork of the Metaphysic of Morals*, trans. H. J. Paton (New York: Harper Torchbooks, 1964).

Kateb, George, *Human Dignity* (Cambridge: Harvard University Press, 2011).

Kavka, Martin, *Jewish Messianism and the History of Philosophy* (New York: Cambridge University Press, 2004).

Kitcher, Philip, *Life after Faith* (New Haven: Yale University Press, 2014).

Krüger, Thomas, "Die Rezeption der Tora im Buch Kohelet," in Thomas Krüger (ed.), *Kritische Weisheit* (Zürich: Pano Verlag, 1997).

Lachter, Hartley, *Kabbalistic Revolution* (New Brunswick: Rutgers University Press, 2014).

Landau, Iddo, *Finding Meaning in an Imperfect World* (New York: Oxford University Press, 2017).

Landau, Iddo, "Why Has the Question of the Meaning of Life Arisen in the Last Two and a Half Centuries?" *Philosophy Today* 41(2) (1997).

Leach, Stephen and Tartaglia, James (eds.), *The Meaning of Life and the Great Philosophers* (London: Routledge, 2018).

Lear, Jonathan, *Radical Hope* (Cambridge: Harvard University Press, 2008).

Levenson, Jon D., *Creation and the Persistence of Evil* (Princeton: Princeton University Press, 1988)

Levenson, Jon D., *Resurrection and the Restoration of Israel* (New Haven: Yale University Press, 2008).

Lycan, William G., "Giving Dualism Its Due," *Australasian Journal of Philosophy*, 87 (2009).

Magee, Bryan, *Ultimate Questions* (Princeton: Princeton University Press, 2016).

Maimonides, Moses, *The Guide of the Perplexed*, trans. Shlomo Pines (Chicago: University of Chicago Press, 1963).

Metz, Thaddeus, *Meaning in Life* (Oxford: Oxford University Press, 2013).

Mittleman, Alan, *Hope in a Democratic Age* (Oxford: Oxford University Press, 2009).

Mittleman, Alan, *Human Nature and Jewish Thought* (Princeton: Princeton University Press, 2015).

Morgan, Michael L., *Interim Judaism: Jewish Thought in a Century of Crisis* (Bloomington: Indiana University Press, 2001).

Morgan, Michael L. and Weitzman, Steven (eds.), *Rethinking the Messianic Idea in Judaism* (Bloomington: Indiana University Press, 2015).

Nagel, Thomas, *Mortal Questions* (Cambridge: Cambridge University Press, 1979).

Nagel, Thomas, *The View from Nowhere* (New York: Oxford University Press, 1986).

Nassar, Dalia, *The Romantic Absolute: Being and Knowing in Early German Romantic Philosophy* (Chicago: University of Chicago Press, 2013).

Neher, André, *Notes sur Qohélét* (L'Ecclésiaste) (Paris: Les Éditions de Minuit, 1998).

Nietzsche, Friedrich, "The Genealogy of Morals," in Walter Kaufmann (ed. and trans), *Basic Writings of Nietzsche* (New York: The Modern Library, 2000).

Nisenbaum, Karin, *For the Love of Metaphysics* (New York: Oxford University Press, 2018).

Novak, David, *Natural Law in Judaism* (Cambridge: Cambridge University Press, 1998).

Nozick, Robert, *Philosophical Explanations* (Cambridge: Belknap Press, 1981).

Oakeshott, Michael, *On Human Conduct* (Oxford: Clarendon Press, 1975).

Pascal, Blaise, *Pensees*, trans. A. J. Krailsheimer (London: Penguin Books, 1995).

Plantinga, Alvin, *Where the Conflict Really Lies: Science, Religion and Naturalism* (New York: Oxford University Press, 2011).

Putnam, Hilary, *The Collapse of the Fact/Value Dichotomy* (Cambridge: Harvard University Press, 2002).

Putnam, Hilary, *Reason, Truth, and History* (Cambridge: Cambridge University Press, 1992).

Quine, W. V., "Mr. Strawson on Logical Theory," *Mind*, 62 (1953).

Rundle, Bede, *Why Is There Something Rather than Nothing?* (Oxford: Clarendon Press, 2004).

Ruse, Michael, *A Meaning to Life* (New York: Oxford, 2019).

Sandberg, Ruth N., *Rabbinic Views of Qohelet* (Lewiston: Edwin Mellen Press, 1999).

Scheffler, Samuel, *Death and the Afterlife* (New York: Oxford University Press, 2016).

Scheffler, Samuel, *Equality and Tradition* (New York: Oxford University Press, 2012).

Scholem, Gershom, *Kabbalah* (Jerusalem: Keter, 1974).

Scholem, Gershom, *Major Trends in Jewish Mysticism* (New York: Schocken Books, 1995).

Scholem, Gershom, *The Messianic Idea in Judaism* (New York: Schocken Books, 1971).

Schufreider, Gregory, "The Logic of the Absurd," *Philosophy and Phenomenological Research*, 44 (1983).

Schwarzschild, Steven S., "The Democratic Socialism of Hermann Cohen," *Hebrew Union College Annual*, 27 (1956).

Schwarzschild, Steven S., *The Pursuit of the Ideal*, Menachem Kellner (ed.) (Albany: State University of New York Press, 1990).

Scruton, Roger, *Modern Philosophy* (New York: Penguin Books, 1994).

Seeskin, Kenneth, *Autonomy in Jewish Philosophy* (New York: Cambridge University Press, 2001).

Seeskin, Kenneth, *Jewish Messianic Thoughts in an Age of Despair* (New York: Cambridge University Press, 2012).

Seeskin, Kenneth, *Searching for a Distant God* (New York: Oxford University Press, 2000).

Seeskin, Kenneth, *Thinking about the Prophets* (Lincoln: University of Nebraska Press, 2020).

Soloveitchik, Joseph B., *Halakhic Man*, trans. Lawrence Kaplan (Philadelphia: Jewish Publication Society, 1983).

Soloveitchik, Joseph B., *The Lonely Man of Faith* (New York: Doubleday, 2006).

Soloveitchik, Joseph B., *Out of the Whirlwind* (Brooklyn: KTAV, 2003).

Sellars, Wilfred, *Science, Perception, and Reality* (Atascadero: Ridgeview Publishing, 1991).

Smith, Justin E. H., *Irrationality* (Princeton: Princeton University Press, 2019).

Sommer, Benjamin D., *Revelation and Authority: Sinai in Jewish Scripture and Tradition* (New Haven: Yale University Press, 2015).

Statman, Daniel and Sagi, Avi, "Divine Command Morality and Jewish Tradition," *The Journal of Religious Ethics* 23 (1995).

Stewart-Williams, Steve, *Darwin, God, and the Meaning of Life* (Cambridge: Cambridge University Press, 2010).

Storey, Benjamin and Storey, Jenna Silber, *Why We Are Restless* (Princeton: Princeton University Press, 2021).

Stroud, Barry, *Engagement and Metaphysical Dissatisfaction: Modality and Value* (New York: Oxford University Press, 2011).

Tartaglia, James, *Philosophy in a Meaningless Life: A System of Nihilism, Consciousness, and Reality* (London: Bloomsbury Academic, 2016).

Taylor, Charles, *A Secular Age* (Cambridge: Belknap Press, 2007).

Taylor, Charles, *Sources of the Self* (Cambridge: Harvard University Press, 1989).

Taylor, Richard, "The Meaning of Life," in E. D. Klemke and Steven Kahn (eds.), *The Meaning of Life* (New York: Oxford University Press, 2017).

Thagard, Paul, *The Brain and the Meaning of Life* (Princeton: Princeton University Press, 2010).

Thomas, Alan, *Thomas Nagel* (Stocksfield, UK: Acumen, 2009).

Tolstoy, Leo, *The Death of Ivan Ilyich and Confession*, trans. Peter Carson (New York: Liveright Publishing, 2014).

Toulmin, Stephen, *The Return to Cosmology* (Berkeley: University of California Press, 1985).

Twersky, Isadore, *A Maimonides Reader* (Springfield: Behrman House, 1972).

Walzer, Michael, *Exodus and Revolution* (New York: Basic Books, 1986).

Weinberg, Rivka, "Ultimate Meaning: We Don't Have It, We Can't Get It, and We Should Be Very, Very Sad," *Journal of Controversial Ideas*, 1 (2021).

Weinberg, Steven, *The First Three Minutes* (New York: Basic Books, 1993).

Weiss, Dov, *Pious Irreverence* (Philadelphia: University of Pennsylvania Press, 2017).

Wiggins, David, "Truth, Invention, and the Meaning of Life," in Geoffrey Sayre McCord (ed.), *Essays on Moral Realism* (Ithaca: Cornell University Press, 1988).

Williams, Bernard, *Moral Luck* (Cambridge: Cambridge University Press, 1999).

Williams, Bernard, *Problems of the Self* (Cambridge: Cambridge University Press, 1973).

Williams, Bernard, *Truth and Truthfulness* (Princeton: Princeton University Press, 2002).

Wilson, Edward O., *The Meaning of Human Existence* (New York: Liveright Publishing, 2014).

Wolf, Susan, *Meaning in Life and Why It Matters* (Princeton: Princeton University Press, 2010).

Wood, Allen, "Fichte," in Sacha Golob, and Jens Timmermann (eds.), *The Cambridge History of Moral Philosophy* (Cambridge: Cambridge University Press, 2017).

Young, Julian, *The Death of God and the Meaning of Life* (New York: Routledge, 2014).

Index

Printed in the USA
CPSIA information can be obtained
at www.ICGtesting.com
LVHW051514111123
763669LV00004B/23

9 781009 098267